54

OPERATION
MAYHEM

STOCKTON BOROUGH

WITHDRAWN

LIBRARIES

D0281388

Steve Heaney joined the Parachute Regiment Juniors at sixteen, then passed Parachute Regiment selection and joined 3 PARA in 1987. Two years later, he successfully undertook selection into X Platoon – more formally known as Pathfinders. He went on to serve with that unit for over a decade, working with almost every Special Forces unit with which the British military has links.

In 1999, he was promoted to Platoon Sergeant. The following year, he was the first non-officer in the unit's history to be awarded the Military Cross for his leadership and courage during Operation Mayhem. He was also awarded the Commanding Officer's Commendation for finding arms caches in Northern Ireland.

Sergeant Heaney left the British military in 2001. He has spent the last decade working as a senior military adviser to one of Britain's key allies.

Damien Lewis has worked as a war and conflict reporter for major broadcasters, reporting from across Africa, South America, the Middle and Far East, and has won numerous awards for journalism. His first book was an international bestseller, translated into more than thirty languages, and made into a film and stage play.

His books *Operation Certain Death*, *Apache Dawn* and *Zero Six Bravo* were all *Sunday Times* bestsellers, as were his previous co-authored military books, *Fire Strike 7/9*, co-written with Sergeant Paul 'Bommer' Grahame, and *It's All About Treo*, co-authored with Dave Heyhoe. Several of his elite-forces books are in the process of being made into movies or TV dramas.

STEVE HEANEY MC
WITH DAMIEN LEWIS

OPERATION MAYHEM

THE TARGET: ONE VILLAGE.

THE DEFENDERS: 26 ELITE BRITISH SOLDIERS.

THE ENEMY: 2000 DRUG- AND BLOOD-CRAZED REBELS.

966.404442

An Orion paperback

First published in Great Britain in 2014
by Orion Books
This paperback edition published in 2015
by Orion Books Ltd,
Carmelite House, 50 Victoria Embankment,
London, EC4Y 0DZ

An Hachette UK company

1 3 5 7 9 10 8 6 4 2

Copyright © Steve Heaney and Damien Lewis 2014

The right of Steve Heaney and Damien Lewis to be identified
as the authors of this work has been asserted by them in accordance
with the Copyright, Designs and Patents Act 1988.

All rights reserved. No part of this publication may be
reproduced, stored in a retrieval system, or transmitted,
in any form or by any means, electronic, mechanical,
photocopying, recording or otherwise, without the prior
permission of the copyright owner.

Quote on p. xi licensed under the Open Government Licence v2.0

A CIP catalogue record for this book is available
from the British Library.

ISBN 978-1-4091-4845-6

Typeset by Input Data Services Ltd,
Bridgwater, Somerset

Printed and bound by CPI Group (UK) Ltd,
Croydon CR0 4YY

The Orion Publishing Group's policy is to use papers that
are natural, renewable and recyclable products and
made from wood grown in sustainable forests. The logging
and manufacturing processes are expected to conform to
the environmental regulations of the country of origin.

www.orionbooks.co.uk

To the Findermen who have paid the ultimate price, we raise a glass in your honour. To those of you who find yourselves once again in harm's way on active operations across the globe . . . be safe and remember always,

'Stay low and move fast'.

'What makes the grass grow? Blood! Blood! Blood!'

RUF rebel chant, prior to battle

'Good men sleep soundly in their beds at night, only because there are rough men willing to do violence on their behalf.'

George Orwell

What Manner of Men Are These
Who Wear the Maroon Beret?

They are firstly all volunteers and are toughened by physical training. As a result they have infectious optimism and that offensive eagerness which comes from well-being. They have 'jumped' from the air and by doing so have conquered fear.

Their duty lies in the van of the battle. They are proud of this honour. They have the highest standards in all things whether it be skill in battle or smartness in the execution of all peacetime duties. They are in fact – men apart – every man an emperor.

Of all the factors, which make for success in battle, the spirit of the warrior is the most decisive. That spirit will be found in full measure in the men who wear the maroon beret.

Field Marshal The Viscount Montgomery

AUTHOR'S NOTE

I have used soldiers' real names in this book when they have been published in the press, or whenever individual soldiers have indicated to me that they were happy for me to do so. I have been asked to use pseudonyms for those serving with Special Forces and other elite units, or for operators who are still involved, or who were involved, in sensitive operations. Otherwise, all aspects of this story remain as they took place on the ground.

I have done my utmost to ensure the accuracy of all the events portrayed herein. Few written records exist covering the events described in this book. Accordingly, I have recreated conversations from how I remember them and in discussions with the others who were involved. No doubt my memory and that of my fellow operators is fallible, and I will be happy to correct any inadvertent mistakes in future editions.

To all other units in the British armed forces – and those of our foremost allies – the Pathfinders' call-sign is *Mayhem*. That is how the unit is addressed over the radio net. The Sierra Leone mission related in this book remains one of the most highly decorated in modern Pathfinder history. Accordingly, and because it seems to suit the actions portrayed in these pages, I have chosen to call this book *Operation Mayhem*.

FOREWORD

by General Sir David Richards GCB CBE DSO
former Chief of the Defence Staff

In January 1999 I led a small team of officers and marines to Sierra Leone. Our task was to assess whether the once proud little army of that tragic but spirited country had any hope of pushing back the brutal rebels of the Revolutionary United Front. I had to assess whether there was anything we could do to help them and present the case to Tony Blair's government in London.

The RUF's signature atrocity was the amputation of the limbs of young and old alike. Designed to intimidate the population, in their warped often drug-crazed minds this also had the advantage of preventing those they 'cut' from casting a vote in any future elections. We watched the Sierra Leonian army, their local Kamajor militia allies and a small contingent of Nigerian troops fight valiantly to push the RUF back out of Freetown. We departed after about 10 days but not before we had successfully persuaded the British government that these plucky people should be helped, financially and militarily.

That experience left a real mark on me and my team. We had been witness to some horrific sights, things we all hoped never to see again. We certainly never thought we would return to Sierra Leone. Little did we know.

By early May 2000, the RUF had reneged on a peace treaty they had signed the previous summer and were once again rampaging their brutal way towards Freetown. This time my ever-ready Joint Force HQ, with 1st Battalion Parachute Regiment group including the Regiment's renowned Pathfinder Platoon and some others under command, were rushed out to Sierra Leone to evacuate

British and other entitled people from the country for fear that they would be butchered by the RUF. It was a race against time. And it was vital that the RUF suffered an early blow to their morale, something that would make them pause and think twice about taking on my limited forces.

This invigorating book tells the tale of the hugely professional and courageous group of men who inflicted that blow on the RUF for me and their inspirational commanding officer Lt-Col Paul Gibson. Deliberately exposed to lure the RUF onto their positions, the Pathfinders lived up to their unrivalled reputation for toughness and professionalism of the highest order. Without a shadow of doubt, their heroic actions that memorable night was the key tactical event in what has been held up as a model intervention operation. It enabled us not only to complete the evacuation in relative security but, more importantly, allowed us to push the RUF out of Freetown and away from the vital airfield without which no operation was tenable. It buoyed up the Sierra Leonean people and crucially bought time for the United Nations forces to recover and rebuild.

Six weeks later, with the RUF essentially defeated and hugely demoralised, we were able to hand over to the UN and wend our way back to the UK. We felt good about ourselves. We had chanced our arm and more than achieved the aim. The generous-hearted people of Sierra Leone had been given their country back and could once again hope for a better future. The Pathfinders had written another stirring chapter in their short but illustrious history and Sergeant Steve Heaney was at the very centre of that story. To great acclaim he was rightly awarded the Military Cross; none can have been better earned.

Steve Heaney captures the confusion, black humour, raw courage, jargon and sheer exhilaration of combat brilliantly in this compelling and simply written book. In my judgement it is the best account of low-level tactical soldiering since Fred Majdalaney's classic *Patrol*, a World War 2 account of a fighting patrol.

But Sergeant Heaney tells a broader tale that has also rarely been captured so well. What makes an elite unit like the Pathfinders so powerful, so special? One that commanders like me loved to have under them. One that their enemies fervently wished was not opposite them. What sort of people join such a unit? What binds them together so closely that they can stay cohesive under the most stressful of conditions? What training do they go through to reach such heights of professionalism? What is the role of humour in keeping morale high when most would succumb to fear and fatigue? This classic book reveals all this and much more. I commend it to the professional soldier and layman alike.

It was people like Sergeant Heaney MC that I was thinking of when I said at my retirement parade on Horse Guards in London 'if I have seen further than most, it was because I stood on the shoulders of giants'. If you don't know what I mean, read this book and you soon will.

General Sir David Richards GCB CBE DSO

PROLOGUE: MAN HUNT

Ahead of me I saw Steve B come to a silent halt.

He dropped onto one knee, his assault rifle covering the arc of fire to the front of us. I went down into a similar stance, my weapon sweeping the arc of fire from Steve's shoulder through 180 degrees around to the operator at my rear.

He in turn did likewise, covering the arc on the opposite side of the patrol, and so it cascaded down the line, such that all areas to either side of us were being watched by a pair of unblinking eyes and menaced by a weapon's gaping barrel. We were a twelve-man seek-and-destroy patrol, hunting a vicious and bloodthirsty enemy – one that outnumbered us a hundred to one.

And right now we were ready for anything.

After weeks of living in the jungle, our unwashed bodies and unshaven faces made us appear like a band of desperadoes. But grimy, soiled uniforms blend in better with the wild terrain, as do layers of dark stubble and beards. We'd smeared thick lines of camouflage cream onto any exposed skin, to better hide ourselves. The whole effect made us practically invisible, but any sudden movement, or any sound at all from our side risked giving our position away.

When hunting an adversary in the bush and the jungle, you have to presume he is out there somewhere, hunting you or waiting in a hidden ambush position. Visibility is limited by the dense vegetation plus the impenetrable shadows. You can rarely see more than a few dozen yards. It makes spotting your adversary ever more challenging. Plus we were acutely aware that an enemy is at his most dangerous when he is injured, bleeding and badly mauled – which is what we reckoned any number of the rebels were right now.

Steve B placed one hand on his head, while the other grasped the pistol-grip of his weapon. It was the signal for me to move up to his shoulder. He raised two fingers and practically jabbed them into his eyes – the hand signal for 'look where I indicate' – then pointed to our left front. Less than a dozen yards away I could see ranks of razor-sharp points poking out from the bush. They continued onwards for a good thirty yards or so towards the ragged fringe of jungle.

It was one of our fields of punji sticks – sharpened bamboo stakes we'd got the local villagers to cut and shape and plant all around our positions, to ensnare the enemy. For a second I wondered why Steve B had pointed them out to me: there were punji pits all around us, so what was so special about this one? But as I studied those vicious bamboo blades more closely I noticed that many were splattered with a sickly red.

Rebel blood.

It had to be.

Steve B swept his hand north, pointing out the ground to the front of the punji field. The terrain was churned into a mishmash of decaying leaf matter, rotten sticks and dark, loamy soil. I could just imagine panicked feet and hands desperately trying to scrabble their way out of the punji field, rebel minds clouded with pain and agony. But it was the thick, gloopy trails of blood running from there towards the forest that really drew my eye.

That marked the way the rebels had retreated.

The path for us to track and to follow.

A wild animal is never more dangerous than when it is badly hurt. From all we'd seen over the past few weeks, the rebels here were worse than wild animals. Ahead of us danger, red in tooth and claw, lurked behind every tree and in the hidden shadows.

No words needed to be spoken between Steve B and me, the patrol commander. Clearly, our plan had worked a treat. Just as we'd suspected, the rebels had charged forward in human waves to attack us, guns blazing. Instead, they'd stumbled into the punji traps. As they'd fought to drag themselves clear of the vicious fields of sharpened stakes, a good many of them had ripped themselves to pieces.

The amount of blood alone was testament to that.

I gave Steve B the nod to push onwards.

As we set off I signalled to the operator behind me to take a good look at the blood-soaked ground, and to pass it down the line. Moving like a silent, stealthy snake we threaded our way through the bush, until the wall of thick forest was right before us – dark, brooding and hostile.

This was the rebels' domain. The Kingdom of the Bad Guys. This was their country, their backyard, the safe haven from which they launched their brutal sorties.

But this was also very much our kind of territory. We're trained to favour those areas that normal mortals shun. Bug-infested swamps, sun-blasted desert, snow-whipped mountains and impenetrable jungle – those are the areas where we expect to find little human presence, which makes them ideal for operators like us to move through unseen and undetected, into the heart of enemy territory.

Right now, we were well behind the rebels' lines. We were moving into terrain that they'd ruled for a decade or more with an iron grip of fear, brute violence and hatred. But I knew for sure that every man on my patrol – each one an elite warrior highly trained at operating in the jungle – felt quite at home here, and ready.

We were taking the fight to the enemy where they least expected it. We'd smashed them in a long and vicious firefight during the hours of darkness. Now, we were going after them in their supposed sanctuary. We'd hit them at night in the open as they tried to rush our positions, and now we aimed to hit them in the hours of daylight, in the heart of the jungle. This way, we'd keep them on the back foot – the repeated blows sending them reeling.

Or maybe not.

Maybe it had all been a feint and a trap.

Maybe the rebels knew we were coming, and were poised to unleash a scything burst of fire as we stepped into the jungle, wiping out our entire patrol.

Only one way to find out.

Push onwards into the shadows.

Steve B took a step into the eerie and claustrophobic forest interior, practically disappearing from my view as the vegetation sucked him in. I followed, each step chosen so as to avoid any detritus that might break or crack underfoot. The humidity beneath the jungle canopy was thick and it hit me like a wall. I could feel the sweat trickling down my back in rivulets, my clammy uniform sticking to the sores and welts that weeks of not washing had caused to erupt on my skin.

Steve paused for an instant, balanced delicately on the balls of his feet. He had his eyes glued to the sun-dappled jungle floor, tracing the thick, congealed strings of red goo that had been left by the rebel injured. In theory, all we had to do was track the enemy through the trees via their blood trails, and we'd have them.

I gave the hand signal for all to double their watchfulness. My adrenaline was pumping in bucket-loads, my heart pounding like a drum. Badly injured men can only move slowly through such dense terrain, so slowing the movement of the entire body of fighters.

The rebels could only be minutes ahead of us now.

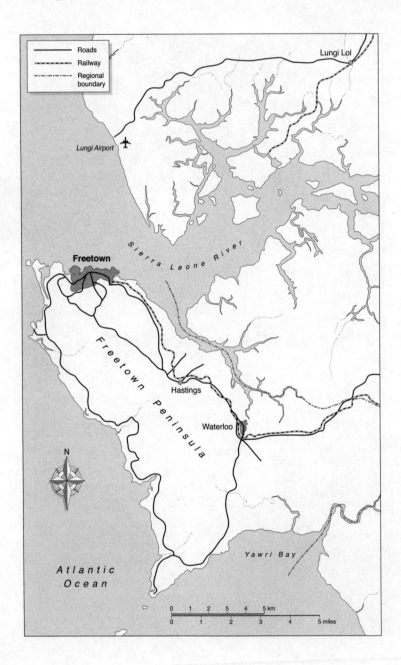

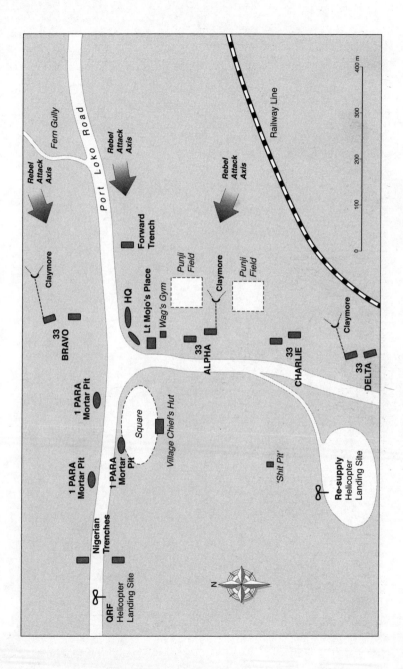

1

The day had begun just like any other. We'd started with our customary early morning run around the perimeter of the base. As usual I'd set the pace, leading from the front.

Each day we'd vary the kit we ran in. One morning it would be shorts, T-shirts and trainers; the next, boots, combat trousers and smocks. Day three we'd be kitted out the same, but carrying a 40-pound Bergen on our backs. Each of the guys had three different rucksacks permanently packed and secured: a desert pack, a jungle pack and one for more temperate climes – mountains, snow and ice.

That way, we were ready for anything.

Always.

We'd mix and match the early morning runs with gym work and sessions in the pool, doing circuit training as a cardiovascular workout and rope-climbs for upper body strength, plus a daily swim to build stamina and endurance.

At thirty-one years of age I was the seasoned platoon sergeant, and each year I led the murderous forced marches and the Endurance stages of Selection. Word was that if you wanted to pass Selection and make it into our tiny, elite unit – the Pathfinders – you needed to stick with Smoggy.

Ever since I can remember, that's been my nickname – Smoggy. I hail from Middlesbrough, a nondescript, grey industrial town in northeast England. A permanent smog seems to hang over the dark landscape, hence the nickname of those born there – 'Smoggies'.

Pathfinder Selection is similar to that undertaken by the SAS

(Special Air Service), only it's shorter – five weeks, as opposed to three months. Many claim that it's more intense, so more punishing. Others say that's bullshit: the shorter duration lowers the attrition rate. I didn't particularly care either way. Pathfinder Selection is Pathfinder Selection: it does what it says on the tin.

It begins with a pre-selection period – days of fierce punishment to weed out the weak and feeble. We'd gather the raw recruits at the Aldershot Training Area and push them through a beasting session similar to the Parachute Regiment's P Company – the fitness and endurance test required to enter the Parachute Regiment. We'd start with an 8-mile run carrying a 55-pound pack, and raise it to a 10-miler – pass time one hour forty minutes maximum. We'd intersperse that with murder runs in full kit – helmet, webbing and weapon.

If you couldn't make it through that first week in Aldershot there was no point going for the real man test – five weeks of hell in the Brecon Beacons, the rain-lashed hills in South Wales where all British elite forces' Selection takes place. Selection proper would start with Walkabout – three days hefting a massive pack across all types of terrain, to test whether individual soldiers knew how to navigate and survive on the hills.

We'd combine the brutal testing with a judicious amount of instruction, as we didn't want blokes getting killed out there – imparting such pearls of wisdom as 'Go low, stay slow; go high, stay dry'. At the end of Walkabout we knew who was capable of going on to the next stages – the Fan Dance, Point-to-Point, Iron Man, Elan Valley – heading out onto the unforgiving terrain alone and for far longer periods of time.

Selection culminates in the killer – Endurance, a 64-kilometre forced march over the highest peaks, under a 55-pound pack (minus food and water) and carrying your weapon.

Endurance has to be completed in under twenty hours.

Needless to say, it has broken many a man.

Both at Aldershot and the Brecons I was the rabbit in all of this.

I set the pace, leading the runs and the tabs. I was hyper-fit and I enjoyed the physical challenge – always have – so it made sense to make me lead man. Hence the saying: *If you want to pass Pathfinder Selection, you need to stick with Smoggy.*

That morning – as with every other 'normal' day at the Pathfinders' Wattisham, Norfolk, base – I'd put a call through to the control tower around 0645 hours. Our base was set in a secure area to one end of an Army Air Corps Apache attack helicopter facility. I'd sought clearance to run the perimeter of the airbase, after which the forty-odd lads of the Pathfinders had gathered for the off.

Oh yeah – plus the one dog.

Ben was a gorgeous chocolate Labrador. I'd had him for a year or so, and every morning he'd join us on the 6.5-mile run. We'd move off as a tight squad – all apart from Ben, who'd be away chasing pheasants and having a ball. For most of the time we wouldn't even see him. Then he'd pop his head out of a patch of bush, give me the look – *You coming, or what?* – and be off again, tracking the scent of a deer.

For the last couple of miles we'd hit open terrain, leaving behind the thick forest and scrub that surrounds the base and heading along the grass fringes of the runway. Ben would complete the last leg by my side every step of the way. First things first, when I got back to base I'd fetch him a bowl of water, then head for the showers.

Together with some of the other old and bold, I'd try to use up all the hot water, so that Grant – Captain Grant Harris, the Second-in-Command of our unit – would be forced to have a cold shower. No matter how many times we did it, it never ceased to amuse us, and Grant – God bless his cotton socks – had the strength of character to see that it was just another ragging from 'the blokes' and to go with it.

The officers who didn't get ragged were the ones we didn't rate.

You only needled the good guys.

But more of that later.

After five months of running the base perimeter Ben was a four-legged hunk of rock-hard muscle and sinew. At times he looked more like a chocolate Rottweiler than a Lab. He'd grown so strong that he'd broken the metal chain that I used to put him on. I'd left him sunning himself one lunchtime, only to get a call from one of the aircrew. They'd found my dog curled up fast asleep in one of the helicopters.

From then on I'd left Ben pretty much free to roam the Pathfinders' part of the base. It was hyper-secure, ringed with razor wire and guards – a fortress within a fortress – so he couldn't get into too much trouble. He'd spend his time lounging with the blokes in the Pathfinders' Interest Room – our clubroom for want of a better analogy – snoozing on top of the grassed-over ammo bunkers, or hanging out with those working on the vehicles in the hangar.

As a unit we were constantly pushing ourselves, but the endless physical training wasn't anything about looking chiselled or Gucci. It was about ensuring we were physically robust enough to take the kind of punishment required of the insertion methods that we specialise in. Get it wrong, and the kind of means we use to get behind enemy lines could seriously injure or even kill you – and that's before you ever put a foot on hostile soil.

During that morning's run I'd been thinking about one particular jump I'd been on recently. We'd paid a visit to China Lake, the vast, one-million-acre Naval Air Weapons Station set amidst the wilderness of America's Western Mojave Desert. With 19,600 square miles of restricted airspace for us to play in, China Lake far surpasses any similar facility in the UK, providing an ace proving ground for the kind of techniques we were pioneering.

We'd been out there working with DEVGRU – America's elite counter-terrorism unit, otherwise known as SEAL Team Six – developing an ultra-high-altitude air-insertion technique, one designed to get a small body of men dropped behind enemy lines in 100 per cent secrecy.

The British military had pretty much pioneered HALO – high altitude low opening – and HAHO – high altitude high opening – parachute jumps. In the former you'd pile out of a Hercules at above 25,000 feet, plummet to earth in freefall and open your chute at around 5000 feet, so getting you fast and direct onto the ground. In HAHO, you'd jump on a static line – your chute opening automatically as you exited the aircraft – then drift for up to seventy kilometres, the idea being that you could 'fly' across an enemy's border and penetrate their airspace undetected.

But those at the helm of Special Forces had decided that a third technique was needed – one that set the 'stealth-level' even higher. This new means and technology had been labelled HAPLSS – the High Altitude Parachutist Life Support System. We were out in China Lake doing what the Pathfinders do best, putting the theory of the concept and the kit to the test of harsh reality.

When jumping at extreme high altitude the air is so thin you have to breathe from an air bottle. But unless the right type of gas is breathed at all the right stages of the jump, you can suffer from Altitude Decompression Sickeness (ADS), more commonly known as 'the bends'. So above 25,000 feet the jump becomes a medical issue as much as a set of physical challenges.

We'd pretty much mastered it for HALO and HAHO, but with HAPLSS we were going even higher and for a very specific set of reasons. Civilian airliners cruise at a much higher altitude, and HAPLSS was a system designed to enable us to jump from that kind of extreme height and survive the devastating cold, G-forces and atmospheric conditions encountered. If we could master all of that, we'd be able to penetrate the airspace of a target country in an aircraft masquerading as a civilian airliner, then jump and drift to earth with no one being any the wiser that we'd ever been there.

In theory we could even pile out of a genuine civvie airliner, leaving unseen from the cargo bay. Or if it was a combat situation, we could catch a lift on a US Air Force B-1B heavy bomber and exit the bomb bay directly after the payload was dropped – so masking our jump as a bombing run. Either would get us onto target totally undetected. But for either means to be workable we had to master jumping from the very roof of the world. That meant taking what the boffins had designed – the space-age HAPLSS survival suit, oxygen mask and protective helmet – and trialling it for real.

With HAPLSS you have to breathe a 'forced air' mixture – so the oxygen is pressurised and pumped into your lungs, as opposed to breathing on demand. You have to start breathing the pure oxygen a good hour before takeoff, to reduce the dangers of getting ADS. The standard British Hercules transport aircraft, the C-130K model, can only depressurise – open the ramp to let you jump – at 25,000 feet or less. At China Lake we'd be jumping at more than 10,000 feet *above* that altitude, and if we tried it in a standard Hercules it would fall apart in midair.

The SEALs were operating the C-130 Juliet (J-model), which had been re-engineered with a completely new set of propellers which would keep turning and providing lift in the thinner air above 25,000 feet. But even the C-130J couldn't go much above 30,000 feet, so the one we were going to be using had been modified to go higher. The only way to trial a HAPLSS jump – at air temperatures of minus 100 degrees Celsius, and in an atmosphere thinner than that on the summit of Mount Everest – was to use an aircraft specifically designed to open its jump ramp at such an altitude.

We'd make all such trial jumps with electrodes and monitors wired up to key points of the body. They'd record stresses on the human frame from G-shocks, how many atmospheres we pulled at exit from the aeroplane, respiratory and heart rate factors, plus the impact of extreme cold on the body as it plummeted through air like ice. In a 'normal' HALO or HAHO jump from 25,000 feet, terminal velocity – the maximum speed at which you freefall – is

320 kph. But the thinner the air the faster you fall. Jumping from 30,000 feet plus, terminal velocity would be considerably faster – around 440 kph.

Even at 320 kph you're plummeting through a thousand feet every five seconds. If you tried to pull your chute at the higher velocity – 440 kph – one of two things would likely happen: either you'd break your back as a result of the impact, or you'd have a canopy explosion. At that velocity, and in such thin air, the chute would come whooshing out of your backpack, and all you'd likely hear would be a massive crack and thump as the individual cells exploded, tearing your canopy to shreds. You'd be left plummeting to earth at a deadly rate of knots, with shards of torn silk flapping uselessly in the air above you.

We knew this because we'd trialled HAPLSS using a dummy – a latex model of your average bloke, laden down with metal weights to around 15 stone, and dressed in the gear you'd normally jump with (a 55-pound Bergen, plus weapons and ammo). From the dummy trials we knew that if you pulled your chute at anything above 25,000 feet, you had little chance of making it down alive – hence the default mode with HAPLSS being to freefall a good 20,000 feet prior to releasing your chute.

There was one problem with that. If you jumped and the turbulence put you into a 'spin', very quickly you'd be in danger of 'blacking out' – so losing consciousness. Ideally, you'd plummet through the turbulence of the aircraft's wake and stabilise yourself, getting into a star shape – arms and legs outstretched – for the freefall. But if you failed to achieve that and went into a violent spin you'd have just seconds in which to save yourself – and the last-ditch option is always to pull your chute before you black out.

You might have to do that at any height after the jump, so we needed to trial doing an 'unstable exit' – something that would put the jumper into a deadly spin, and possibly force him to pull his chute. We didn't even know if an operator could get out of a spin while wearing all the cumbersome HAPLSS gear ... but we still had to try.

Prior to heading for China Lake I'd gone through the necessary medical trials at the JATE – the innocuously-named Joint Air Transport Establishment; the body that oversees such high-end, James-Bond-type military air techniques – to ensure that I was physically fit and robust enough to go ahead with the trials. Hence why running the base perimeter every morning was so necessary.

The JATE is based at RAF Brize Norton. My medical trials passed, I'd got the brief on what exactly the JATE boffins wanted from me out at China Lake. They were asking me to go higher than any British military parachutist had ever gone before – so jumping from well above 30,000 feet – but that wasn't the half of it.

'Steve, we want you to do the jump, make an unstable exit and hold it for twenty seconds,' they told me. 'Then we want you to try to get out of it and we'll track whatever problems you incur.'

They made it sound so easy.

What they really meant was this: Steve, pile out of the aircraft, go into a spin, allow the spin to escalate for a good twenty seconds – or 5000 feet – of freefall, then try to save yourself. It went without saying that I'd be close to blacking out by then, so the last-resort option would be to pull the chute, with every likelihood of it exploding. But hey, the only way to perfect such techniques was to trial them, and eventually you had to switch from a dummy to a real person – i.e. muggins me.

In a way it was fair enough. As the long-serving Pathfinder Platoon sergeant I was one of the most practised military freefall parachutists in the British Army. Airborne insertion is the bread and butter of what we do: we train for it more exhaustively than any other unit in the armed forces. I had over 1200 jumps under my belt, plus I was one of only a handful of military freefall tandem masters – meaning I could freefall with another human being strapped to my person, or a piece of high-tech weaponry, or a specially-designed canister packed with 1000 pounds of ammo.

Arguably, there was no one better qualified to trial HAPLSS over China Lake.

So it was that the modified C-130J had droned up into the hot and thin air high above the wildlands of the Mojave Desert. As we neared the predetermined altitude I started to make ready. There was only one way to ensure I did what was required of me – I had to achieve an immediate 'unstable exit'. Normally you'd leap off the ramp front first, in what amounted to a long dive, arms and legs outstretched to anchor yourself in the air. By shifting an arm or a leg – drawing it closer to, or moving it further away from, your body – you could slow down or accelerate, and steer your fall.

This time, I was going to plummet from the heavens curled up into a tight ball – getting into a streamlined water-droplet or bullet shape.

The SEALs had zero idea of what would happen if a jumper was forced to pull his chute above 25,000 feet, in a desperate attempt to escape the spin. They made it clear they thought it was pretty messed-up to try, though they appreciated that we needed to know. They were pretty used to how the Brits operated by now: we had all the human potential, guts and expertise, if little of their kit or their airframes. Hence a Brit was today's fall guy, and the Yanks were providing the jump platform and the space and freedom of China Lake in which to push the limits of the known and the possible.

As I hunched on the edge of the ramp in the foetal position, the wind gusting and buffeting me like a giant tennis ball in a wind tunnel, I reflected upon how I really wasn't getting paid enough for this kind of shit. Being a Pathfinder, I didn't even get the extra £45 a week pay uplift that the UK Special Forces got. The Pathfinders don't sit within the UKSF family. We were formed as a completely black, off-the-books outfit, one that officially didn't exist. We had no budget, no personnel – every man officially remained with his parent unit – plus no kit, weaponry or ammo other than what we could beg, borrow or steal from other units.

Hence the unofficial name given to us: the X Platoon.

I couldn't see anything much while hunched into a tight ball, but I knew the red 'prepare-to-jump' light must have flickered on, for the two Parachute Jumping Instructors (PJIs) had grabbed hold of me. The PJIs are dedicated specialists whose only role in life is to oversee military parachute jumps. Right now I was going out blind, and these guys held my life in their hands.

The light must have flicked from red to green, for over the deafening roar of the slipstream I heard the voice of the lead PJI guy yelling: 'Go! Go! Go!'

I scrunched tighter into a ball, as I felt the PJIs manhandle me forwards and roll me out into thin air. For an instant I plummeted, then I felt myself sucked into the maw of the slipstream, the violent turbulence throwing me over and over and over.

Spat out of the aircraft's wake, I began to fall vertically towards earth, twisting around and around like some crazy, messed-up, man-sized spinning top. I was counting out the seconds in my head, but in the back of my mind a voice was already muttering my prayers.

'One-thousand-and-three, one-thousand-and-four, one-thousand-and-five ... God get me out of this shit alive ...'

I counted off the seconds and prayed for some kind of deliverance, as I tumbled through the thin, freezing blue.

The only means I had of assessing how fast I was spinning was by trying to monitor how rapidly the air around me turned from blue to yellow to blue to yellow to blue again. Blue meant I was facing the sky, yellow meant the Mojave Desert, and so on and so forth.

Had I been able to pause for the barest instant I'd have seen the clear curvature of the earth below me, but right now I was struggling to remain conscious, let alone having a spare moment to admire the view.

Being scrunched into a tight ball I was massively aerodynamic, which lowers drag and increases terminal velocity still further. I just kept accelerating and spinning faster and faster and faster, my air speed and the G-forces growing with it, the wind howling and tearing at my head like a raging hurricane.

Imagine going at one hundred kilometres an hour on a motorcycle. If you've ever done it, you'll know just how intensely the wind rips into your face and your torso, as the pressure tries to slam you out of the saddle. Now imagine going at over *four times* that speed, without even the benefit of a full-face helmet, or a set of handlebars and a seat to keep a grip on. Imagine doing so in minus 100 degrees air temperature, and with the following strapped to your person: a bulging parachute pack, a massive Bergen, your webbing stuffed with ammo and grenades, a pistol strapped to your thigh, plus your main weapon – your assault rifle – slung over your shoulder. Now imagine all of that when you're spinning crazily like a top, without the faintest clue which way up you are . . .

Sickening, right?

I was ten seconds into the freefall and the spin just kept getting worse. I could feel myself gasping for breath, as my burning lungs struggled to drag in enough gas from the bottle. My sensory awareness – my ability to judge where I was exactly, which way up I was, or who I was even – was slipping away from me.

Blue-yellow-blue-yellow-blue-yellow-blueyellow-blueyellow-blueyellow-blueeeeellooooow . . .

Argghhhhh!

The air pressure was tearing at the oxygen bottle fixed to my front, plus it was trying to rip away the heavy Bergen strapped across my lower body. I could feel my weapon slamming around in the air at my side, the butt like a baseball bat cracking blows into my helmeted head. I was on the verge of vomiting. The pressure on my heart and lungs was unbearable, and I was seconds away from losing consciousness.

At which stage I'd be dead.

With my pulse juddering inside my skull and my mind reeling horribly from dizziness and disorientation, I tried to focus on the count.

'One-thousand-and-fifteen, one-thousand-and-sixteen, one-thousand-and- ...'

Three seconds to go and I had to try to break free and get into a stable freefall position, face to earth. I counted out the last seconds. Snap! I thrust my arms and legs into a rigid star shape, arching my back against the unbearable forces that were threatening to tear me limb from limb. I strained my muscles against the pain and the pressure, letting out a cry of agony at the top of my voice – one that I knew no one would ever hear, for I was alone on the roof of the world here.

My limbs were thrust out rigid to make four air-anchors, as I tried to grab at the thin atmosphere and slow my seemingly unstoppable whirlwind of a fall. Gradually I sensed the revolutions decrease, as the air howled all around me and my body screamed in pain. But I still didn't know which way up I'd eventually come to a halt – facing the sky or facing the earth.

Finally I stopped spinning.

I forced my frazzled mind to concentrate.

I was facing blue.

Blue meant the sky.

Wrong way round.

I was plummeting at a murderous speed with my back to the earth. If I pulled my chute in the position I was in now it would open below me and I'd fall through it. It would bag around me, doing a fine impression of a sack of damp washing, and I'd plummet to earth like a corpse entombed in a shroud of tangled parachute silk.

Not good.

I brought my right arm in close to my side and threw my opposite shoulder over, trying to flip myself so I'd end up facing yellow. *Yellow = earth.* But for some reason it just wasn't working. All it achieved was the very opposite of what I wanted – to send me back into the spin again.

For a moment I was on the verge of panic. My hand reached involuntarily for the release cord of the chute. I forced myself to stop. I forced myself to remember how we'd trialled this repeatedly with the dummy, and every single time the chute had ripped itself to shreds.

Don't pull the chute.

Pull the chute and you're dead.

There was one more thing I could try. My last option before blacking out was to do what I did now. I dragged in both arms tight by my sides, rammed my legs out straight behind me and got my back locked and arched. I was now in the Delta Track position, which should bring me into a head-down dive.

Like this I hoped to remain conscious long enough for the thickening atmosphere to slow me down to the point where pulling my chute – and survival – was a real possibility.

That at least was the plan.

2

I was three minutes into the freefall when I finally risked pulling the chute. I was at 3500 feet and I'd just completed a mega death-ride to earth. It was the Delta Track that had done the trick, getting me into a stable enough position to flick out into the star shape again, and ready myself to send 360 square feet of the finest silk billowing out above me.

It takes six seconds for the chute to deploy fully, so in reality I was at 2500 feet by the time I broke my fall, drifting silently beneath the canopy over the hot Mojave Desert. The other way to look at it was like this: I'd deployed the chute when I was a bare fifteen seconds away from ploughing into the earth at plus-320 kph. At that speed there wouldn't have been a great deal of me to scrape up amongst the cacti and the tumbleweed, so my parents – and Ben my dog – could bury what was left of me.

Still, at least now we knew.

We knew what happened when you flipped into a death spin at well above 30,000 feet while doing a HAPLSS jump.

Once I was 'safely' down I gathered up my chute and the pick-up wagon trundled over to collect me. I was driven to one of China Lake's 2000-odd hangars, halls, laboratories and other assorted buildings. There the boffins unplugged the wires, and sensors and data-recorders, to check on all the readings made during the jump.

It turned out that I'd pulled more G-forces than a top-gun fighter pilot does when putting a state-of-the-art F-15 Eagle fighter jet through its paces – and I hadn't had the luxury of a glass-and-steel airframe wrapped around me to shield me from the bitter ice and turbulence, plus the punishing air pressure and the wind speed.

Still, that was what being a Pathfinder was all about.

It went with the territory.

The day after the jump of death I felt as if I'd been in a boxing bout with Godzilla – only it had been held in a giant washing machine set to maximum spin. You only get out of shit like that when you are at the absolute peak of physical condition, hence the runs around the Wattisham airbase, plus all the other daily workouts and the intense training.

I upped the pace as we hit the final leg of that morning's run, thanking the gods or the fates or whoever for getting me through China Lake in one piece. We surged as a pack through the lines of the Army Air Corps, Ben out front, his fur sleek and glistening, his fine muzzle leading the way. This early morning ritual was known as 'running the fence', and the Apache gunship pilots had long grown used to the Pathfinder Express Train steaming through.

Of the forty men on that morning's run, twelve were at Ready Status One (R1) – which meant they were able to deploy instantly on missions anywhere in the world. Another dozen were on R2, meaning they could deploy anywhere within twenty-four hours. The rest were on R3, which meant deployment within thirty-six. On R3 you could be on a training course or on leave, as long as you could get back to the base and be good to go within thirty-six hours.

After a steaming hot shower I came into the ops room to find Graham 'Wag' Wardle, our Ops Warrant Officer, glued to the phone. From the few words that I caught of the conversation I knew that something was up. Wag and me understood each other instinctively and were the best of mates, in spite of him forever needling me about having the world's biggest ears, and me going on about him having been hit real hard with the Ugly Stick.

Wag was short and stumpy with the body of a Hobbit. He hailed from Burnley, and spoke with a thick Lancashire accent. He was shaven-headed and a walking advertisement for the world's dodgiest tattoos: there wasn't one that wasn't misspelled, off-colour or misaligned. In short he looked and sounded like a football hooligan in uniform.

To make matters worse he wasn't the biggest fan of military freefall, which was the bread and butter of our business. I used to joke that Wag had been born with four left arms. What redeemed him was that he was a total stalwart. The Pathfinders was his life. Wag was hard, robust and fit, but his real gift lay in his powers of dynamic lateral thinking. In thinking the unthinkable Wag pretty much had no equal.

At thirty-seven years of age, he was also the 'old man' of the unit. I used to joke that I'd put myself through the Military Tandem Master's course purely so I could HALO Wag in on a mission, for he was never going to make a high-altitude low-opening jump on his own. That summed up the fierce, piss-taking rivalry between us, and under our guidance the X Platoon had thrived.

As Wag came off the phone I called over to him. 'Before you get started, mate, quick question.'

'Yeah, what?'

'How did you get to be so ugly with just the one head?'

'Fuck off, go play with Noddy, Big Ears . . .'

To the rear sat Captain Grant Harris, our 2iC, and by now his shoulders were rocking with laughter. I'd made Grant sit behind me, because in contrast to Wag he was the pin-up of the unit. A youthful twenty-six, Grant was blessed with classic dark good looks and he had the gorgeous girlfriend to go with it. I hated him for it, though only in jest. Still, Wag and me were forever ribbing Grant and hitting him with the wind-ups.

The slagging stopped just as soon as Wag gave us a heads-up on the phone call he'd just had. 1 PARA had been warned off for immediate deployment to some obscure African nation none of us had ever heard of before – *Sierra Leone*. Their mission was to make a last-ditch effort to evacuate British citizens from the nation's capital, which was under threat from a bunch of rebels threatening wholesale murder and mayhem.

None of us knew the slightest thing about where or what the country was exactly, except the obvious – that this was the dark, chaotic, war-torn heart of Africa. But the best news of all was this: 1 PARA's CO had asked for as many Pathfinders as we could spare to deploy on the mission.

When I'd started that morning's run I'd had not the slightest inkling that this might be in the offing. I hadn't even known we had a spot of trouble brewing in one of the ex-colonies. But needless to say this was a very pleasant surprise. It was a golden opportunity for the Pathfinders to get some operational action in a far-flung, war-blasted, benighted corner of the world.

Top news.

Eddie 'The White Rabbit' Newell, the Platoon's Colour Sergeant, joined us in the office. Like me and Wag, The White Rabbit was a long-serving member of the unit. His role as Colour Sergeant made him a glorified stores man, but it was a necessary stepping-stone to him getting Ops Warrant Officer, once Wag moved on. With his pale, spooky, almost albino look there was no guessing how Eddie had earned the nickname; his hair was as white as snow, and his skin looked as if it never got to see any sunlight.

The White Rabbit measured five-foot-ten, weighed 15 stone and worked out in the gym a lot, but he was known as something of a tortoise-like plodder on the runs. He was no speed athlete or racing snake, yet you'd be sure of Eddie always getting there in the end. He was the third unshakeable pillar of our outfit – one of a three-cornered pyramid formed by Wag, Eddie and me.

Along with Eddie, Captain Robert Donaldson, the Officer Commanding (OC) of our unit, pitched up. They were like beauty and the beast. Tall, suave, with swept-back blond hair, Donaldson had been OC Pathfinders for the past several months, and he was approaching the halfway point in his two-year posting.

From the very first Donaldson had reminded me of Prince Charming from the movie *Shrek*. Needless to say, he and I couldn't fail to rub each other up the wrong way. Early on I'd been sent away to do a two-month Arctic survival cadre with the Swedish Special Forces, plus some other elite units. By the time I'd returned Wag had confirmed my worst fears: the verdict of the men was that Donaldson was struggling to make the grade as the Pathfinders' OC.

A quiet tension simmered just below the surface whenever we were in the same room. But right now we put our differences to one side, for we had some urgent number crunching to do on the Sierra Leone mission. The twelve men on R1 couldn't deploy. They were on standby for emergencies that constituted a direct threat to the UK. Barring those who were sick or on training, that left twenty-seven Pathfinders ready and able to go.

I headed down to the Interest Room to brief the blokes. The moment the warning went out that we were about to deploy, we'd cut all communications with the outside world. We'd go into strict isolation, with no calls or emails allowed to wives, girlfriends or family. That morning fathers had kissed their kids goodbye and gone into work expecting it to be just another day. Now all of that was about to change. This could be the start of a six-month deployment – for that's what you signed up for when you joined the Pathfinders.

I started the briefing by outlining what we knew about the mission, which was pretty much bugger all. Then I dropped the bombshell – those who were and weren't going.

'R1 guys, you know who you are – you're staying. The rest of you fit and able blokes not on R1 – *get ready.*' I read out the list of names.

The sheer elation on the faces of the chosen was a picture. By contrast, those slated to be left behind instantly started trying to jockey for a position. I silenced the lot of them with a wave of the hand. Plenty of time for that after the briefing was over.

'Right, patrol commanders,' I continued. 'Get away and get some background on Sierra Leone. Get a bloke up to the Maps Room. Do we have 1:25,000 or 1:50,000 scale, or air maps only? You'll need another guy on the local flora and fauna, plus any climatic conditions that'll dictate what kit we take. Medics – I need to know about disease types, prophylactics, malaria, and if we have the right drugs to hand . . .'

The Pathfinder medics had all attended the Patrols Medics cadre – four weeks of intensive training on how to deal with gunshot and shrapnel wounds, plus whatever else might hit us in the types of terrain in which we operate. After that, they'd completed a six-week attachment in an Accident and Emergency unit at a hospital in the UK – dealing with cuts, lacerations, burns, breaks and the like. Finally, they'd done a stint at the Army Dental Corps, learning emergency dental work – chiefly how to use Cavit, a temporary, press-in filling that hardens in the mouth.

At our Wattisham base we had a fully-fledged medical store, complete with a safe stuffed full of morphine, so we could deploy with that to kill the pain of injuries. But with Sierra Leone being cloaked in dense, steamy jungle, it was sure to offer a plethora of venomous snakes, blood-sucking bugs and nasty tropical diseases that we needed to be ready for. No point deploying to war if we all went down with cerebral malaria the moment we set foot on the ground.

If a 1 PARA guy suffered a snakebite in the field, more often than not it could be treated at his headquarters. By contrast, we'd very likely be deployed deep in the jungle where there are no such luxuries. We had to be 100 per cent self-sufficient – hence the high level of medical training, and the kind of kit we had to carry on missions. While on operations we had to presume we could only treat ourselves with what we carried on our persons.

We'd also need water purification kits, to cope with extended periods spent drinking from rivers. We'd need water purification kits such as Millbank bags, plus machetes and mosquito nets. The signallers would need to work out the right radio antennae for use under the deep-jungle canopy, likely battery life in such conditions, and how to keep such delicate kit dry and workable.

The list went on and on.

I finished my briefing with this. 'Right, we basically know bugger all about this deployment. I want blokes running down every rabbit hole exploring every possibility, so we have all kit possible good to go ... Everything else stops. Get on it and get it done.'

I had barely finished speaking when the first dissenter grabbed me. It was Roger Holt, a cracking soldier who'd taken an injury during a recent stint of training, which meant he was off the list to deploy.

'Mate, get me on it,' he begged. 'I don't care if I'm injured – with morphine and a bandage I'll muddle through.'

Our unit is a meritocracy. Those who lead do so by dint of their experience, skills and ability, regardless of rank. Everything's done on first name terms, and it's the lack of formality and Regular Army bullshit that draws a particular kind of soldier to the Pathfinders. There is no better foundation on which to build an unbreakable *esprit de corps*.

I told Holty I appreciated his fighting spirit, but he was too badly injured and he'd have to sit this one out. He gave me a look like he'd just been given a death sentence. I knew how he was feeling: a mission such as this one came along seldom, if ever, in most soldiers' lifetimes.

As blokes bolted from the room, I caught the expressions on their faces. Those who were single were buzzing. This was the chance for what they craved most – *operational action*. But for the married guys it was all just starting to sink in. It was a Friday, and God only knew what they'd got planned for the weekend. Instead, they were about to disappear with barely a word to their families. Needless to say, being a Pathfinder wasn't a recipe for a long and happy marriage.

The chirpiest bloke seemed to be H. Lance Corporal Joe 'H' Harrison – also known as 'Tackleberry', a gun-toting, shit-kicking redneck in the *Police Academy* movie series – was young, free and single. He was already counting the beer tokens, for we'd be spending nothing while out in deepest, darkest Africa. Or maybe H was dreaming about what new guns he could buy with all the money he'd save up while we were away.

H was five-foot-eleven and had a rock-hard physique, topped off with the Freddie Mercury shaven-headed droopy-moustache look. Most of the time he'd wander around base wearing nothing but a pair of shorts and a couple of belts of shotgun ammo wrapped around his person. He only seemed to own one set of 'going out' clothes – a pair of battered jeans, plus a faded green bomber jacket. Where others might buy a new set of threads, H would invest in a new gun magazine, and his room was stacked high with them.

Like many of the vagabond collection of misfits that made up our unit, H had a wicked sense of humour. Hailing from Doncaster, he spoke with a thick Yorkshire drawl. He spunked all his money on guns, gun mags and real ale, and normally he couldn't afford to drink beyond happy hour. This deployment might change all of that – at least for the few short days immediately after he got back from the mission.

H was also a superlative operator. He was a L96 AW sniper rifle guru, and the most accomplished shot in the unit. He was fit, hard and totally reliable, plus he was a demon with the general purpose machine gun (GPMG). When operating the GPMG, H was known as the 'Death Dealer'. If it all went tits-up he was the bloke you wanted by your side.

H was thick as thieves with Corporal Nathan 'Nathe' Bell, his patrol commander. Nathe was a short, stocky turnip farmer from Lincolnshire. He'd had his front teeth knocked out while playing rugby, and he wore false ones, which added a slight lisp to his slow, country bumpkin 'aarg-aarg-aarg' accent. Nathe had a boyish, prankster sense of humour. His party trick was to drop his false teeth into your glass when you weren't looking, so when you drained your pint all was revealed.

Nasty.

Nathe and H were like Laurel and Hardy. They permanently ripped the piss out of each other, but they were actually the best of mates. As two blokes heading up a Pathfinder patrol they were about as good as it gets – though it hadn't always been that way.

As a young lad on selection Nathe had missed the final check-point on Endurance, due to horrendous weather conditions. Being unable to pinpoint his location, we'd launched the safety proce-dure, which included calling out the mountain rescue team. The 'lost procedure' for those on Endurance was to head for the A470 Brecon to Merthyr Tydfil road, and tab towards the nearest check-point. En route Nathe had managed to find a friendly local farmer, who'd allowed him to make a call to alert us to his location.

Finally, we'd found him sitting by a roaring fire in the farmer's cottage, tucking into a bowl of his wife's finest home-made soup. From such memorable beginnings Nathe had risen to his position of patrol command admirably, becoming a superlative operator, and with H as his right-hand man he ran a tight, unshakeable unit.

The Pathfinders' numeric call-sign is *33* – so as HQ patrol, Wag, The White Rabbit, Grant and me were *33*. Nathe and H's patrol was *33 Alpha* – so the lead patrol – with the others being *33 Bravo*, *33 Charlie* and so on. Whatever shit we might be heading into in Sierra Leone, I'd put *33 Alpha* at our point of greatest vulner-ability, for I had absolute confidence in them. H was extremely capable and I knew he could take over patrol command if any-thing happened to Nathe.

In preparation for the coming mission Grant, Wag and me broke down the blokes into four fighting patrols – with a patrol commander, a sniper, a demolitions expert and a lead scout, plus a medic and a signaller in each. That done we tried to garner some bigger picture ground truth. First off, we needed to know where the hell Sierra Leone was and what was the best weaponry to take, and whether we'd be able to use the vehicles.

Our *raison d'être* being behind enemy lines ops, that was how we had to figure Command would use us in Sierra Leone – *that's if we got used*. We needed to know the type of terrain over which we'd be operating, and the possible means of insertion. Would we be going in by helicopter, or on foot, or by HALO or HAHO means? It wouldn't be via HAPLSS, that was for sure, for we'd yet to perfect HAPLSS for use on operations.

Right now this was an 'Operation Blind' – we were preparing to deploy with next to zero Intel, and little sense of who the enemy might be, or their number or capabilities. All we knew was that it was a non-combatant evacuation operation (an NEO) and from that alone the five of us – me, Wag, Grant, The White Rabbit and the OC – tried to work up potential scenarios.

We might be inserted into the jungle to overlook named areas of interest (NAIs); in other words, positions from which rebel attacks might be expected. We might be sent forward as an early warning force, to watch for a rebel advance. With British and allied nationals needing to be evacuated from the capital, we had to presume the rebels were poised to seize it, so we might well be tasked to call in air power or artillery, raining down death on the bad guys.

Having scoped out our likely tasks, we figured we'd need specialist observation post (OP) kit – like SOFIE thermal imaging sights, night vision goggles and GPS units, plus infrared fireflies and TACBE emergency comms beacons in case we were forced to go on the run through the jungle. The list of goodies being drawn up by The White Rabbit just kept getting longer, as we tried to think of every potential piece of kit we needed to unearth from the stores.

The Pathfinders' armourer, Pete Brewster, was busy racking up a growing pile of the kind of hardware we might need when fighting in thick tropical bush. Trouble was, he had bugger all Intel to go on. Did the rebels have armour? If so, did we need LAW 80s – our 94 mm shoulder-launched light anti-armour weapons? Did the rebels have heavy machine guns? If so, we'd need the wagons with their vehicle-mounted .50 calibre Brownings to answer their firepower.

Ideally the 50-cal isn't used against human targets. The GPMG is the weapon of choice against advancing troops – used properly, it rakes down their number. The 50-cal has a slower, thumping rate of fire, and we'd normally use it with armour-piercing explosive incendiary rounds – perfect against soft-skinned or light armoured vehicles, optics or radio antennae, thermal imaging kit, satellite dishes, brick buildings and command and control nodes, and out to 1800 metres range.

It was midday when we got the call to deploy via road to the Air Mounting Centre (AMC), at South Cerney, near Cirencester – the muster point for all British military operations going out by air. There we presumed we'd get issued with our ammo and food rations, plus extra mission-essential kit prior to departure.

Heading to the AMC didn't mean that the mission was totally a 'go'. We could still get stood down. It was never actually happening until you dived out of the aircraft over the drop zone, or drove over the border into hostile terrain.

But this sure took us one big step closer to going in.

3

The modern day Pathfinders was formed in the mid-1980s to perform a role that was seen as lacking in the British Army: covert insertion deep behind enemy lines to recce drop zones and guide in the main force, and for capture, sabotage or direct-action missions. While the SAS and SBS (Special Boat Service) are trained for such tasks, their remit is multifaceted: they have to be ready to perform sneaky-beaky espionage, hostage rescue and anti-terrorist and anti-insurgent missions, plus a host of other taskings.

A guy in the SAS's Air Troop – their airborne ops specialists – has to master all disciplines required of him, which means he has limited time to train for airborne missions. Our role being purely behind enemy lines ops, we'd be doing six HALO jumps to his one, and that simple fact makes us unbeatable at what we do.

In part due to its 'black' nature, the Pathfinders has a more fluid, opaque kind of identity than Special Forces, but with that comes real downsides. Black status means no official budget. Typically, the MOD want an elite asset without having to pay for it. That means we have to fight tooth and nail for any specialist kit, training or weaponry that we need. We don't always get it – just as the Sierra Leone mission was about to prove.

Recently, we'd taken to signing off our comms with the piss-taking acronym: PF PL SFOW PMSAS. It stands for 'Pathfinder Platoon; Special Forces Or What; Poor Man's Special Air Service'. I'd done so once with a brigadier. He'd come to pay us a visit at our Wattisham base, riding his flame-red Ducati and dressed in a full set of leathers.

I'd greeted him with this: 'Sir, welcome to PF PL SFOW PMSAS.'

'Erm . . . sorry?' he'd said, shaking his head in bemusement.

I'd spelled it out for him and he'd taken it in pretty good humour.

As with all our operations, we'd deploy to Sierra Leone wearing no unit flashes or marks of rank, or anything that might identify us as an elite British military outfit. We'd sanitise ourselves still further, removing anything that might give away who we were, or what country we hailed from: photos of family, wallets, clothing brand labels, ID documents of any sort – all of it would have to go, just in case any of us got captured or killed by the enemy.

Our unit had only recently returned from a lengthy deployment to Kosovo. Tony Blair was in power, and he'd made no secret of his desire to wage 'righteous wars', as he saw them. In due course Sierra Leone would become known as 'Blair's War' – and we were about to head to Africa with no clearance to do so other than a private nod from the British prime minister.

The commanding officer of 1 PARA, Colonel Paul 'Gibbo' Gibson, had led the Kosovo mission, winning the DSO for it. He'd made a ballsy move now by launching the deployment to Sierra Leone – getting an entire British battle group, Pathfinders included, under way pretty much on the fly. He'd as good as told us he had no clear authority to move to the Air Mounting Centre, but we were going anyway, 'cause it got us one step closer to going in.

'Let's just do it,' Gibbo had told us. 'Let's just go. Get yourselves down there, Pathfinders.'

I'd barely had time to say goodbye to Ben before we swung out of our Wattisham base and hit the road. Heaping his bowl with dog-biscuits, I'd promised him I'd be back home as soon as, and in truth I'd have loved to be taking him with us. There would have been nothing better than my rock-hard chocolate Lab to give the rebels a good bite on the arse – though I had a sneaking suspicion Ben was more of a lover than a fighter kind of a dog.

Scores of military vehicles were now en route to the AMC – our open-topped Land Rovers and Pinzgauer all-wheel-drive vehicles amongst them – without anyone knowing we were on our way. Normally, some 800 men at arms undertaking a road move to deploy requires clearance from HQ Land. It requires an escort of Military Police, for live ammo is in transit, and it needs rakes of formal permissions. Colonel Gibson had had to work around all of that. Recognising that hundreds of British citizens were on the verge of getting chopped to pieces or kidnapped, he'd found the means to get the mission under way.

It was typical Gibbo: decisive action in a very unclear and fast-moving situation.

Gibbo had his priorities dead right.

Taking the bull by the horns.

Respect.

The colonel was tall, skinny and gaunt, with the physique of a long-distance runner. I'd served under him in Kosovo, and at first I hadn't warmed to him much. But with time Gibbo had proved that he knew how to play the game, and Kosovo had ended up being very good for all of us. The 1 PARA battle group had acquitted itself well, and I'd developed a grudging respect for the man. He could make gutsy, timely decisions; he was not a ditherer. His calls might be right or wrong, but either way they were timely – which was about all you could ask of a senior commander. Right now he was riding the crest of a wave, and with the Sierra Leone op we were going to have to ride it with him.

It was dusk by the time we reached South Cerney and we had to bluff our way onto the base. Normally the guard at the main gate would be told what was on its way. But right now a massive military convoy had turned up from out of the blue, and the poor corporal had not the faintest idea of what was happening. We sat in this humongous queue that snaked along a leafy country lane, as the guy tried to make up his mind whether to let us in or not.

He stood in front of the barrier with one-hundred-plus vehicles ranged before him, pumping out the diesel fumes. By now it was getting dark, and the headlights wound into the distance as far as the eye could see. Gibbo fixed the hapless bloke with a gimlet eye. The corporal quailed under the colonel's stare, eyes flicking nervously to his clipboard – like somehow he'd missed the fact that an entire battle group was scheduled to come through his gate that very evening.

'Son, open the barrier.'

No one was about to naysay Gibbo. The convoy was let through.

South Cerney is only fully staffed when there's an official airmove under way. Right now it was like a ghost town: there was no one to organise the chaos. The 1 PARA convoy got itself seriously gridlocked on the tarmac that lies between the main hangar and the runway. That done, Gibbo got the 1 PARA lads into the massive hangar and lined up by company: B, C and D in three rows, the blokes' kit piled beside them. The poor lads from A Company were on exercises in Jamaica, so they were missing out on this mission.

On the far side was the so-called 'black hangar' where we would normally gather in isolation, along with any other elite units that might be mustering. But right now the black hangar was locked, so we parked up on the approach road and kipped down beside the vehicles. I was hoping for a proper briefing on the coming deployment, but it turned out that the British military had no one on the ground in Sierra Leone. The Pathfinders were likely to be first-in, and consequently there wasn't much that anyone could tell us.

It's the Pathfinders' role to get in on the ground early and establish an intelligence picture – that way you risk sending in a few good men, as opposed to an entire battalion. Even so, it would have been nice to know the basics – the size of the rebel force we were up against, their level of training and operational capability, their weaponry, and their positions in relation to the nation's capital.

Unfortunately, no one seemed to know a thing.

HMG had been caught with her proverbial pants down.

In fact, the entire force now preparing to deploy had no maps of any sort – apart from the few that we had managed to grab from our Maps Room. There were no photos of the rebels or their bases, there was no aerial or satellite surveillance, and little info on the enemy's make-up or likely modus operandi. Worse still, no one had any food rations *or even any ammo*, because no formal orders had been given to issue any.

Each of us had packed a 'follow-on' bag, one that contained goodies to leave at a forward operating base: books, PT kit, iPods, snacks and so on. We broke out whatever scoff we had in those and got a brew going on our foldable 'hexy' stoves – ones that burn solid hexamine fuel blocks similar to firelighters. But there was sod all we could do about the lack of ammo.

No bullets with which to go to war.

It was a typical Army SNAFU – Situation Normal All Fucked Up.

Captain Donaldson, our OC, was in and out of conference with Colonel Gibson. Predictably, the mission was 'on', 'off', 'on', 'off' all night long. The rest of us got our heads down as best we could. It was the golden rule of good soldiering – always grab the chance of a feed or a sleep.

At around dawn The White Rabbit shook everyone awake, telling us there was a scoff-on in the cookhouse. From somewhere the South Cerney boys had managed to rustle up some food and someone to cook it. The queue circled several times around the cookhouse, and we were two hours waiting in line. It was like being on a conveyor belt: fifteen minutes to get as big a plate of fried bread and eggs swimming in grease down you as possible, before you were spat out the door so some hairy-arsed PARA could take your seat.

Shortly after loading up on the grease and the carbs we were given the news we'd all been waiting for: our lot would be on the first flight to Sierra Leone. We were to go in 'light order' – personal weapons, belt kit and Bergens, and no vehicles. And still we hadn't been issued with any ammo. We joked that maybe it was a good thing. Our main weapon was the SA80, a universally reviled assault rifle of sorts. When loaded, it could pose as much danger to the user as to the enemy.

The SA80 suffered from any number of horrendous faults. Worst of all was the habit the magazine had of falling off. The SA80-A1 had the magazine release button set just above the magazine housing. Because of the location and the fact that it was raised a good inch, all you had to do was go into a tight fire position and the release button would get accidentally hit, at which moment the magazine would fall to the ground, spewing out the rounds.

We joked that this was why we hadn't been issued with any ammo for Sierra Leone – so we couldn't go wasting it. But in truth, being lumbered with the SA80 wasn't very funny.

It was unbelievably prone to rust, especially around the moving parts that force the rounds into the breech. If the air was moisture-laden – if there was fog or mist even – those parts would rust up before your very eyes. Not good when we were about to deploy to a jungle with one of the highest annual rainfalls on earth. With the two main rivals – the M16 and the AK47 – if any dirt or rust got into them it would rarely prevent the internal parts from working. With the SA80 one speck would jam it every time.

As if that wasn't enough the SA80 had a safety catch that wasn't fit for purpose: it kept getting knocked one way or the other accidentally. Worse still, the weapon couldn't be operated left-handed. The cocking handle was positioned so it could only be used by a right-handed person, as opposed to the M16 or AK, which are either-handed. Once we'd been issued with the SA80 all the Pathfinders who were lefties – and we had a good number of 'em – were forced to retrain so they could shoot cack-handed, as far as they saw it.

From its earliest beginnings our unit had been issued with the M16, the superlative American assault rifle. The M16 knocks the socks off the SA80, as does the AK47. But over time our M16s had become old and worn. When we'd lobbied to get replacements we were told we were getting the SA80 instead. It was just one more example of the downside of not being part of UKSF: the SAS and SBS had a lightweight, gucci variant of the M16. We Pathfinders got lumbered with the SA80.

The SA80 was designed and built by Royal Ordnance at a cost of £850 per rifle. At the same time the M16 was actually being produced in the UK under licence at £150 a throw, but somehow the MOD had felt it better to saddle us – plus the rest of the British Army – with a costly crock of shit like the SA80.

So it was that we boarded the ageing RAF Tristars to go to war in Sierra Leone with zero ammo and decidedly dodgy assault rifles. In spite of this our morale was sky-high. Every man amongst us wanted this mission. It was an operational deployment. A combat tasking. It was a chance to get our hands dirty, to put into practice all of our specialist skills and knowledge, and to test ourselves for real against the enemy.

It was about as good as it got.

I appreciated what a blinding move Colonel Gibson had pulled here. By getting all of 1 PARA plus a good number of the Pathfinders gathered at South Cerney he'd forced the MOD's hand. As much as anything else, the force of warriors now boarding the Tristars was Gibbo and the PM's Trojan Horse. With the rebels poised to chop up a large number of British nationals, the MOD had had no option but to give us the green light. The media would have had a feeding frenzy if it had leaked out that a force such as ours had been poised to fly to the Brits' aid, but had been stood down by the penny-pinching bean counters at the MOD.

I was certain the SAS and SBS would also be deploying, though hopefully we would pip them to the post. The Sierra Leone capital, Freetown, was a hub of MI6 activity, from where they were monitoring drug-runners, Al Qaeda operatives and the trade in uncut diamonds. Al Qaeda were known to have a growing interest in so-called 'conflict diamonds' – those mined from war zones

– for money-laundering purposes, turning their dollar millions into untraceable, raw stones.

British Embassy staff – and agents from our Secret Intelligence Service – were going to be at risk if the rebels overran the Sierra Leonean capital. US nationals were bound to be working along-side the Brits, and they would be equally threatened. Securing or evacuating the British diplomatic mission was a classic SAS task-ing, so the boys from Hereford were bound to deploy. It had now become a race to see which unit would get boots on the ground soonest, and be first into the action.

After a six-hour flight the Tristar touched down on a sun-blasted runway fringed with dilapidated terminal buildings and feathery palm trees. As yet we still had no ammo, so it was hardly as if we could bomb-burst out of the aircraft ready to unleash hell. In truth, I'd slept most of the flight and as we tumbled down the steps of the Tristar I had no idea where on earth we'd landed, and neither it seemed did anyone else.

This operation was moving at such a speed we were going faster than the information envelope – not to mention the ammo. We figured the Tristars wouldn't have put down in the heart of the Sierra Leone jungle, so we were likely in a transit point. But Kenya, Mauritania, Uganda – it could have been just about any-where in Africa. Then someone spotted a sign above the control tower announcing this to be 'Dakar Airport'. Someone else fig-ured out that Dakar was the capital of Senegal, a neighbouring West African country of Sierra Leone.

Senegal: that's where we were.

To our left two C-130K Hercules transport aircraft were turn-ing and burning, turbines thrashing in the hot, breathless air. We were ordered to mount up the right-hand side of the two aircraft, so we sprinted across the runway with machetes in one hand and assault rifles in the other – leaving someone else to bring on our Bergens. The C-130 ramp whined closed, the turbines spooled up to speed, and we were airborne once more.

Still we had no ammo, but at least we'd got a steer as to our next destination. As we'd rushed aboard the Hercules, the aircraft's loadmaster had told us we were heading for an airfield called Lungi, which was on the coast of Sierra Leone. Other than that we had not the slightest clue what we were flying into here.

For what felt like an age the C-130 roared across the jungle low and fast, before I finally felt the lurch and the thump as it touched down. The top half of the ramp was already open, and I could see a baking hot stretch of tarmac out of the aircraft's rear, fringed by a thick, impenetrable-looking wall of green – the jungle.

The aircraft slowed, and we did a classic tactical air landing operation (TALO) – bursting out of the ramp and peeling off to either side of the still-moving warplane. By the time the twenty-seven of us Pathfinders – plus the forty-odd 1 PARA lads with us – were on the ground, the C-130 was accelerating again and was very quickly airborne.

It was midday by now, and the heat hit us like a furnace.

We made for the shallow ditches that flanked either side of the runway. I'd gone left and found myself facing a mass of brooding, tangled vegetation some fifty yards away. Wag had gone right, so towards the dilapidated and sagging airport terminal building. With bugger all ammo there was precious little we could do if the rebels were poised to smash us, but at least we looked the part.

The second Hercules came in tight on the back of us, disgorging an extra sixty PARAs. All of C Company, 1 PARA, was now on the ground, plus us lot.

I scanned the airport. There was the odd African soldier wandering about, wearing the light blue beret of a United Nations peacekeeper, plus one or two airport officials dripping in braid. There was even the one civvie airliner crouched on the baking hot runway, with passengers preparing to board. This was Sierra Leone's main hub, it seemed, and it was still in use by those trying to flee the rebel advance.

Colonel Gibson marched over to the terminal building and took command. The locals were staring at him with this slack-jawed expression, like he'd just beamed down from the Planet Zog. The airport terminal was a mass of drooping fans, broken conveyor belts and sagging plastic chairs. Gibbo seized the annexe to the fire station as his ops and briefing room, one of the few vaguely clean and functioning parts of the airport.

Within thirty minutes he had things up and running. Wag, The White Rabbit, Grant, Donaldson and me – the Pathfinders' head-shed – joined him. Gibbo ordered us to fan out onto the main tracks leading through the jungle, to get eyes-on possible routes of rebel advance. Luckily, a C-130 had just landed with a – very limited – supply of ammo, and each Pathfinder was to grab his allotted share: two mags, so sixty rounds per man.

It left us with nothing for our secondary weapons – our Browning pistols – or for our heaviest firepower, the GPMGs. But some ammo was better than no ammo at all. From somewhere a white United Nations Toyota pick-up truck had been requisitioned, to ferry us into the jungle.

'The truck will drop patrols at positions no more than two kilometres out,' Donaldson briefed us, putting some flesh on Gibbo's basic orders. 'I need *Alpha*, *Bravo*, *Charlie* and *Delta* at points west to northeast on the northern side of the runway. If the rebels are out there, that's the direction from which they'll try to hit us.'

The UN vehicle ferried us out of the airport and into the jungle. Donaldson, The White Rabbit and Wag were staying put to form our HQ element, so I set out with Grant plus four others, to form our command patrol in the field. After leaving the airport by the southern gate, we hit a dirt track lined with ramshackle stalls selling bunches of bananas, mangoes, battered cans of Fanta and sun-bleached packs of Winston cigarettes.

We drove for a good few minutes, skirting the southern edge of the runway, and the habitation petered out. We turned north into the deserted bush, following a dirt track maybe ten feet wide, hemmed in on both sides by a thick wall of jungle. We followed that track until we hit the main road leading north from the capital city, Freetown, into the country's interior. This was the Sierra Leonean equivalent of the M1, but it consisted of little more than a hard-packed gravel road maybe fifty feet wide.

We were the last patrol out and it was approaching dusk by the time we were dropped at our destination. After waiting for the UN vehicle to leave, we pushed into the jungle until we were one hundred metres or so off the main highway. From there we could get eyes-on the dirt road without being seen.

The highway had been carved out of the virgin jungle – a sandy-yellow slash cut right through it. Our mission as delineated by Gibbo was to report on any movement seen – but what movement exactly? No one doubted that the capital was under threat of rebel mayhem, but right now life seemed to be continuing pretty much as normal. There would doubtless be goat-boys, cow-herders, market traders and others moving on the road, and we had zero idea of how to differentiate the civvies from the rebels.

Colonel Gibson had only C Company plus us lot in-country, so around 125 lightly-armed soldiers. He was at his most vulnerable, for C Company had not yet had the chance to dig in and get fully armed-up, or to form any meaningful defensive positions around the airport. With an entire battalion scheduled to fly in, Gibbo would get 600 1 PARA blokes on the ground, plus 125 from 2 PARA who were coming in alongside them.

That would be a force to be reckoned with.

But right now he had 125 British soldiers in-country, and the rebels were rumoured to number in their thousands. None of us had the slightest idea what they looked like, or what might mark them out as rebels. Did they wear any form of uniform, such as armbands, a rebel flash, a badge, a logo, or any specific type of headgear?

Gibbo must have realised just what he'd flown into here, and that now was the point of maximum threat. He needed someone out there in the jungle as his early warning, in case the rebels made a rapid move on the airport.

And for better or worse, we were it.

4

We settled into our positions, each of us belly-down under the forest canopy, facing the road. Darkness comes quickly in the jungle. With it, the hordes of biting insects arrive – which right here and now included ravenous mosquitoes, eerily pulsating fireflies, and these giant flying beetles that kept cannoning into our heads, ones that we quickly nicknamed 'basher-beetles'.

I lay on the dark, musty forest floor in nothing but my combats, the scent of rot and decay seeping into my nostrils. I could feel the mozzies feasting on my blood as they forced their tiny insect jaws through my trousers and shirtsleeves and drilled into me. What made it all the more frustrating was that we'd yet to be issued with any anti-malaria pills. We knew which ones we'd needed, but no one had managed to get their hands on any prior to leaving the UK.

Still, at least we were out on active operations, and it was great to know we were first into the country ahead of any other British force.

'Any idea what's happening?' I whispered to Grant. 'What we're looking for?'

'Not a sausage, mate,' came the hushed reply.

As the darkness thickened around us even our night vision goggles (NVGs) couldn't help much. Come sundown the light level beneath the jungle canopy quickly drops to nothing. NVGs work by collecting and boosting ambient light, but with next to no illumination filtering through the vegetation above us they were barely able to function. They offered at best an unclear, wavy, fuzzy vision of the highway – little better than using the mark one human eyeball.

As far as we could tell there was zero movement out on the road anyway. Come last light everything seemed to have stopped. There were no cars, trucks, people, animals or anything. If we could have taken away the deafening beat of the insects – the rhythmic *preeep-preeep-preeep* of the cicadas above all – it would have been eerily silent. I could only presume that the rebels preferred to operate at night, so everything else stopped during the hours of darkness.

Technically speaking, what we'd formed here was a DPP – a defensive perimeter post – as opposed to a standard OP. An OP is there to observe and report; a DPP is there to observe, report and engage and fight if necessary. If we spotted any rebel movement, doubtless Gibbo would order us to slow them down as much as we possibly could, bearing in mind our tiny number – four patrols of six Pathfinders, so twenty-four men in all – plus our pitiful supply of ammo.

As I lay there in the hot and humid darkness, being eaten alive by the mozzies, I reflected on when any of us lot had last got a good feed. After fried eggs and bread that morning at South Cerney, our only other meal had been a butty box on the Tristar. Mine had consisted of a couple of soggy cheese sarnies, a packet of prawn cocktail flavour crisps, a Kit Kat and a can of Panda Cola – the cornerstones of any British Army nutritional meal. The growling in my stomach would have been audible from the bloody road, were it not for the cacophony of the insects.

Still, I loved being in the jungle. I always have. Generally speaking, it's love or hate at first sight with such terrain. As Pathfinders we'd done rakes of jungle training, and we'd tailored our tropical kit to just such a theatre of operations as this.

Each of us was wearing a very weird-looking set of headgear. The nearest you'd ever get to it in the civvie world is a beekeeper's helmet. It's basically a head-and-neck mozzie net. You pull it on like a giant sock, the fine-mesh netting bagging out around the face and fastening via elastic around the neck. We'd slapped insect repellent cream on any exposed skin, plus our combat trousers were tucked into jungle boots, to stop leeches, ants or other nasties crawling up our legs and doing damage to our manhood.

But none of this could stop the mozzies getting lock-on and chewing through our clothing – and the mosquitoes here in Sierra Leone were monsters. I could see them circling around me like mini Apache gunships, each intent on wreaking blood-sucking, disease-ridden mayhem. It wasn't as if I could keep swatting whenever I felt a bite. The golden rule of such DPP work is to remain absolutely still and silent, so as to observe the enemy without being seen.

I glanced at Grant. 'Nice here, innit, mate? We've got sixty rounds per man, we're being eaten alive, and our last feed was a butty box back on the Tristars . . . '

Grant's teeth grinned white in the faint moonlight. He eyed me through the fuzz of his mozzie net. 'They can't keep us out here forever. If we don't get eaten to death we'll bloody starve . . .'

Come daybreak we'd seen practically nothing, and certainly no movement of armed men out on the road. We needed to get a report radioed into HQ, and dawn was the time to make our first regular 'Sched' – scheduled radio call. When out on operations our patrol – headquarters – was supposed to make two daily Scheds, one at dawn and one at dusk. If we missed a Sched, that was the trigger for HQ to consider us compromised and on the run.

Miraculously, our signaller, Neil 'Tricky' Dick, managed to get a radio call through to headquarters pretty much on the first attempt. We reported what we'd seen, or rather the lack of it.

It was a marvel that Tricky had got the comms up and running amongst the thick tropical vegetation, but he was pure genius with such kit. The only way to set up our archaic Clansman 319 high frequency (HF) radios was to tie a length of string onto the end of a flexible wire aerial, fix a rock onto the string and hurl it into the treetops. When the forest canopy was up to a hundred feet or more above us that took some doing.

I'd once been on a joint exercise in the US with American elite forces. We'd been inserted via HALO parachute drop alongside a unit of Marine Corps Force Recon operators. Our mission was to mark a drop zone (DZ) for the largest airborne force parachuted by NATO since the Second World War. We'd made the long tab into the DZ, during which one of our sister units, a Navy SEAL team, had a guy badly mauled by an alligator.

When we finally got eyes-on the DZ, we prepared to radio in reports to our respective headquarters. The Force Recon signaller pressed a button on his lightweight radio backpack, flipped out a helix antenna – a collapsible, space-age dish-like aerial – and within a matter of seconds his commander was able to call in his report. By the time he was done Tricky was still trying to hurl his rock into the nearest tree, to snag a branch.

It was all the more reason to be thankful for having a guy like him with us here in Sierra Leone. A trustworthy and totally solid operator, Tricky never let the shit state of the comms kit get to him. It was all just a challenge to his ultimate professionalism.

Tricky hailed from 216 Signals Squadron, a specialist communications unit, so he was an absolute master at his chosen discipline. Pathfinder Selection is open to any soldier regardless of unit or rank. Although 216 Signals isn't a fighting outfit as such, Tricky was still a hard-as-nails operator. Five-foot-ten and blond, he was good-looking in a tough, Jason Statham-lookalike way. He could drink like a fish, smoke like a chimney and run like the wind. He loved a punch-up, but he was a thinking man's scrapper. He'd analyse a fight carefully before wading in.

Tricky was cat-like, agile and cool – a float like a butterfly, sting like a bee kind of an operator. No one ever heard or saw him coming. If I was forced to go on the run here in Sierra Leone I'd most likely choose to do so with him. Wag would get you out in the end, but Tricky would do so quickly, stealthily and in style.

Orders from Gibbo were to return to headquarters, for a re-tasking. By the time we got back there, Lungi Airport had become like a mini version of London Heathrow. Hercs were flying a relay of further men and *matériel* from Senegal. By now we'd got eight flights in, and already they were taking out the NEOs – the first British and allied civilians to be evacuated from the war-torn country.

Those who'd realised what was about to happen – that Free-town was on the verge of being overrun by thousands of rebels who had the darkest, most savage reputation of any in the world right then – had made their own way to Lungi Airport, planning to jump on whatever flight might be available to anywhere other than here. They were being shovelled onto the Hercs as fast as possible and flown out to Dakar.

To either end of the runway I could see the 1 PARA lads dig-ging in, as they formed proper defensive positions. At the furthest western end of the runway I spotted a small vehicle-mounted unit setting up what had to be a separate, discreet base. I knew in-stinctively it had to be the lads from the SAS or the SBS, or maybe both of them.

It turned out it was the SAS. I knew a bunch of them, as did some of the other 'old and bold.' They drove past us in their Pinkies – lightweight, open-topped Land Rovers, simi-lar to the ones we had been ordered to leave behind in the UK – and there was the odd wave and yelled greeting between us. We'd beaten them into the country, but now the lads from the Regiment were here it was going to be a race to see who got tasked with the first and the best of whatever missions were going.

Stacked to one side of the terminal building was a pile of British Army ration packs, so we made sure to grab some of those. That done we got issued with our first operational maps – 1:50,000 scale, showing Lungi Airport and the surrounding terrain. There were only enough for one per patrol, but that didn't stop the blokes from getting down to some serious map study and ground orientation.

In the Pathfinders, navigation is a collective art. Every man on a patrol has to know exactly where he is at any time, so as to be able to take the initiative if the patrol commander gets hit, or a patrol gets split up. Using the maps we did our first IPB – Intelligence Preparation of the Battlefield – noting key ground and vital terrain, defensive positions, routes to and from those defensive positions, likely avenues of enemy approach, possible routes of escape, and ambush points along the way.

That done, Wag, Grant, Donaldson and me got called in for mission briefing. It was given by Lewis Carson, the 1 PARA Operations Officer, and a former 2iC of the Pathfinders. It was no secret that Lewis was angling for Donaldson's job, once Donaldson had finished his two-year stint. I for one couldn't wait for him to take over. He'd proved himself a superlative operator when he'd served with us as 2iC, commanding the respect of all the men bar none.

Lewis's brief was punchy and to the point. If anything it reinforced just how little we knew: the rebels were closing in on Freetown; there was a very real fear of looting, horrific rapes and massacres if they seized the city; all British passport holders and citizens of 'allied nations' – Americans, Europeans, Aussies, Kiwis and Canadians – were to be evacuated from the country as soon as.

All of that was pretty much as we knew it. But Lewis did have one vital new element of Intel for us. Apparently, the rebels had heard about the arrival of British forces in-country, and they were determined to 'take' Lungi Airport and drive us out – and that meant that our primary objective had to be to hold it.

But for the Pathfinders mission priorities were about to change dramatically. Apparently, no one was available to secure the British Embassy or evacuate its staff – despite that being a classic SAS tasking. Hence we were to be airlifted across to Freetown, on the far side of the Freetown Estuary, in order to do so.

On hearing this we were lit up. It sure beat lying in the jungle starving hungry and getting munched on by ravenous insects, with not a rebel fighter in sight. But for some reason it didn't seem as if Donaldson shared our joy at the coming tasking.

'I really can't see the need for us,' he announced, from out of nowhere. 'I've spoken to the CO, and I've told him I don't understand the need for the Pathfinders. There's no real task for us, and we have training commitments back in the UK, and that's where we should be right now. We're wasting valuable training time and I've told the CO as much.'

Wag and I caught each other's eye. I could see the disbelief written across his features. Even Grant was struggling to hide his frustration at what he'd just heard. But as usual it was left up to me – mouthy old Smoggy, reliably blunt to the point of rudeness – to voice our collective disquiet.

'What d'you mean, boss – *we should be in the UK, training*? We're on ops here. This is an operational deployment to a war zone. This is what we live, eat, breathe and train for.'

'Smoggy's right, boss, we need to stay,' Wag added. 'We need to stay 'cause who knows what the next few hours and days may bring.'

Every bloke in the unit knew where we needed to be right now – mixing it here in Sierra Leone. But Donaldson seemed to have his mind set on getting us back to the UK, regardless. He left to go speak with Gibbo some more, leaving Wag, Grant, The White Rabbit and me to talk it over. We agreed to keep a close eye on him. If he tried doing the unthinkable and getting us off this deployment, then Donaldson would have to be stopped.

Two Chinooks from the Special Forces Flight had arrived in-country, after a truly epic journey out from the UK. They'd set out from RAF Odiham under their own steam, the UK military lacking any aircraft large enough to fly them out to theatre (C-17 Globemasters, or the equivalent). The aircrew had flown out, refuelling en route, via France, Spain, North Africa and into

West Africa. It was a 4800-kilometre flight, and it would turn out to be the longest self-deployment by helos in British military history.

We mounted up those newly-arrived Chinooks and were whisked across the water to the nation's ramshackle capital, Freetown. We touched down at the Mammy Yoko Hotel, which had been designated the rallying point for all civilians seeking to get evacuated from the country. The Mammy Yoko looked like a classic run-down, white-walled colonial-era establishment. The gardens were grand but tired and ill-kept, pretty much reflecting the look and feel of the hotel itself.

The main advantage of the Mammy Yoko was its flight facilities. Set on the ocean front the hotel has a flat, oval, gravelled area facing the sea: a helipad. It came complete with two massive refuelling bowsers, the hotel being one of the UN's main centres of operations in the country. As we'd flown in we'd noticed two massive Soviet-era Mil Mi-8 (named HIP by NATO) transport helicopters sitting on the helipad, painted in white and with 'UN' emblazoned in massive black lettering on their sides.

While the Chinooks were tasked with all military movements around the country, the HIPs were ferrying the civilians out to Lungi Airport, for onward evacuation.

From the Mammy Yoko we sent out an eight-man patrol en route to the British Embassy. It was led by Corporal Sam 'Dolly' Parton, the commander of patrol 33 Bravo. His position of patrol command had come about by dint of his natural leadership abilities. The average face in a crowd, Dolly was married with two kids. He was a softly-spoken, quiet family man and an utterly solid operator. After Nathe and H's patrol, Dolly's was my next most capable unit, and they constituted a great backstop to 33 Alpha.

Once Dolly's patrol had got the Embassy staff relocated to the Mammy Yoko Hotel, we'd airlift them out to Lungi Airport and onto a waiting C-130 Hercules. In the meantime, we settled ourselves in as best we could. A path from the helipad led to the centre of the hotel grounds, where there were some tennis courts, sur-rounded by twelve-foot-high chain-link fencing. The courts were overlooked by the hotel's bar and swimming pool, one that was built in an abstract kind of a splodge shape.

Set some seventy yards back from the pool was the hotel build-ing itself. It looked to be about a dozen floors high, with a curved façade facing the sea. The rooms had to offer an amazing view over the Freetown Estuary, not that I figured there were many guests with the time or inclination to enjoy it. Right now, anyone with any money or sense and the right passport was getting the hell out of Freetown.

Colonel Gibson had also shipped himself over to the Mammy Yoko, and he had seized one of the hotel suites as his ops room. Donaldson disappeared to liaise with the colonel, the rest of us setting up a makeshift camp. By now our Bergens had reached us, so we were able to rig up ponchos lashed to the chain-link fence – making a series of waterproof lean-tos, which lined the edge of the tennis courts.

Our ponchos were US Army issue, for the British military didn't possess such kit. We had to buy rakes of our own equip-ment, including boots, rucksacks, torches, waterproofs, ammo pouches and the ponchos. The British Army doss-bag weighed in at 10 pounds. It was fine for a Regular Army unit, for their Ber-gens would be brought up to their lines by vehicle. For us it was 8 pounds overweight. Accordingly, every Pathfinder had a civvie sleeping bag, one that weighed in at 2 pounds and stuffed down to nothing.

If I stood every man of our force in line, I figure 10 per cent of our kit would have been standard British Army issue. Each bloke carried around £1500-worth of personalised gear, and all bought with his own money. It was a powerful testament to their dedica-tion to the unit that each had made such an investment, and most on a private's wage of some £650 month.

Camp set, we broke open the twenty-four-hour ration packs,

got a scoff-on and waited for some kind of an update from Donaldson. I killed time chatting with Wag. We were determined that Donaldson would deliver the right kind of an update – *that we were staying, and that we were getting ourselves a peachy tasking.* The Embassy job was clearly an interim kind of a mission. Time was ticking, and we needed something we could really get our teeth into.

Our determination to stay was just about to get a huge boost, as we got our first detailed briefing on the rebels. A military intelligence specialist gave us a good talking to in the hotel grounds. The rebels were known as the Revolutionary United Front, or RUF for short. Led by an ex-Sierra Leonean Army (SLA) sergeant, Foday Sankoh, they espoused no coherent political or other ideology. Their sole aim seemed to be to spread terror and mayhem across the country, and in that they had been spectacularly successful.

The rebels' 'signature' was to lop off the hands of women and children, offering them 'long-sleeve' or 'short-sleeve' style – the former being amputation below the elbow, the latter above it. They did so simply to spread sheer and utter terror across the land. Typical rebel 'tactics' involved surrounding an isolated village at night, killing all the able-bodied men, raping and mutilating the women, and then rounding up all the kids of 'fighting age' – the would-be child soldiers.

Boys of eleven and twelve were forced to rape their own mothers and kill their own fathers, or get macheted to death on the spot – and do so in front of the rest of the village. Thus, horribly traumatised and alienated from their surviving family and community, they were sucked into the rebel ranks. With no way back to their homes or their villages, the RUF became their only 'family'. Young girls were taken in a similar way, as rebel fighters' 'wives'.

Once they were so 'recruited', the would-be rebels were fed a cocktail of crack cocaine, heroin and other drugs – 'injected' directly into the blood stream via cuts made in their foreheads. The nascent child soldiers quickly became drug-addicted. To cap it all they were bathed in vats of voodoo medicine by the rebels' 'high priestesses', supposedly to make them 'bulletproof' and 'invincible' in battle.

RUF terror sorties were invariably led by these child soldier shock-troops, high on drugs and voodoo gibberish. More often than not they sported the most bizarre of 'uniforms': frilly dresses, fluorescent pink shell-suits, women's wigs, and even animal costumes made from real animal skins. Yet in spite of all of this they were a force to be reckoned with. Several times during the decade-long civil war they had seized control of the entire country, including the nation's capital, in an inconceivably dark and brutal orgy of violence that had cost over 70,000 lives.

After ten years of such warfare the Sierra Leone Army had been left largely impotent. Recently, some 17,000 United Nations peacekeepers had been drafted into the country, supposedly to keep the peace. They hailed from the Jordanian, Indian, Nigerian and other armed forces, and they very often lacked boots, radios or even weaponry to carry out their duties, not to mention a basic modicum of co-ordination, discipline or morale.

UNAMSIL – the United Nations Mission to Sierra Leone – was the largest UN peacekeeping force in history, but it had proved an utter debacle. The RUF had kidnapped dozens of peacekeepers, seized their armoured vehicles and looted their ammo dumps and their weaponry. Indeed, it was via seized UN trucks and armoured personnel carriers that the rebels were now making their final push on Freetown.

Some 800 PARAs, a handful of SAS and we Pathfinders were heavily outnumbered by the rebels. There was also increasing evidence of the RUF's links to darker forces hailing from outside the country. Sierra Leone was blessed – or possibly cursed – with a surfeit of alluvial diamonds, which occurred near the surface and could be easily mined by hand. If anything, it was lust for the diamond wealth of the country that was driving this crazed war.

Recently, terrorist franchises like Al Qaeda had started popping up in the country, looking to buy up these illicit 'conflict diamonds' and so launder their millions. Diamonds represent the ultimate fungible asset – a handful of tiny rocks that are essentially undetectable at airports and borders but remain a store of enormous wealth to whoever holds them. Factor in the hard drugs being run through West Africa, and it was a dark and dangerous mix.

It was these concerns that had prompted Tony Blair to launch the present deployment. In fact, Blair had deeply personal reasons for intervening in Sierra Leone, for his father had worked in the country as a teacher and he felt personally compelled to act. And with Colonel Gibson having moved heaven and earth to get an entire battle group in-country, we had made a half-decent start.

At the same time the overall force commander, Brigadier David Richards – who would go on to become General Sir David Richards, chief of the Defence Staff – had very much nailed his colours to the mast. In a meeting with Sierra Leone's embattled president, Ahmad Kabbah, Brigadier Richards had just made a signal promise: *he had pledged that the British military would end the war in Sierra Leone once and for all, by knocking seven bales of shit out of the rebels.*

After learning all of this I was doubly certain that this was not the time to contemplate withdrawing the Pathfinders from the country. Quite the reverse: there was a war to be fought here for all the right reasons, and against an enemy that needed to be given a right bloody nose.

I knew full well that if we jacked this mission we'd never live it down. The stigma would plague the Pathfinders for years to come, plus we'd never get another job like this. So it was just as well that we were about to get a top priority tasking – one designed to make Brigadier Richards' promise of knocking seven bales of shit out of the rebels a reality.

As the Pathfinders' platoon sergeant, I got to shape and form this tiny, bespoke unit in exactly the way I wanted. Kit failures and deficiencies apart, I didn't think there was a unit out there that could touch us in terms of the elite skills we specialised in. You needed to build a special brotherhood to succeed at our level. After the countless hours spent sprinting around the base perimeter or tabbing in the Brecons, the long overnights in OPs and on recce taskings, not to mention all the HALO, HAHO and HAPLSS jumps, I reckoned the bonds formed between us were unbreakable.

Which was just as well, for in the coming days the Pathfinders were to be tested to the limits and beyond.

5

Things began to move lightning fast. We were ordered to break camp and mount up a waiting CH-47, to be flown back to Lungi Airport. Upon arrival we were rushed in for an emergency briefing with Colonel Gibson, who'd flown back alongside us.

Humint (human intelligence) sources had reported a huge rebel force massing some seventy kilometres or so to the north of Lungi Airport. The rebels were planning to attack just as we had the NEO in full swing, loading confused and frightened evacuees onto waiting aircraft. That way, there would be hundreds of British and allied civilians milling about in the airport, and they'd be easy game for the rebels.

The RUF's intended route of advance was the dirt highway that threaded south through the swampy jungle – the one we'd kept watch over during our first night. We were getting flown far upcountry to an isolated clearing that straddled that track, near a village called Lungi Lol. The village was believed to be 'friendly', though nothing was ever certain with the ever-shifting allegiances that defined this war. Our role was to act as an early warning force, and to hold up the rebel advance for as long as was humanly possible.

The village was set deep in the jungle some sixty kilometres inland, so way beyond any British forces, which were massed around the airport and Freetown.

This was more like it. This was a classic Pathfinder tasking: an insertion ahead of British lines to recce, harass, sabotage and destroy. Colonel Gibson rounded off his briefing with this. 'Your force is very much on its own, but I have every confidence in the Pathfinders. There will be a 1 PARA QRF on standby, for I understand the danger you are going into here. If it all goes pear-shaped, make your way back to British lines by whatever means possible.'

At least we had a QRF (Quick Reaction Force) of PARAs on standby, if it did all go to rat-shit. We gathered in the ramshackle terminal building over a map, so Donaldson could brief the patrol commanders in more detail. Thankfully, the OC seemed to have got some of his mojo back, now that we'd landed such an out-there kind of a mission.

'We're going in as a platoon to form an early warning group,' Donaldson told the men. 'Intel suggests rebel forces are moving to take the airport, or at least to attack and capture British soldiers and evacuating citizens. The CO wants us out there at his furthermost point, to put a clear stop to them.'

As the blokes digested what they'd just been told, the atmosphere was electric with anticipation. This was the kind of tasking every Pathfinder dreams of.

'Our intention is to move by helo some sixty klicks northeast,' Donaldson continued. 'We'll take vehicles to give us mobility on the ground. The CO wants us in situ at this point – Lungi Lol – before last light, so we need to move it and begin liaison with the pilots. We could be going into a hot LZ. So prepare to E & E in case it does go loud. If we do need to E & E we'll move to the coast, using this dirt track, and link up with the SBS who will be patrolling the coastline.'

E & E is short for escape and evasion – our bug-out plan if we were forced to go on the run. I was hunched over the map, shoulder to shoulder with Wag and Grant, but as I traced Donaldson's proposed E & E route I didn't like what I saw. We'd be heading southwest to a chokepoint, leaving our backs to the sea, and if the SBS lads failed to show we'd have nowhere to run to but the water.

I glanced at Wag, my finger tracing the route. 'It doesn't look like we can move any further than there,' I muttered, speaking out of the corner of my mouth. 'If we get there and we're being followed by the rebels we're fucked.'

'Yep. Agreed.'

'It's not like SBS will be parked up waiting for us. It could be hours before they're tasked to us or available.'

'Agreed.'

Donaldson finished his briefing and asked for any questions.

'Yeah – just the one,' I volunteered. 'The option to move south-west to the coast if we have to E & E ...'

'Yes, what of it?'

'Boss, you do realise if we do that we're moving to a chokepoint leaving our backs to the sea. If we're being pursued and we hit the sea with no pick-up ...'

'Steve, that's what's been agreed. Move on.'

Agreed by bloody whom, I wondered? A unit like the Pathfinders operates as a meritocracy. Every bloke, regardless of rank, gets to have his say. We had a way of doing things, a collective means of decision-making that meant there were checks and balances.

'Boss, I've got to agree with Steve,' Wag volunteered. 'We'll be pinned with nowhere left to go.'

Donaldson now had his platoon sergeant and his Ops Warrant Officer voicing concerns. Between us, Wag and me had over twenty-five years' experience of elite force operations.

'It's agreed with the boss,' Donaldson countered. 'Move on. Sort the kit. Let's get on with it.'

With that he strode off to the ops room. The looks on the faces of the rest of us said it all. Small unit operations rely on command and control decisions cascading down. Officers need to trust their NCOs and patrol commanders to highlight faults in plans and identify how things can be done better. They need to earn respect. Donaldson's reluctance to use the expertise and experience of the men ran counter to everything the Pathfinders stood for, and the very soul of the unit.

I could feel Nathe, Dolly and the other patrol commanders eyeing Grant, Wag and me.

'You need to get this bloody sorted,' Nathe grumbled.

'Go brief your patrols and we'll deal with it,' I reassured him.

'Nathe, we know,' said Wag. 'Leave it with us. Go back, brief your blokes on the mission. We're going in light order for a forty-eight-hour tasking, so twenty-four hours' worth of food and water in belt kit, then a further forty-eight hours in your daysack . . .'

Once Wag was done the patrol commanders split. Tricky headed off to liaise with the signallers from other units, to sort call-signs, frequencies, timings of the Scheds, and the use of the Crypto – cryptographically encoded communications systems. That left Grant, Wag and me to chew over the E & E issue.

'Grant, mate, at some stage soon you need to go talk to Donaldson,' I told him. 'Officer to officer. You need to get him to listen, 'cause this is crucial shit.'

Grant nodded. 'I know. I'll have words.'

Grant was still a relatively young and inexperienced officer. I had five years in age over him, plus a decade of elite soldiering, and Wag had more. His reluctance to go against a fellow officer and the unit's OC was understandable. As NCOs, me and Wag would simply get a bollocking if we fronted up to Donaldson. If Grant was seen as undermining the command of a fellow officer it could seriously harm his career, but someone needed to get Donaldson to see sense.

It was around 1300 hours by now, and we were scheduled to get airborne at 1500 hours and on the ground at the LZ thirty minutes thereafter. In the interim we had a shedload to organise. We had to sort an air-plan with the Chinook pilots, gather all our kit, rations and water, sort the comms and the wagons – we'd just had two Pinzgauers flown in on a Hercules – load and secure them in the CH-47s, and get ourselves good to go.

But the chief worry for me right now – apart from the faulty E & E plan – was this: as the platoon sergeant I was acutely aware of our appalling lack of ammo and weaponry with which to go up against several thousand rebels. We still had just the sixty rounds per man for our SA80s, plus nothing whatsoever for the GPMGs. And there was a shedload of other assorted weaponry and explosives I'd very much like for a mission such as this one.

It was now that Wag had one of his brainwaves. Mick Robson was the 1 PARA RQMS – Regimental Quartermaster – and a guy we knew well. He was six-foot-four, blond, wiry and he was nobody's fool. Near the edge of the runway he'd established a makeshift ammo dump. He'd driven metal pickets into the ground and stretched razor wire between them, fencing off an area some twenty metres by twenty metres.

A couple of 1 PARA privates had been set to guard the ammo dump, but as Wag pointed out that didn't mean that we couldn't go on the scrounge. We hurried over. We found Mick in the centre of the Kingdom of Mick, overseeing more ammo supplies that had just been flown in. He glanced up at us with a look on his face – *here they come again, the Pathfinder likely lads on the scrounge.*

I gave him my best winning smile. 'Mick, mate, long time no see. We're heading upcountry, mate, and we could well end up in a firefight. Trouble is we've got fuck-all to fight with, so we need whatever ammo you can spare us ... mate.'

Mick stared at the two of us, then gestured at the palettes ranged all around him. 'How long's a bit of string. Any idea exactly what you're after?'

I ran my eye around the Kingdom of Mick feeling like a kiddie in a sweet shop. One palette was piled high with metal boxes of 5.56 mm ball ammo: SA80 rounds. Next to that was a mound of 7.62 mm belted link: GPMG ammo. Two dozen LAW 94 mm anti-armour rockets were laid out nearby, along with crates of 51 mm mortar rounds.

But the real Aladdin's Cave lay on the far side of the razor wire fence: *the demolitions and explosives enclosure.* PE4 plastic explosives, timers, detonators, detonation cord – Mick would have the works in there. Being a true pro he'd sorted his ammo dump so as not to exceed the NEQ – the net explosive quantity. Under British Army rules you could only store a certain amount of explosive material – the NEQ – in one dump, hence the demolitions enclosure being placed to one side. It was set under a poncho, to keep the sun off the stuff that goes bang.

I licked my lips, wondering just how hard to push things. I opened with this. 'Mick, we've got five guns: how much ammo can you spare us for each?'

'Guns' is military speak for the GPMGs.

Mick rolled his eyes. '400 rounds.'

'How about six?' I countered.

'All right. Six – you're done. What else?'

I told him we had sixty rounds per man for the SA80s – but I wanted 330 rounds per man, so over five times that amount. Each man needed to have six mags of thirty rounds each, plus a bandolier containing an extra 150. The bandolier is a long green sleeve that you sling around your torso, consisting of five compartments each containing thirty rounds.

Mick nodded. 'Yeah, okay. Suppose you can have that. Next?'

I eyed the LAWs. 'What about four of them – them LAWs, Mick?'

He ran a hand across his sweaty forehead. 'Fuck . . . Well, okay. Take 'em. Just keep it quiet. Next?'

'Mick, any L2s or Claymores in-country?'

The L2 is the British Army's high-explosive fragmentation grenade, the Claymore a curved anti-personnel device of devastating lethality.

Mick shook his head. 'Nope. Next?'

I'd brought with me a 51 mm mortar tube from our armoury, but as yet I had no ammo. 'What about 51 mm rounds?'

'There's illume, but no HE.'

Illume are flare rounds, ones that burst high in the sky to illuminate a battlefield. Not quite high-explosive (HE) rounds, but better than nothing.

'Okay, great: how many can I have?'

He pointed to a nearby crate: 'Here – just take that bloody box while no one's looking.'

I'd open that crate later to discover eighteen rounds inside. I had no idea right now what a total lifesaver they would prove to be.

'Right, Mick, what else have you got?'

He stared at us for a long second. 'You're fucking joking me.'

I pointed to the second enclosure – the demolitions dump. 'What's that, Mick, under that poncho?'

'You lot are never bloody satisfied. It's the demms kit.'

'Let's have a look, then.'

Mick hesitated, then he stepped between Wag and me, moving towards the gate. Out of the corner of his mouth he muttered: 'You two wankers coming, or what?'

We moved around the corner to a tiny gate, then stepped inside the sacred enclosure. I pointed at a box of PE4. 'Mick, how much of that have you got?'

'About fifteen pounds.'

My mind was racing. PE4 comes in a block like a thick cigar. It's off-white, smells a bit like marzipan, and is wrapped in a kind of greaseproof paper. Fifteen pounds equalled thirty sticks.

'Mick, can I have ten sticks?'

'If I give it you, will you fuck off?'

'I will if we can have some dets as well ...'

Behind Mick, Wag was on his knees levering open boxes. He was laying stuff on the floor, piling up a ready-made war in a box. I tried to keep Mick occupied while Wag mounded up his heap of swag.

'Mick, can we have this lot as well?' Wag piped up.

Mick turned and saw what Wag was doing. He raised his arms and cut his hands across the air – like *cut-it; cut it out; no more*.

'That's it,' he hissed. 'The fucking shop is shut – go!'

I grinned. 'Fair enough, the shop's shut. Sold out. Cheers, Mick, anyway.' I turned to Wag. 'Mate, bag that lot up before he changes his mind and I'll go get the patrol commanders. We'll need a good few blokes to carry it all.'

I called the blokes over and we began to distribute the goodies around the patrols.

I would have liked to have got our hands on a few of the folding-stock Minimi light machine guns, which the SAS had in theatre, for the GPMG was big and clumsy when patrolling through thick vegetation. I'd have liked M203 grenade launchers, although the 40 mm rounds can get deflected by thick jungle and rebound to hit your own side. But most of all, I'd have liked M16 assault rifles as our main weapon.

Yet Blair was winging it, Colonel Gibson was winging it and Brigadier Richards most certainly was – so I figured there was no reason why the Pathfinders shouldn't wing it alongside them. And with Mick's help, at least we now had the kind of ammo and explosives we needed to take the fight to the rebels.

We loaded up the waiting Chinooks, each with the one Pinz-gauer strapped down in preparation for a seat-of-the-pants kind of a ride. The 'Pinz' is a four-wheel-drive all-terrain vehicle, with a cab sitting over the front wheels and an open rear. The two vehicles were there to provide us with a fast and mobile means to escape and evade, with greater reach than going on the run on foot. Wag, Grant and me got our heads together with the Chinook pilots over the air maps. There looked to be nowhere to land to the south or west of the village. The best bet seemed to be a small clearing to the northeast, adjacent to the road. We figured it was just about large enough to land the pair of Chinooks, but by anyone's reckoning it was going to be a tight fit. We decided they'd go down as a pair facing northeast, ramps open towards the village.

We agreed actions-on if the LZ turned out to be 'hot'. If the pilots encountered heavy ground fire, we'd abort the landing and search for an alternative LZ. If we put down, disgorged and took heavy fire, the helos would fly a holding pattern, providing cover with their door-mounted, six-barrelled Miniguns. We'd only call the helos back in to extract us if the resistance proved too fierce, and if they stood a decent chance of getting in and out without being shot down.

As the aircrew readied themselves to get airborne, Lewis, the 1 PARA Ops Officer, pulled me off for a last word.

'Steve: over here, mate!'

'Wag and Grant?' I yelled back.

'Yeah, bring 'em too.'

We gathered in a huddle, Lewis with a worried expression in his eyes. 'Look, guys, just to warn you, 'cause you need to know: Donaldson's still arguing to the CO to get you sent back to the UK. He's saying he doesn't see a role for the Pathfinders and that you've got training scheduled with air assets cued. Guys, you're on the verge of being pulled out. Be wary.'

Having given us the warning Lewis split, leaving Wag, Grant and me to digest the news. Donaldson had seemed reinvigorated, our unit having landed the present mission. There was no way we could allow ourselves to get pulled off this one at the eleventh hour.

I eyed Grant. Wag was staring at him too. He held up his hands in a gesture almost of surrender. 'All right, guys, it's out of order and don't I know it. But look, we're flying out of here and once we're airborne we're committed . . .'

Donaldson was scheduled to fly in with us, this being a platoon-level op. The White Rabbit had drawn the short straw and was remaining here as our liaison with Colonel Gibson, along with one of our radio operators. We figured we needed to get Donaldson on the Chinook and airborne as quickly as possible, at which stage we were pretty much past the point of no return.

As we waited on the apron for the final 'go' an unmarked HOOK helicopter flew in low and fast. It looked exactly like the HIPs the UN were using, except it had a shorter body and was painted a dull khaki green. It landed beside us, and eight operators dressed in black jumpsuits dismounted, each carrying an AK47. The only clue as to who they were was the American flag sewn onto the shoulder of each of them.

We'd had no warning they were inbound and I presumed they had to be either Delta Force or from the CIA's Special Activities Division (SAD), its paramilitary wing. I figured they'd be here to help deal with any US nationals holed up in Freetown. Being Pathfinders, we'd trained with Delta, but there was zero time to go have words with the new arrivals. Our priority was to stay on the helos and get out of Lungi Airport before anyone could put a stop to us.

At 1500 we got the final 'go'. The Chinooks' giant twin rotors spooled up to speed and finally we were airborne. We were whisked over the thick jungle that fringed the runway, clipping the treetops in an effort to avoid being detected by the rebels or getting hit by any ground fire. I felt this massive surge of elation as we left Lungi Airport behind us: at least now the mission was a go.

We had fourteen Pathfinders on our Chinook, ranged in two ranks of seven, seated to either side of the aircraft's hold. The Pinz was fastened to the metal lugs at the front of the hold, tight against the metal compartment that sealed off the cockpit. Beside me the Chinook's loadmaster was strapped to the aircraft's side, hanging out of the two-part rear ramp, the upper half of which was folded inwards to offer a view over sky and jungle.

As the Chinook gathered speed the ground sped past beneath the open ramp. I gazed out. The terrain below looked utterly horrendous – patches of thick, dense forest interspersed with wide expanses of tropical swamp and mangroves. Here and there water glinted in the blinding mid-afternoon light, revealing the bend of a river, a lagoon or a quagmire. Away from the one dirt highway there looked to be no easy way through such terrain.

I'd plugged into the Chinook's comms system via a set of

headphones, ones that linked me to the cockpit. I could hear the pilot and co-pilot calling out landmarks and flight details to each other plus the navigator, who was perched on a fold-down seat to the rear of the cockpit crouched over his air maps.

Pilot: 'Boomerang-shaped turn in dirt track, port side of aircraft, three hundred metres.'

Navigator: 'Check. Thirty klicks out of village.'

Pause.

Co-pilot: 'Speed: a hundred and fifty knots. Direction of travel: zero three five degrees.'

Pause.

Pilot: 'Passing moon-shaped lagoon to starboard side of aircraft, two hundred and fifty metres.'

Navigator: 'Check. ETA LZ twenty minutes. Look for bend in track five hundred metres on left, then clearing a hundred and fifty metres ahead of that.'

Pilot: 'Roger that.'

By now I'd pretty much realised there was no end to the swamp, wetlands and mangrove forests flashing past below. This wasn't the odd, isolated patch of waterlogged terrain that you could skirt around. I'd trained and operated in the lowland forests of Belize, Brunei and elsewhere, so I'd experienced wet jungle ground before – but I'd never set eyes on anything like this.

With the terrain to either side of the road being impassable, the only viable escape route was going to be that one dirt highway. It snaked south, passing through a series of villages, ones that were totally uncharted territory: they could be friendly or they could be rebel bases. Even if we got the Pinzgauers going on the road and could get through the villages okay, we couldn't load all twenty-seven of us onto the wagons, because they couldn't carry that many.

It would be easy enough to get into the dense, waterlogged terrain to either side of the road and disappear on foot. We could go to ground and hide, but what then? No one was about to come into that kind of terrain to lift us out, and at some point we'd be driven to leave – by hunger, disease, or the snakes and crocodiles that would infest the badlands. In the meantime the rebels would be able to motor ahead on the dirt road and get us outflanked and surrounded.

We were twenty-seven against God only knew how many thousand rebels, and we were heading into a green hell.

6

We closed in on the LZ. There was a high-pitched whine and the bottom half of the helo's ramp folded down, hot jungle air and burning avgas fumes barrelling in through the opening. On the port side of the Chinook the hatch was open, the door-gunner manning the six-barrelled .50-calibre Gatling gun readying himself for action. If there were hostiles on the LZ we were relying in part of his firepower to provide cover for our extraction.

I took one last look at the terrain as we thundered in. We were hammering along at fifty feet above the jungle canopy, below which there was an endless seam of glistening swamps and rivers feeding into the Freetown Estuary. I glanced around the faces of the men, trying to give them the kind of reassuring look that I figured they expected from their platoon sergeant. The lads were utterly silent, and I could feel the tension and apprehension sparking in the air.

No one was breathing a word, but we all knew. It was a water-logged, jungle hell down there and we had not the slightest idea of what we were going to encounter at the LZ. But over and above the fear and apprehension, I sensed something else – a real confidence and self-belief. Every man aboard the Chinook shared a unique bond: each of us had made it through the brutal Pathfinder Selection course, bonding us as brother warriors. There was an inner strength, one grounded in the conviction that we could take care of ourselves come what may.

We were also acutely aware of how Colonel Gibson had shown absolute belief in us by sending us on this mission: *Your force is on its own, but I have every confidence in you, Pathfinders.* Those words were balanced by what we could see of the ground now, but we were determined to prove the colonel right in putting us out here as his vanguard.

He could have sent another unit forward. He could have chosen to use the SAS boys operating out of Lungi Airport. He hadn't. He'd chosen us.

That was what we had to live up to.

The loadie raised two fingers and waved them in front of the faces of the blokes: we were two minutes out from the LZ. The guy allotted to drive the Pinz mounted up the vehicle and the engine coughed into life. To either side of him, guys prepared to loosen the quick-release straps and get the wagon rolling.

The loadie held up his thumb and index finger in a sideways U-shape, signalling we were half a minute out.

'Thirty seconds!' he yelled above the noise of the screaming turbines.

The guys were on their feet now, ready for the go.

I could feel the Chinook descending through the hot and humid air, the arse-end of the helo dropping more quickly than the front. The pitch of the turbines changed as the pilot feathered back on the rotors, the beat going from a rhythmic *thwoop-thwoop-thwoop*, that sliced the air apart, to a crazed *brrrrrrrrrrrzzzz*, as we flared out to land.

As the Chinook dropped, I felt a series of powerful, juddering shock waves reverberating through the airframe. For a moment I feared we were taking fire, before I realised what it was: the rotor blades were slicing into the jungle at the outer edges of the LZ, the space was so tight. This weird, rhythmic ripping sound bounced back at us – as if some giant chainsaw were tearing into the vegetation to either side of the aircraft.

I prayed the rotors held up. If they hit any major trees then they'd shear, sending us into the hell of a crash-landing. All of a sudden there was a massive *Bang*! – as if the rear rotor had struck a tree trunk. An instant later I realised it was our back wheels slamming into the deck as we landed. I felt the aircraft pivot forwards, and then the front pair were down.

The instant they were the loadie was screaming: 'GO! GO! GO! GO! GO!'

We piled off in two sticks, those on the left-hand side of the aircraft going left, and those on the right going right, until we had a ring of blokes strung around the Chinook, guns levelled at the jungle to their front, the twin rotors thrashing in the air above us. The Pinzgauer followed on our heels, roaring out of the Chinook's belly and onto the rough ground, the two blokes who had released the fixing straps piling down the ramp last-out.

Thirty seconds after touching down the loadie yelled into his intercom: 'Troops off! Ramp clear!' It was the call for the pilots to get airborne. Turbines screamed into a deafening howl as the pilots hit full throttle, and the pair of Chinooks rose as one, rotors tearing at the air as they clawed skywards, banking towards the east. We were left in a wind-whipped chaos – vegetation, grass, leaves, rotten wood and dirt howling all around us.

The bellies of the helos were swallowed up by the dust storm. We stared down the barrels of our weapons into a blinding whirlwind of debris.

I couldn't see a bloody thing.

Gradually the air cleared, revealing the wall of vegetation that surrounded the clearing, rotor-strikes clearly showing in the white scars of shattered branches.

The helos weren't taking any fire above us.

We weren't taking any fire on the ground.

Not a muzzle sparked amongst the shadows.

Right now, there was zero sign of the enemy.

As far as we could tell there wasn't a thing moving out there. We were down on our belt buckles 300 yards to the north of the village of Lungi Lol, and there wasn't a soul to be seen – villager or rebel fighter.

The patch of ground that we'd put down on looked as if it had been cleared via slash-and-burn – a method by which locals cut the jungle, leave it to dry, fire the vegetation and plant crops in the ash-rich residue. The first things to move off were the Pinz-gauers, bumping and lurching across the uneven ground. They made for the dirt highway some thirty yards from where we'd landed.

We joined the Pinzgauers on the main track. They began chugging their way towards the village, as we skirmished through the jungle to either side on foot. All the while I was thinking: *Where the hell is everyone? The locals must have heard the Chinooks come in, so where the hell are they?*

We hit the northern edge of the village. I noticed the first of these mud-walled and grass-thatched huts lining the road, interspersed with cleared areas for gardens and patches of thicker vegetation. Then I spotted the first of the locals. Here and there wide, frightened eyes peered out of a shadowed hut doorway. They were staring at us like the Martians had just landed.

We reached the T-junction of dirt tracks that marked the centre of the village. I gave orders to the patrol commanders to take up positions facing the wall of jungle to the northeast of us – the most likely line of any rebel attack.

We went firm.

To the east I could hear the pair of helos flying their pre-arranged holding pattern. They'd orbit there for five minutes, in case we needed to call in their fire support. We checked the vegetation to our front for anything untoward: the glint of sunlight on gunmetal; a muzzle flash; urgent or rapid movement through the trees. Our eyes scanned for targets, all the while knowing that just as the villagers had heard us fly in, so would any rebels – that's if there were any hereabouts.

While the villagers wouldn't have a clue as to who we were or where we'd come from, one thing would be crystal clear: *we weren't rebels.* We were clearly foreigners and we were clearly soldiers, but that would be about as much as they could know right now. It was no surprise that they were keeping to the cover of their huts: in a country such as this, men with guns were so often the bad guys.

For a good five minutes we scanned silently for targets. It was starting to look like ours had been an unopposed landing, as if the rebels hadn't reached this far south yet. We'd touched down at 1530 hours, so we had around three hours remaining until last light. The village was now loosely secured. We were in occupation, we'd yet to get shot at and we were not aware of any immediate threat.

Wag, Grant, the OC and me decided to do a walkabout, to get a sense of the lie of the land. We got the Pinzgauers parked up on an open area of hard-packed dirt, one ringed with huts, just to the west of the T-junction. I figured this was something like the village square. There was a clutch of ramshackle wooden stalls ranged down one side, which had to be the marketplace.

A smaller track branched off from the main highway, slicing south through the jungle. That had to be Donaldson's intended E & E route. The track ran for 12 kilometres, before it reached a dead end – the sea. Our flight over the jungle had only reinforced in my mind how defunct was any escape plan based upon heading that way. We'd be hemmed in on three sides – by sea and impenetrable jungle – and with the rebels at our backs.

Walkabout done, Wag and me began siting the individual patrols, while Tricky, Grant and Donaldson established comms with headquarters back at Lungi Airport. All we had to go on when choosing patrol locations was the lie of the land. We needed maximum cover from view and from fire – from being seen and being shot at – while at the same time being able to put down rounds on the most likely avenue of enemy approach – the dirt highway. With the terrain being impassable off-road, we presumed the rebels would have to come at us straight down the main drag.

We sited the HQ patrol in a couple of shallow craters, some thirty metres to the east of the village square. That way, we'd be pretty much at the heart of things so we could co-ordinate any action. We put Nathe and H's patrol – *33 Alpha* – some ninety yards to the east of us, facing down the throat of the dirt track. From there they could put down accurate fire onto the road, as far as we could see to the front of us.

Dolly's patrol – *33 Bravo* – we sited in a patch of thick bush a hundred yards or so to the far side of the highway, so protecting our left flank. The patrol commanded by Dale 'Ginge' Wilson – *33 Charlie* – we placed a hundred yards to the south of Nathe's patrol, with *33 Delta* – Taff Saunders' patrol – a hundred yards to the south of that. We now had the entire front of the village covered by our defensive positions.

Ginge Wilson, *33 Charlie*'s commander, was a northerner with a distinctive Mancunian accent. Around five-foot-ten, with a whippet-like runner's physique, Ginge had the impulsive ways typical of a 'racing snake'. He had only recently been promoted to patrol command, and was one of the least experienced and most excitable of the lot – hence my decision to sandwich his patrol between Nathe and Taff's, putting an experienced pair of hands to either side of him.

Taff Saunders – *33 Delta*'s commander – hailed from the Royal Regiment of Wales, and he was a five-foot-ten, 15-stone, hard-as-nails Welsh rugby player. He had a thick Welsh accent – he called everyone 'bud' – and he would only ever refer to God's own country – England – as 'the annexe', a carbuncle on the otherwise unblemished face of the Welsh motherland.

Taff hailed from the Rhondda Valley – the heart of the land of myths and dragons. The blokes ripped the piss constantly: *How can you be under cover behind enemy lines with an accent like that? Guys from the Rhondda all marry their sisters.* We did a lot of our training in South Wales, and you have to cross the Severn Bridge to get there. It's a toll bridge, but you only pay the one way, going from England into Wales.

Taff would torture us with that. 'Hey, bud, you only pay to get into Wales, not the other way around. No one pays to get into England.'

I referred to Taff as my 'yeah-but' man. He was a natural-born brawler and great in a bar fight, but he always had an answer for everything. A typical conversation with Taff went like this.

Me: 'Right, Taff, what I need from you is . . .'

Taff: 'Yeah, but, it'd be far better, bud, if we . . .'

I'd sited Taff out on our right flank – one of our most isolated and vulnerable positions – for a very good reason: I knew that the tough little Welsh git would never back down from a fight.

Wag and me left the lads to dig themselves some hasty shell-scrapes – the fastest way to get a bunch of soldiers below ground. A shell-scrape is a hole some two metres long, one and a half wide and three-quarters of a metre deep. It's big enough for two men to lie side by side facing the enemy, along with their kit – Bergens, webbing and weaponry. Shell-scrapes provide decent protection against fire, and limited protection against a nearby ground-burst explosion.

If the men had the time, they'd create additional cover by building up a 'bullet mantle' – using the soil they'd dug out of the hole to mound up around the front and sides – and then camouflaging that with local vegetation. That would provide the kind of defence that is our minimum for a twenty-four- to forty-eight-hour mission such as this one.

For the moment everything was going like clockwork. From an insertion onto a potentially hot LZ we'd formed a front line of defence across a village that seemed to be largely peaceful. Having sited the patrols, Wag and I made our way back to the HQ position. But before we could get much of a heads-up with Grant and Donaldson, the first figure to appear emerged from the bush.

He wasn't quite what we had been expecting.

He was tall and ebony-skinned, and dressed in a spotless set of combat fatigues, topped off by a pair of enormous mirror shades, plus a distinctive light blue beret. It seemed as if there was at least one UN peacekeeper based here in the village of Lungi Lol.

We beckoned him to approach. His sunglasses were so completely black that you couldn't see his eyes, and they had massive Foster Grant golden frames. They covered his face from his eyebrows to his cheek-bones, but other than that he was parade-ground smart. He was freshly shaven, his combats had sharp creases down the front and his boots were polished to a gleaming, mirror finish.

Impeccable.

He opened his mouth to introduce himself and out came this educated, public school English. He sounded posher than any of us lot – Grant and Donaldson included.

'Good afternoon, gentlemen. I am Lieutenant Oronto Obasanjo, from the Nigerian Army, forming up part of UNAMSIL, the United Nations peacekeeping mission here in Sierra Leone. You are most welcome. You are from which nation's military – Her Majesty's Armed Forces, if I am not mistaken?'

Grant and Donaldson recovered pretty well from the shock and did the introductions. Meet and greet done, we asked him for a ground orientation brief – a talk around the position. He proceeded to outline the lie of the land. The village was maybe eight hundred yards from end to end, with some fifty huts scattered along its length. There was little evidence of furniture or other material possessions amongst the villagers, and between each of the huts lay a swathe of thickly-vegetated farmland, where they grew most of their food.

Our two Pinzgauers parked up on the village square were the only vehicles in the entire place. At the southern edge of the square was a more substantial hut, and that was the village headman's place, the lieutenant explained. It was something like the mayor's office, and from there the chief oversaw everything that happened in his domain.

That was about all Lieutenant Obasanjo had to tell us. Apart from this: he'd been deployed to Lungi Lol six months earlier leading a force of sixteen fellow Nigerians. In the entire time he and his men had been here they had received not one visit from their commanders in UNAMSIL or even a set of orders. They had no food rations, they hadn't been paid for months and they had very limited supplies of ammo. In short, this was a typical UNAMSIL operation – chaotic, dysfunctional and forgotten by everyone in command.

Under the circumstances, what the lieutenant told us next was hardly surprising: his men had gone native. They'd discarded their uniforms in favour of T-shirts and sarongs, and shacked up with local village ladies as 'wives'. It was only Lieutenant Obasanjo, it seemed, who had refused to let standards drop. A true blue officer, he was determined to keep up appearances come what may.

'What, if anything, has happened in the village in terms of the rebels, the RUF?' Donaldson asked him, once he'd finished telling us about his posting. 'Have you had any encounters with the RUF while you've been here?'

The lieutenant shook his head. 'No. We have seen no sign of the RUF. In fact, we have had very few if any visitors.'

This was bizarre, way out left-field kind of shit. We'd flown into what we'd been warned was potentially a hot LZ, only to be met by a Nigerian officer fresh from the parade ground, with seemingly not a worry in the world. More bizarre still, his was no UN checkpoint keeping watch for rebel movement: it was sixteen blokes who'd discarded their uniforms, got married to the locals and become a part of village life. And if the lieutenant was to be believed, he and his men were quite happy thank you being left here to rot by the UN.

In a sense you had to take your hat off to the guy. He wasn't moaning or feeling sorry for himself. He and his men had adapted to the situation as they'd found it. Abandoned by all, they'd done what they had to in order to survive. And if the lieutenant didn't have a local wife then he was up all night washing and starching his uniform and polishing his boots, which I didn't think was very likely.

'Can you fucking believe it?' Wag remarked, once the lieutenant had left us. 'Fucking Lieutenant Mojo and his Gone Native Crew – chilling out in Lungi Lol?'

I laughed. *Lieutenant Mojo.* That was it – the name stuck.

We set about building an ATAP at the HQ position – a simple wooden frame thatched over with branches and leaves. It was a temporary structure designed to last the next forty-eight hours – the supposed duration of the mission – and was for shelter and camouflage only. Then we slung our hammocks from the nearby trees. Sewn from parachute silk, they are incredibly strong, lightweight and versatile. But as with so much of our gear we had to buy the raw materials and get a wife, girlfriend or mother to sew it for us, for the British Army didn't possess such kit.

The cost of getting one of those para-silk hammocks made was a considerable burden and many – especially the married blokes – simply couldn't afford it. They came complete with a para-silk mozzie net, one that pulled over the top, and a waterproof poncho above that. Half a squash ball threaded onto the cords at either end stopped any water running down or insects getting in. The hammocks were perfect for deep-jungle missions, yet the entire lot weighed less than two pounds.

The hammock situation typified how ludicrous was the British Army's kit-procurement system – the same system that had endorsed the SA80 over the M16. The British Army did issue hammocks, but they were made from thick nylon, came complete with collapsible aluminium struts, and were designed to double as a stretcher. Great idea on paper. Shit in reality. They were impossibly heavy, rattled as you moved and took an age to erect and take down.

They typified the Army's egghead mentality, whereby kit was rarely if ever tested by those who would use it at the hard end of soldiering. The trials and development unit of the British Army

should have been manned by soldiers who'd served on operations, and had the experience and ingenuity to make kit workable
in the field. Instead, it was staffed by SO1 (staff officer 1) colonels
who'd rarely if ever been out at the dirty end of ops.

Normally, we'd set trip flares around positions such as those
we'd taken up at Lungi Lol, to warn of any hostile forces creeping
forward under cover of darkness, plus we'd position motion sensors on the ground to detect any movement. The motion sensors
consist of a transmit–receive module that looks like a transistor
radio, plus eight individual sensors each the size of a 12-bore shotgun cartridge. You'd hollow out a small hole and bury each sensor
just below the surface, in areas you couldn't cover by fire, or to
plug gaps in your defences.

There are eight LEDs on the transmitter–receiver. The buried
sensors can detect seismic activity – so ground disturbance
within a twenty-metre radius. If someone walks past, the sensor
picks up the movement and transmits a message back to the receiver, at which point the LED corresponding to that sensor lights
up. With each sensor's location plotted on your map, you'd then
know you had something moving at position X.

But with none of that kind of kit available in Lungi Lol, it was up
to human watchfulness to detect any rebel approach.

Just prior to last light we called the patrol commanders in for
'prayers' – a communal heads-up, and to set the routine for the
coming night hours. We gathered in a circle – Nathe, Dolly, Ginge,
Taff, Wag, Grant, Tricky, Donaldson and me. Prayers is a concept
that lies at the heart of the Pathfinders: it's supposed to be a
time when all ranks are free to contribute to whatever is being
planned.

Donaldson began by outlining our mission. 'Now, the reason
why we are here is to observe for any rebel movement and to stop
them infiltrating further south,' Donaldson began. 'The threat is
from rebel attack, which makes holding the village key. We need
to presume the rebels' approach will be via the main track from

the northeast. They've got the same constraints as us, so they can't move unless using that dirt highway. We'll set stags through the night keeping watch, two on and two off...'

'We need to make the ERV west along the main track,' Grant piped up, once Donaldson was done. 'Then we can E & E to Lungi Airport that way.'

ERV stands for Emergency Rendezvous – the point at which we'd come together if we were on the run. Behind Grant's seemingly innocuous comment lay a whole change of plan. He was suggesting that we E & E down the main highway to Freetown and Lungi Airport – in other words, abandoning Donaldson's plan that pitched us directly into the sea.

Donaldson stared at his fellow officer for a second, before nodding his assent. 'Okay. Good one, Grant. We'll do that.'

A silent sigh of relief went around the men. At least we'd got the E & E sorted.

We discussed actions-on if the rebels hit us in overwhelming numbers and we couldn't hold on for the QRF. If we had to bug out we'd try to use the vehicles and keep together as a unit. We'd move fast down the main drag, using the Pinzgauers to carry our wounded, and with the rest of us beasting it on foot. If we got split up the ERV was set as a point on the map 1.5 klicks down the dirt highway. Those already gathered at the ERV would sit on a standoff bearing, allowing them to watch the ERV unobserved, and check if any new arrivals were 'friendlies'.

We'd keep the ERV 'open' for two hours following the time of first contact with the enemy, giving every man that long to make it – at which point everyone gathered there would bug out. Our next ERV was the 'War RV' – the point at which we had entered the country as a unit – so Lungi Airport itself.

'To help keep watch on the main highway I want some early warning out front of the patrols,' Donaldson announced. 'Steve, Grant: you two take a couple of blokes and a Pinz and push forward five hundred yards out on the track.'

I glanced at Grant, worriedly. We'd sited the patrols well and got our defences sorted. We were ready. Sending four guys alone and unsupported at night into unknown terrain, and into the teeth of a rebel advance – it didn't make any sense. Not in my book, anyway.

I gritted my teeth. 'Boss, in light of everything we know, do we really want four blokes five hundred yards out there and at night? Especially as that's the way the rebels will come. We'll be isolated, unsupported, and in unknown territory.'

'Yes, we do. I need eyes out there.'

'I understand that, boss, but any movement to our flanks and we'll be cut off.'

'No, 'cause you'll be covered from the village.'

Covered from the village? We'd be a good half a kilometre out from our forward positions. The accurate range of an SA80 is far less than that, even if the lads could see in the darkness to aim and to shoot properly. More to the point some three hundred yards out from the village the track kinked northwards, putting it out of sight beyond. I figured we'd be unseen, out of range, and cloaked in darkness.

To my mind, we'd be lacking proper cover and support.

If an order or direction is delivered in a way that is rational and sensible, and I can understand why it needs to be done, I will embrace it. But as far as I was concerned this was none of those things. Pathfinder prayers always ends with 'going around the bazaars' – getting input from each of the men present.

'Anyone got anything else to say?' Donaldson asked. 'Dolly? Taff? Ginge? Nathe? Nope? Okay, get ready in your positions for stand-to.'

At first and last light we do stand-to. Militaries the world over have worked out that those times are the best at which to launch an attack. At first light men are likely to be sleepy and less alert, but there is enough light to see and fight by. At last light they are likely to be tired from the day's activities, and looking forward to a good feed and a rest. Accordingly, we get locked and loaded and on high alert at first and last light, with every man ready to rumble.

After stand-to we'd adopt 'night routine', with sentries set all through the hours of darkness. We'd have two men in each patrol standing watch, with the changeover times staggered, so there was always one set of eyes out on stalks. Staggering sentry changeovers also provides for continuity, so one sentry can report to the next all that has been seen.

But as for Grant and me, it was time to head east into the brooding darkness and the unknown. Donaldson ordered us to push out in one of the Pinzgauers, in case we had to make a 'rapid withdrawal'. We chose to take Mark 'Marky' Lewis and Steve B with us, a couple of solid operators whom we'd pulled in from Nathe and Dolly's patrols.

To my way of thinking it made little sense to send four men into the unknown with several thousand rebels massing. Right now Donaldson was ignoring one of the cardinal rules of the Pathfinders – that critical decisions are discussed and decided upon collectively, and based upon experienced-based reasoning, using the input of all the senior blokes.

But making an open stand against Donaldson now, in front of the others, would only damage us, and at the very moment when we needed to perform at 101 per cent. We prided ourselves upon tight cohesion, trust and faith in each other, brotherhood and *esprit de corps*. Having made it through Selection, the aspiration of every man was to become a patrol commander, and then make platoon sergeant. If right now they were forced to witness Sergeant Heaney ripping into their OC – that would be very bad news indeed.

So we mounted up the Pinzgauer, pushing north, with dark walls of jungle hemming us in on either side.

7

Half a kilometre out from the village we pulled to a halt.

We'd made the drive showing no lights, and navigating by the faint moonlight that filtered through to the dirt track, so as to have a greater chance of remaining unseen by any watching enemy. Our natural night vision had kicked in. We'd spotted a small, open area to one side of the track, one devoid of any vegetation. It was maybe ten feet by twenty and it formed a kind of a lay-by.

Using that we spun the Pinz around and got the nose of the wagon pointing back down the track towards the village, in case we had to make a run for it.

The cleared area had a bank of earth about four feet high running around it, where the bulldozers had pushed back the dirt and vegetation. Grant and me said we'd take the first stag, leaving Steve and Marky to try to get some sleep. The back of the Pinz was lined with bench seats, making it too cramped to doss in. So Steve and Marky bedded down on the dirt, lying in the lee of the earthen bank, which at least provided some cover from fire.

On the far side was the jungle.

It loomed before us like a dark and impenetrable cliff-face – one-hundred-foot-high forest giants, fringed with smaller palm-like bushes, tree-ferns and vines, where the dozers had torn a jagged edge through the mass of vegetation. Mature rainforest – growth that has remained undisturbed for centuries – generally consists of a high forest canopy, with little greenery on the dark forest floor. But where such virgin jungle has been disturbed – like having a highway slashed through it – secondary vegetation springs up in the sunlit clearings so formed.

The dirt highway had cut a tunnel of sunlight through the forest, and on each side of the road was a riot of greenery. While it is relatively easy to trek through mature jungle, such secondary vegetation is thick, tangled and more often than not full of horrendous thorns and spines. If the rebels hit us, it would take an age to cut through it with our machetes. In reality the only escape route was to drive hell-for-leather back the way we'd come.

With Steve and Marky bedded down on the deck, Grant and me took up a position by the rear of the wagon, weapons pointing eastwards – the direction from which we presumed the rebels would come – eyes scanning the night-dark terrain.

'I know why I'm here,' I muttered to Grant, not taking my gaze from my weapon's iron sights. 'Gets mouthy old Smoggy out of the way.' I jerked my head in Marky and Steve's direction. 'But why are those two here, plus you?'

Grant shook his head imperceptibly, eyes showing white in the darkness. 'I've no idea. None, mate.'

We were keeping our voices low, partly in case any rebels were within hearing distance, but partly so we wouldn't be overheard by Marky and Steve. We didn't want our doubts and apprehension cascading down to the blokes. They had to believe the links in the chain of command were strong, although none of the guys were stupid. They would know there were tensions.

I tightened my grip on my weapon. 'You know, this doesn't make any sense ... Sending the four of us out here ...'

'Mate, don't I know it,' Grant cut in. 'But right now there's not a lot we can do about it.'

Having talked it over some more, we agreed that the only thing to do was for Grant and the senior NCOs – me, Wag, The White Rabbit – to go direct to Colonel Gibson if this continued. And with Gibbo a whole world away back at Lungi Airport, we were pretty much stuck with things as they were right now.

It was far from perfect, but what other options were there?

The night proved warm and sticky, with a lot of ambient light from the moon and stars. It meant our view northeast up the road was pretty good, without having to use any NVG. No one could make much progress through the jungle or down the road without making considerable noise, so we'd most likely hear 'em before we'd see 'em.

Or so we hoped.

If they skirted by us undetected in the deep jungle, they could get between our position and the village, at which stage we were toast. We'd be surrounded by rebels on all sides. We'd be killed or captured – and if the latter, presumably we'd be offered amputations, 'long-sleeve' or 'short-sleeve' style. Or maybe something even worse. But there was sod all we could do about that now – four blokes set a half a klick out from any support.

We focused our every molecule on our senses – chiefly hearing and sight – our early warning systems. The key to survival here was watchfulness in every sense of the word, and tuning in to the natural environment. Once we'd familiarised ourselves with the regular beat and rhythm of the jungle, we could filter out those sounds and scan for ones only a human might make: the crunch of boots on leaves; whispered voices; the *clatch-clatch* of a bolt being pulled back on an assault rifle.

It was like a form of meditation, this tuning in to the night environment. I opened up my mind and senses to any changes in the setting here, and I was hyper-alert to any sense of threat. If my ears caught the faintest sound – anything distinct from the deafening night-time beat pulsating out of the forest shadows – my eyes immediately swivelled around to focus on that point.

We had with us one Clansman 349 VHF radio, which was set to 'listening watch'. This meant we had an open line of comms to Tricky, back in the HQ ATAP, and we'd keep it live all night long. That way he would hear if we were under attack the moment it happened. We'd only speak to him if we had to – if there was something vital to report – and vice versa.

All that night the tension rippled back and forth, as we sensed movement out there in the darkness. Every noise from the brooding bush sent my pulse racing. I'd soldiered in many of the world's jungles but this was something different. We were four against several thousand, and we stood out like the proverbial dog's bollocks with the wagon parked on the dirt roadway.

First light was about the most welcome sight that any of us had ever seen. Imperceptibly the jungle brightened, and I felt the tension of the long night's watch draining out of me.

Almost as the first rays of sunlight filtered over the horizon, Tricky came up on the air. '33, Zero. Move back into village.'

Zero was the OC's call-sign, 33 was us.

'Roger, out.'

Never has a short drive down a dirt track been so enjoyable as that one back into Lungi Lol.

We parked the Pinz on the village square and made our way to the HQ ATAP, leaving Marky and Steve to head back to their patrols. We'd been out there for nine hours straight and I'd managed four hours' fitful sleep, lying in full belt kit on the dirt with my weapon only ever a hand's reach away. With the constant buzzing of the mozzies that were feeding on me, plus the tension, I'd never really been fully asleep. There was always an edge of wakefulness.

After stand-to we got a brew on, tucking into some ration packs over a nice cup of tea. All around us I could hear the village starting to come to life. None of the patrols had much to report, our first night in Lungi Lol being seemingly a quiet one.

Around 0800 hours Donaldson gathered the head-shed. 'Right, I'm heading back to Lungi Airport,' he announced. 'I need to speak to the CO. I'll need a driver, so I'm taking Marky with me.'

Utter silence.

No one said the barest thing in response. This was so totally and utterly unexpected we were at a complete loss for words. The OC radioed for Marky to join him, and the two of them made their way across to one of the Pinzgauers. With barely another word they mounted up the vehicle and drove west out of Lungi Lol.

The four of us in the HQ ATAP – Grant, Tricky, Wag and me – were stunned. It was as if we were all waiting to see who was going to be the first to break the silence and say something.

It was Wag. 'What – the – *fuuuuck*?' he asked, incredulously.

I shook my head in disbelief. 'Mate, I have no idea.'

'But what the *fuck* is that all about? Tricky – has he said anything to anyone on the comms?'

Tricky shook his head. 'Nope. Not said a word all night long.'

There weren't the words to express how we were feeling right now. We were utterly dumbfounded. The ramifications of this were unknowable. Was Donaldson gone for good, or just paying Gibbo a temporary call? Did command now pass to Grant, or not? Was Grant now *Sunray*, the OC Pathfinders' call-sign? Or was Donaldson somehow still in command – just that he wasn't with us any more?

Who fucking knows?

Why did Donaldson need to speak to the CO in person anyway, instead of via the radio? No one had the faintest idea. Equally importantly, would they even make it? They had several dozen kilometres of uncharted territory to get through, with no known friendly forces between us and Lungi Airport. Plus we were left with just the one vehicle in Lungi Lol, which greatly lessened our ability to escape and evade via the wagons, for one Pinz could carry no more than a dozen men.

We took stock. We had another thirty-six hours max of the mission ahead of us, and we were determined to make the best of it. We decided to use the time well. First off, we'd get the patrols to build up their defences still further. Wag and I got them busy doing that, then we went to have a further chat with Lieutenant Mojo, to try to get a better sense of whether his men might be of any use to us in a fight with the rebels.

Just to the south of the HQ ATAP Mojo had his own quarters,

encircled by a palisade of wood driven into the ground. We'd yet to see inside, for the fence was ten feet high and blocked all view. It was around 0900 hours when we knocked on the small wooden door. Mojo appeared dressed as immaculately as he had been on day one, and gestured for us to join him.

'Please – this is where I live.'

We poked our heads inside. Immediately to our front was a large hut, one made out of a wooden frame plastered in mud and with a grass-thatch roof. To the right was the weirdest sight of all – a rickety post, with the distinctive light blue flag of the United Nations hanging limply. The palisade was so high and the flagpole so low that you couldn't actually see the flag from outside. But what struck me most powerfully was what was *lacking from the place*: I couldn't see a single radio antenna, no sign of any radio, nor any solar panels with which to charge one.

It looked as if Mojo and his men had no way of making comms back to UN headquarters, that's presuming the UN had such a thing. They had no way to receive orders, Intel updates, schedule resupplies or to get relieved, and no way to call up reinforcements when several thousand rebels came charging down their throats. In the circumstances, going native – as Mojo's men had done – seemed about the smartest option in terms of trying to stay alive.

Having been shown around the Kingdom of Mojo, it struck me that the lieutenant mightn't even know that a battalion of British PARAs – plus elite forces – had jetted into the country. We invited him over to our place for a brew and a chat. It quickly became clear that Mojo had not the slightest idea about pretty much anything: he had no idea that the British military had intervened in the war, occupying Lungi Airport and most of Freetown. He'd presumed we were British soldiers somehow working with the UN, as fellow peacekeepers.

He knew of the RUF's existence, but he had zero idea of their proximity, or that they were massing to assault Lungi Airport and Freetown – so aiming to usher in another dark chapter of murder and mayhem across the country. In fact he had absolutely no idea of the kind of danger he and his men were in – largely because he had no way of making contact with, or getting updates from, the UN.

Incredible.

Grant proceeded to enlighten him. 'Lieutenant, you need to know that there is an imminent threat and that this village is in danger. There are several thousand RUF advancing on Freetown and the only way they can get there is via here. Right now they could be any distance away – from a few dozen kilometres to spitting-distance close. The updates we're getting are that they're on the move, and we thought we were flying into a hot LZ.'

Lieutenant Mojo looked suitably taken aback. He'd had six months of a peaceful posting, without the slightest hint that the villagers of Lungi Lol were about to get butchered, along with all of his men.

'Ours is only a forty-eight-hour tasking,' Grant continued. 'We envisage we will be gone in two days maximum. We're here as a blocking force, to provide security while we evacuate our nationals from Lungi Airport. But while we're here we'll assist you with your mandate, which I presume is securing the village.'

Mojo gave a confused shake of the head. 'I had heard reports of villages getting attacked, of women being raped and of villagers being put to work by the rebels – but this was all upcountry and a very long way away. If the rebels are poised to take Freetown that means the UN operation here ... well, it has been a very big failure.'

'That's as may be,' Grant replied. 'It's not our concern. You're the UN and you have your roles and responsibilities. Our tasking is to ensure that the ongoing evacuation of civilians from Freetown goes ahead unhindered. We are not – *repeat not* – a peacekeeping force. We will use lethal force if fired upon or if the need arises. Do you understand the difference between us?'

Mojo glanced at Grant. 'I do. But it doesn't seem as if there is much peace to keep any more.' He paused, then fixed Grant with this earnest look. 'If things are as serious as you say, you need to meet the village chief. Let me take you to him. He needs to know this.'

We figured this was a smart idea. The more local connections we could forge here in Lungi Lol, the more Intel we might garner.

Mojo led the way to the village square. It was around 1030 by now and the marketplace was getting busy. People were milling about carrying baskets of mangoes and trays of tomatoes and bicycles were criss-crossing to and fro. There was even the odd guy on a moped pootling about. To one side of the square lay a larger building raised up three feet or so on wooden stilts. Its walls were made from a woven latticework of branches plastered with mud, and it had the obligatory grass-thatch roof. Six wooden steps led up to a veranda that ran along the front of the building, plus a wooden door.

To the left of the door sat an old, balding, wiry-looking man on a straight-backed wooden chair. His poise and bearing marked him out as a man of substance. The chair faced onto the village square, plus the T-junction. From this vantage point he could observe all who passed through his domain. To the right of the door was a younger dude – clearly the village chief's lackey.

It struck me as odd that the chief hadn't been over to see us yet, to ask what we were doing in his village. But we'd learn with time that the chief never stirred from his chair. Everyone went to him. People came to ask a favour, or to air a grievance, or to sort a feud, whatever.

Grant, Wag, Mojo and me gathered at the bottom of the steps, with Mojo slightly in the lead. He began to address the chief, speaking some language that we couldn't understand. I caught the odd English word, but otherwise it was gibberish. We'd learn in time that this was Pidgin English, a blend of English mixed with Creole – a West African dialect dating back to the times of slavery.

The chat went on for a good few minutes, Mojo doing the talking and the chief listening. I saw him gesture at the three of us, as he gabbled away. Every now and then the chief would glance at his lackey, the lackey would say a few words, and then the chief would nod for Mojo to continue.

I gave chiefy a good long study. I figured he was around seventy-five years old and thinning on top, with wispy hair flecked with grey. He was lighter-skinned than Mojo and several of his yellowing teeth were missing. An all-in-one robe fell from his shoulders to his feet, which were shod in worn leather sandals. In his right hand he had a lighted cigarette and every now and then he took a drag.

We were doing our best to be culturally sensitive – hearts and minds stuff and all that – but still Wag couldn't resist making the odd comment.

'What d'you reckon he's saying now?' he muttered, out of the corner of his mouth. 'Let's kill 'em all?'

Mojo still had his massive Foster Grant shades on – in fact I'd never seen him without them – but his tone and attitude was now one of total respect. When the chief raised his hand in a gesture for silence Mojo shut it immediately, leaving the big man free to talk. The chief said a few words, his eyes flickering from Mojo to us and back again, and Mojo translated.

'Okay, he says he is happy that you are here. He welcomes you on behalf of the village. He says if you need anything while you are here you must come to him. He is very glad you have come.' Mojo paused. 'So, he would like you to introduce yourselves.'

Grant glanced at the veranda. 'Hi, I'm Grant.'

Mojo: 'Grant!'

I was trying not to crack up. 'Right, I'm Steve.'

Mojo: 'And Steve!'

'Aye, and I'm Wag,' said Wag.

Mojo did a double take: 'Wag?' he queried, in a high-pitched voice of surprise.

'Mate, just this once how about being Graham?' I muttered.

Wag glared at Mojo. He was crouched there like a Hobbit, his weapon in one hand and his torso wrapped in bandoliers of ammo. Correction. Right now he didn't remind me so much of a Hobbit, as of Gimli the Dwarf in *The Lord of the Rings*.

Wag scowled. 'Not Wag like that,' he said, mimicking Mojo's high-pitched whine. 'It's *Wag*,' he growled. 'Wag.'

Mojo turned to the chief and shrugged: 'And . . . Wag.'

The chief nodded gravely. Introductions done, Mojo chatted some more, then turned to us. 'Okay, so we're done. Let's go.'

On the way back to HQ ATAP Mojo told us it had all gone very well. 'Any assistance the chief can give – anything – just let me know.'

'We're fine for the time being,' Grant replied. 'We've got the men on the ground and the patrols are well bedded in.'

'How many of you are there?' Mojo asked.

'Twenty-seven.'

Mojo stopped dead in his tracks: '*Twenty-seven*?'

We'd spent all morning warning him about the danger of getting massacred by thousands of rebels. I guessed he'd imagined several hundred British troops had thrown a wall of steel around Lungi Lol. Now we'd revealed our true numbers – *twenty-seven*. Correction: twenty-five with Marky and Donaldson gone.

Mojo hurried off towards the Kingdom of Mojo looking decidedly worried. We turned left to where Tricky was hunched over the radio. Right now he had a bunch of kids crowded around him. Our ration packs contained bags of boiled sweets, and Tricky had started doling them out to the boys and girls of Lungi Lol. Each time he handed some out a kid would start cavorting about and yelling for joy. *Yippeee!* Compared to back home in Britain these poor little sods had next to nothing, and the looks on their faces would have melted the hardest of hearts.

'So, how did it go with the chief?' Tricky asked.

'Yeah, we just met The King,' Wag replied. 'He never said a lot. Happy for us to be here . . . yada, yada, yada.'

Tricky grinned. 'I've just sent the morning Sched. Told 'em we are on the ground with nothing to report on rebel movements . . . so far.'

It was a good three hours since Donaldson had left us, so unless he and Marky had been hit en route and were lying dead in a ditch they would be back at Lungi Airport by now. I checked with Tricky if he'd had any news, but there was none. There was bugger all we could do about it, so we settled down to priority number one – stopping the RUF at Lungi Lol.

Grant, Wag and me got our heads together, talking through how best to cement our positions. First priority was to map the ground over which we would be fighting. That done, we could hone our defences to better suit the threat. We'd need to ensure each patrol knew its left and right arcs of fire, beyond which they shouldn't put down any rounds – for they'd be straying into the neighbouring patrol's domain. That way, we'd have interlocking arcs of fire covering all potential avenues of approach.

There was no way we could target any rebels massing in the tree line – the fringe of jungle that hemmed in the village on all sides. It was too dark and vegetated to see clearly, and that meant we only had a limited amount of open ground in which to stop them. That in turn meant that we'd have to make every shot count once the rebels were in the kill zone.

We got Dolly, Nathe, Ginge and Taff to draw up detailed sketches of the terrain within each of their patrols' arcs of fire. Any landmarks or reference points – a burned tree stump, a distinctive termite mound – were marked up. That way, fire could be called in instantly: 'Bring to bear, twenty yards right of burned tree!' Everyone in the patrol would know exactly where the enemy was.

Range cards were put together, on which we measured out the distance to each marked point. Below 100 yards the trajectory of fire isn't affected by wind or distance, but above that it is. With the range cards, we'd know exactly when to compensate and by how much: we'd automatically aim off the correct fraction for wind speed and distance. Finally, a 'dead ground' study was added to the mix – identifying areas that were hidden from view and from fire, where the enemy could go to ground, regroup and attack.

Those areas were shaded on the sketches, with the entry and exit points identified and named. Fire could then be called instantly onto any of those points. The GPMGs were repositioned to cover the dead ground, while the SA80s would be used to hit individual targets in the open. This was all about increasing the accuracy and intensity of the fire we could bring to bear.

In spite of our mega-blag with Mick back at the Lungi Airport weapons dump, Wag and me were painfully aware of our limited supplies of ammo: there would be no 'fire for effect' on this mission. So at its simplest, this was also about ensuring that every bullet found a target.

When the rebels hit us we needed to make sure one shot equalled one kill.

8

We figured we also needed to up our profile and our visibility with the locals. All morning we'd had people moving along the main highway into and out of the village – presumably traders, family visitors, farmers, whatever. Everyone stopped to stare at these strange white soldiers who'd occupied Lungi Lol. But it was clear as day that any number of them could have been rebels posing as villagers.

The rebels might be recceing our positions, or even infiltrating the village so they could hit us from the rear. Their ranks were made up of scores of child soldiers, so in theory even the kids could be the bad guys. We knew they had used villagers as human shields – forcing them to march in front of their fighters – in previous battles. We had to presume they were pretty much capable of anything, and if they were getting in amongst us undetected it wasn't good news.

As a priority we needed to push out roving foot patrols to keep a watch on the comings and goings, and to establish stop and search checkpoints. The more we could get the patrols on the move the more ground truth we'd garner, plus the harder it would be for any of the bad guys to figure out our exact positions or our numbers.

That afternoon Wag and me did a walkabout to check on the patrols. It was the hottest part of the day by now, and out from under the tree cover the sun was merciless. We headed first for Dolly's position – *33 Bravo* – on our left flank. By the time we had reached the shade of the thick bush we were soaked with sweat. I had beads of it dripping off the rim of my jungle hat in a constant stream.

What made matters worse was that we'd been issued with just the one litre of drinking water per man per day. As with ammo, weaponry, maps, anti-malarials and so much else, someone had forgotten to add water to the list of supplies we might need in Sierra Leone. While we had the kit to filter and purify water, the village appeared to be totally dry. We figured they'd built it on a patch of the highest land available, so that it didn't flood too badly during the rains. But that meant there wasn't a ready supply of water anywhere nearby.

Ideally, we needed to drink several litres per day, to keep properly hydrated. Dehydration causes listlessness and the lack of ability to focus. Right now we'd not had a single shot fired at us or seen the slightest sign of any rebels, and village life seemed to be proceeding pretty much as normal. We needed to get around the blokes and reinforce the need for watchfulness.

The threat was very real: we just didn't know when or where exactly they'd hit us. We needed heightened alertness, measured with sustainability. The blokes couldn't be staring down their rifles all day long or they'd go stir crazy. We needed to balance getting good rest, eating properly and trying to keep actions to a minimum during the heat of the day, with a permanent readiness to do battle. That was the message we spread around the patrols.

The plan in the case of an overwhelming assault was to hold the village for as long as possible. We agreed three trigger points for us to go on the run. The first was taking unsustainable casualties (i.e. more than we could evacuate). The second was facing the serious danger of being overrun. The third was when two-thirds of our ammo had been exhausted. If that stage was reached we'd be left with around a hundred rounds per man with which to do a fighting withdrawal.

It was late afternoon by the time Wag and me were back at the HQ ATAP. Mojo must have had a word with his blokes, for several of them had pitched up, dressed in a hodgepodge of mixed combats, T-shirts and sarongs. In contrast to their leader's parade-ground perfection, these guys were tatty and unkempt, and their weapons looked similarly ill-maintained. They carried Belgian-made FN assault rifles, but one look at them and I doubted if they would be much use in battle.

Wag was obviously thinking along the same lines. He approached one of them, feigning interest in his weapon, as if he'd never seen the likes of it before. In reality Pathfinders are trained to use just about every kind of small arms invented, in case we have to disarm the bad guys, or scavenge their weaponry and ammo when in a situation like the one we were in now.

'What kind of gun is that, then, mate?' Wag asked. I wondered if the Nigerian would understand his thick Burnley accent. 'Can I have a look at it then, mate?'

The Nigerian handed it across. The FN looks like the old British Army self-loading rifle (SLR). It has a fully-automatic function and packs a 7.62 mm round. Wag removed the magazine, unloaded the weapon, cocked it and got a good look at the working parts. Simply by listening to the action as he moved it back and forth, he'd be able to tell if it was smooth and well-oiled, or stiff and gravelly.

'Oh yeah, this is a nice weapon, like,' Wag remarked. He turned it around as if admiring it, before replacing the magazine. 'Is it yours like? All yours?'

The Nigerian smiled proudly as he took back his weapon. It was his all right, and by the look on Wag's face it hadn't seen a clean or an oil in the six months the Nigerians had been here.

'The mag was dented and battered,' Wag reported, once Mojo's men had gone. 'Looked to be about half a dozen rounds in it, max. And did you hear the crunching of the working parts? Horrendous . . .'

We could assume that if one was like that, they likely all were. If and when the rebels hit us, we'd not be relying on Mojo's men for back-up, that was for sure.

Prior to last light Tricky radioed through the second Sched

of the day. We got a surprise message from The White Rabbit in return: '*Sunray* will not be returning to your location. Repeat: *Sunray* will not be returning to your location. There will be a re-supply tomorrow morning: send HLS grid.'

Sunray was the code-name for Donaldson. As no further information was provided, no one had a clue what had happened. But we could make a good guess about how Donaldson's surprise reappearance would have gone down with Colonel Gibson. In any case, he was gone and we had a job to get on with here.

During that afternoon's walkabout we'd realised there was a far better HLS – helicopter landing site – than the one we'd flown in on. Due west of Taff's position was a large, open, sandy bowl some seventy metres across. The surface was hard-packed like concrete, and there was little vegetation to obstruct a landing. That was now the preferred HLS. Tricky called through its grid to The White Rabbit, and we got confirmation that a Chinook would be inbound the following morning.

We didn't know what the resupply flight was for exactly, as we were scheduled to be out of Lungi Lol sometime tomorrow. The White Rabbit rounded off the comms with an Intel update for us.

'Information suggests significant rebel movement towards Freetown, and that *it will have to come through you*. Repeat: rebels moving in significant numbers and coming via your location.'

Comms done, we took stock. We could easily have been scouted by the rebels posing as villagers during the day. Even if they hadn't infiltrated Lungi Lol, we had to presume that word of our presence had spread like wildfire. In Lungi Lol and its environs we had to be this year's biggest ever news.

The rebels would know we were here. For certain.

And now we were doubly sure that they were coming.

We called prayers. Having passed the new Intel around to the blokes, Grant delivered the news that Donaldson was gone. He did so in as easygoing a tone as he could muster, but the looks on the patrol commanders' faces said it all.

Nathe gave a snort of derision 'So where's he fucking gone to, then ...'

'It doesn't matter where he's gone,' Grant interjected. 'He's gone, so let's kill it there. Let's get on with it.' He paused to let the words sink in. 'Right, night-time routine, and I don't need to warn you about the threat level ...'

No one appeared to dwell on the OC's departure too much, and morale seemed high. This was the 'train hard, fight easy' mentality: the more you drilled down into your skills, the more confident you became in your abilities. When you trained relentlessly, when you were twenty-five guys at the zenith of your abilities, then you could have total faith in those to either side of you. And you could face odds like these with steel in your eyes – not to mention losing your OC.

With dusk came all the noises from the jungle. But tonight there seemed to be more than the normal amount of weird squeals and squawks from out of the tree line. No one had a clue what they were exactly, but we knew of the rebels' habit of signalling to each other at night, using the calls of jungle animals.

'What the fuck's that?' Wag muttered. We'd taken the first stag. 'Was that an animal? Doesn't sound like any I've ever 'eard of.'

To our left people were trickling down the darkened road into the village. We spotted a crowd of a dozen or more moving steadily towards the square.

'Who the hell're that lot?' Wag growled.

I studied them via my NVG. 'Can't see any weapons. I can see a kid, plus a couple of women.'

'Right, well if it's blokes only we stop and search 'em. Agreed?'

'Agreed.'

By the time Wag and I came off stag the village square was filling up. We did a short walkabout, and it turned out that more people were expected. Word had spread on two fronts: one, that the RUF were poised to launch an attack characterised by all the usual bloody murder and mayhem; two, that the British Army were in Lungi Lol to stop them. People were flooding in from all around and kipping down on the village square, *for protection*.

The village chief was vetting each new family arrival, giving them permission to stay, and allocating an empty space for them to sleep. Most were women and children and they were terrified of the horrors they feared were coming. They bedded down on straw mats that they'd carried with them, with blankets thrown over families huddled together, for the added sense of security. The village square was some seventy yards wide and it was already half-full.

It was our second night in Lungi Lol, and we were counting down the hours until our withdrawal. But in truth, no one was particularly keen to leave. Hardened from years of soldiering in Northern Ireland, where so many of the locals hate British soldiers, it felt great to be on the side of the angels for a change.

We returned to the HQ ATAP. In addition to our sentries, our patrol had a 24/7 watch to keep over the radios. New orders, plus intelligence updates on rebel movements, might be radioed through at any time, and it was vital to keep a listening ear.

Those of us not on watch dossed down, fully dressed in boots and belt kit and with a machete strapped to our side. A grab bag made a passable pillow, with any extra kit stuffed inside it in case of the need to go on the run.

At the crack of dawn I got Tricky to radio Nathe's patrols and get a couple of blokes sent to me. We then headed down there. At 0700 hours dead the distinctive form of a Chinook swooped in low over the treetops and put down in the clearing. The White Rabbit came off the open ramp, along with Marky, the guy who'd driven Donaldson out in the Pinzgauer. I ran across in a crouch to meet them.

'Mate, this is open-ended now!' The White Rabbit yelled in my ear-hole, above the deafening noise of the helo's turbines. 'No idea how long you'll be here!' He jerked his thumb towards a heap of stores lying under a cargo net in the hold. 'Load more supplies in there – water jerries, food, anti-malarials . . .'

I signalled to the guys to get unloading. Eddie and I moved away from the helo, whose rotors were still turning and burning, as the blokes started ferrying kit out from under the downwash of the thrashing blades. We got ourselves a good twenty metres away from the noise and the dust, so we could get a proper heads-up. Even so, Eddie still had to yell to make himself heard.

'Steve, Donaldson's gone. He flew out on a Herc yesterday back to the UK. He's on a compassionate. Jacko's been made stand-in OC Pathfinders.'

A 'compassionate' is military speak for going on compassionate leave – so if you had extraordinary personal or family reasons that meant you had to get home. If Donaldson had gone on a compassionate, at least that would help make some sense out of all that had happened.

Jacko – Mark Jackson – had been the 2iC of the Pathfinders prior to Grant taking over. He'd served under Johnny Allem, the superlative OC we'd had prior to Donaldson. He was the son of Sir Mike Jackson, the high-profile ex-commander of KFOR (Kosovo Force), the force that had liberated Kosovo in 1999. Needless to say, we were in good hands if Jacko had taken over command.

'Mate, the NEO is almost done,' Eddie continued, 'but the op is evolving and the Intel we're picking up indicates serious rebel movement towards your position. The CO wants you here for the duration.'

Intel was flooding in thick and fast, Eddie explained. Largely it was from humint sources – paid informers – within the rebel ranks, but also due to our electronic warfare people having cracked the rebels' communications, so we could listen in on their conversations. From that they figured some 2000 rebels were massing to the north of us. They were armed with small arms, rocket-propelled grenades, light machine guns, and 12.7 mm DShK heavy machine guns, plus they had captured UN armoured personnel carriers and trucks.

'Make no mistake: holding this place is key to everyone's plans,' Eddie continued. 'The rebels have to be stopped here, otherwise they'll make it into Freetown and we all know what follows. The CO doesn't have anyone else who can do the job.

'Now that you're here for the duration, the SAS lads will come through you and recce your flanks. That's about it. Oh yeah, apart from this.' Eddie handed me a large, bulky mobile-phone-like device. 'We figured you might need this. We've got another back at base so we can do satphone-to-satphone comms, just in case the radios aren't working.'

Our 319 HF radios were dodgy as hell. All it generally took was a good soaking and the 319s would stop working. By contrast, the Thuraya satphone that Eddie had handed me was a bulletproof system. A purely civvie piece of kit, it was 100 per cent reliable, versatile and fast. A tenth of the size and weight of our 319s, it was also perfect for going on the run. They were like gold dust, and getting our hands on one meant the nightmare scenario of getting hit by the rebels and not being able to call in the QRF was pretty much over.

Eddie and me chatted for a few seconds more as the blokes finished unloading, running through various scenarios of how the twenty-six of us lot were going to stop 2000 rebels armed to the teeth.

He signed off with a bemused shrug. 'Mate, fuck knows.'

With that he turned and took a crouching run back up the Chinook's open ramp. The loadie hopped on after him, gave the thumbs-up, and almost before the ramp started to whine shut the Chinook lifted off. They'd been on the ground for four minutes max before they were heading back towards Lungi Airport.

The White Rabbit had flown in with three days of rations per man – all they could spare from stores. He also had a few jerry cans of fresh water. Being Pathfinders, no washing was allowed when on operations, so this was for drinking only.

The reason you don't wash is if you cut your face shaving you can get an infection, which in conditions like these could turn nasty very quickly. Plus our aim on a mission such as this one was to take on the look, the feel and the smell of the jungle, so as to become invisible to the enemy. If we were forced to go on the run we would be living like animals anyway, so the transition would be that much easier if we'd started it early.

In short, we didn't have the water to waste washing and couldn't take the risk of doing so. The only exception to the no washing rule was teeth. The body can cope with being dirty – just. But gum disease or rotting teeth is an endex (end of exercise) issue – you'd be pulled off the mission.

I fetched the Pinzgauer. We loaded up the supplies and drove back to the HQ position. It was the start of our third day in Lungi Lol, and we'd been in-country for six. Finally the British Army had managed to get its act together on the medical front: the resupply included some packs of Lariam, an anti-malarial pill.

I sent the guys back to their patrols, then gave Wag, Tricky and Grant the news.

'The op's evolving and we're here for the duration, to protect the only viable route into Lungi Airport and Freetown. The task is open-ended, and this is it: the rebels stop here. Oh yeah, and Donaldson's gone back to UK on a compassionate, and fucking Jacko's taking over as acting OC.'

As I was telling them about Donaldson being gone for good, I was watching the guys' expressions. Wag's face would become all puckered-up whenever he was annoyed, which was exactly what it had done now. He looked like a size ten bloke in a size eleven skin. As for Grant, he actually seemed relieved.

'At least now we can get on with the job in hand,' he announced.

Wag grunted a bunch of curses in agreement.

Tricky, meanwhile, was in sheer ecstasy at having got himself a Thuraya.

We called the patrol commanders in and Grant briefed them in turn. They took the news about Donaldson's compassionate pretty well. No one spared much of a thought about the OC any more. There were other priorities right now. We were twenty-six against two thousand, and we'd be here until battle was joined.

We had no heavy weapons, one thin-skinned vehicle, and with only two Chinooks in theatre we suspected the QRF might take a little longer to get to us than the thirty-five minutes we'd been promised. The chances of a helo plus a platoon of PARAs being kept permanently on standby to come to our aid were just about zero – especially with the evacuation of hundreds of civilians under way.

To make matters worse we had no access to any fire support. We had no air assets in theatre capable of doing danger-close air strikes in the thick of the jungle. And while we did have British warships steaming off the coast, ones boasting guns with the range to reach Lungi Lol, there was no one in theatre capable of orchestrating such complex naval fire support. In short, we were pretty much unsupported and on our own out here.

Eddie's Intel brief had contained one other, distinctly worrying, snippet of info: one of the chief aims of the rebels was to capture some British soldiers. No one needed telling what would happen to any so taken. If they could capture some elite operators like us, it would serve to humiliate the entire British military. It would also big-up the rebels' own reputation, and very likely turn public opinion in the UK against intervening in such a far distant war.

As the rebels had advanced towards Freetown they had already started to achieve their aims. They'd surrounded and laid siege to some 500 Indian peacekeepers upcountry in an isolated UN base. Parachute Regiment Major Andy Harrison had been captured, along with fourteen Indian troops. Major Harrison had only just been posted to Sierra Leone. He'd been sent here to try to turn the UN mission around, but before he could get to work the rebels had struck.

That was only one in a wave of such kidnappings, all of which were being targeted chiefly at British troops. The RUF had surrounded and laid siege to a second UN base, this one staffed by seventy Kenyan peacekeepers. Inside the base were Royal Marine Major Phil Ashby, plus Royal Navy Lieutenant-Commander Paul Rowland and Major Andrew Samsonoff of the Light Infantry. It was those British soldiers that the rebels were hell-bent on getting their hands on.

The RUF had vowed to spill British blood in Sierra Leone. As of yet, no British soldiers had been killed, but Andy Harrison had fallen directly into their hands, and had been savagely beaten and threatened with execution. The rebels had a habit of giving their missions darkly bizarre names: Operation Cut Hands; Operation Kill All Your Family; Operation Kill All Living Things. They had named their present mission 'Operation Kill British'.

The overall aim of Operation Kill British was apparently to turn Sierra Leone into 'Britain's Somalia' – a reference to the American military's defeat in the Somali capital, Mogadishu, immortalised in the book and the movie *Black Hawk Down*. Via Operation Kill British the rebels would drive us out of Sierra Leone, and their victory – plus the humiliation of Her Majesty's Armed Forces – would be complete.

And all that stood in their way right now were the twenty-six of us.

9

In light of Operation Kill British we figured better and stronger defences were in order, and for what we now had in mind we'd need the village chief's help. Around midday we paid a visit to the Kingdom of Mojo. The lieutenant invited us in – his gate was always open – and Grant proceeded to brief him on how we were here for the long-term.

'We need to go see the chief, 'cause we need a workforce,' Grant told him. 'The incentive for him to provide one is that there are two thousand rebels moving on Freetown and they are coming through his village. For us to be able to help him and his people, he is going to have to be ready to help us.'

Mojo must have realised the seriousness of the situation. He seemed more alert and his whole pace had quickened. 'Okay, I understand. Let's go.'

We made our way directly to the chief's place and found him already holding court. Two women with a young boy were in a conflab with him.

Mojo held out a hand to stop us butting in. 'Okay, just wait.'

We took a ticket and joined the queue.

When they were done Mojo launched into one. He was the most animated I'd ever seen him, and while I couldn't understand what he was saying I could sense the urgency, as if he was really trying to drive his points home. He finished speaking and the chief had a few words with his lackey.

Then: 'Okay, we will help.'

Via Mojo we told the chief we'd work out exactly what we needed, now we knew he was able to assist. Then we said our thank yous and returned to the HQ ATAP.

Tricky got a brew on – he was the master of the brews – while Grant gave Mojo a good talking to. Bearing in mind the state of their rifles and their drills, we didn't want Mojo and his men anywhere near us when the bullets started to fly. But we did need some kind of force to man a line of defence to the rear of the village, in case the rebels managed to get around the back of us. We didn't have enough men to mount a 360-degree defence, so maybe the Nigerians could act as an early warning force if the rebels were attacking from the rear.

'Once we sort out the battle plan we may need you and your men to be involved,' Grant told Mojo. 'No longer can you just sit on the sidelines.'

Mojo's response was muted. He knew full well that the long, lazy months of summer were over and that he and his men were going to have to either shape up or ship out. But still he seemed reluctant to get involved.

'But we are here only on peacekeeping duties,' the lieutenant objected. 'Our role is to keep the peace . . .'

Wag and me waded in. We soon convinced Mojo that there was no f-ing peace to keep. If and when the rebels hit Lungi Lol it was kill or be killed – and that was the same for the Nigerians in their natty blue berets as much as for us. Grant told Mojo we'd come back to him on exactly what we needed, when we'd worked out the wider plan.

With that Mojo left, shoulders bowed and heading for the privacy of his compound. Presumably, he was trying to think up the words to tell his men that the Lungi Lol Sunny Vacation was over, and that Armageddon was only just around the corner.

With Mojo warned off, Grant, Wag and me gathered over the maps. It was time to drill down into the threat – to establish exactly what it was and where it would come from. As always, we would afford the enemy the ultimate respect until proved otherwise. We had to think along these lines: *If I was advancing with*

2000 men and that kind of firepower, how would I launch an attack?

If the rebels chose to rush us in a full-frontal assault we'd face 2000 coming at us in human waves. With 300 rounds per man, we could in theory kill 7800 enemy fighters – but that's if every round equalled a kill. As it was, we'd have to average one kill per 6.66 rounds fired, if we were to account for 2000. But *my* favoured plan of attack would be far more sophisticated than that, and we had to work on the presumption that the rebels would come up with something equally subtle and sinister.

By now we'd had foot patrols out, pressing into the edge of the forest. One of those patrols had stumbled upon a feature that worried me perhaps more than anything. To the far side of Taff's position – so on our right flank – there was a railway line. It wasn't marked on any maps and we figured it was disused. But it constituted a clear line of advance through the jungle, and it ran pretty much parallel to the main highway.

In short, it provided the rebels with a second line of march, in addition to the dirt track. If I was attacking Lungi Lol, I'd put a force on the main road and make it look as if I was launching a full-frontal assault. But at the same time I'd send a second force down the railroad, moving silently and stealthily through the jungle. I'd use that to outflank us, and hit us from the side and the rear – just as the feint from the front drew all our fire.

From all that we could see, the first thing that was obvious was that we needed Claymores. They could be planted covering key avenues of approach – the worrisome railroad first and foremost. Triggered by a command wire, a mass of shrapnel would fire out in a 180-degree arc, scything down anything in its path. Claymores would be a game-changer. We didn't have any, of course, but with the chief's help we figured we could likely cobble some together.

Top of our shopping list with chiefy went: 'Find raw materials for making Claymores.'

With a 1 PARA QRF being thirty-five minutes' call away – plus add another ten to muster them – we'd need to hold out for forty-five minutes before a platoon of PARAs flew in to reinforce us. We needed to block enemy approach routes with Claymores and channel the rebels into massed groups, where we could mow them down with our heaviest firepower – the GPMGs. That should hold them off for long enough to get the QRF in.

In order to channel them we needed to create obstacles that would slow them down and cause injuries, and put large swathes of terrain off-limits. We needed to squeeze them into kill zones. We needed to clear the vegetation around those kill zones so they had not a scrap of cover to hide, and so we could see them to shoot them.

Second on our shopping list with chiefy went: 'Get villagers to clear kill zones out to forest edge.'

But the biggest challenge was how to channel the rebels into those kill zones. The Claymores would stop them in their tracks on the main approach routes. From there we needed physical barriers to corral them into death traps. The question was, what raw materials were available in and around the village to create such barriers? We had an abundance of wood. Most of the village buildings – Mojo's palisade included – were built out of one particular type: bamboo. This wasn't like the bamboo you get in your garden back home: here it grew to sixty feet in height and the thickness of a man's arm.

We had an abundance of bamboo, plus we had machetes and knives, and from what we'd seen the locals knew how to work with bamboo to build pretty much anything. It was Wag who first gave voice to the idea that was coalescing in our minds: *could we get the locals to make and plant fields of 'punji sticks'?* Done properly, they'd trap and injure the rebels, corralling them into zones where we could cut them to ribbons with the guns.

Wag and me had been on several joint training exercises with the SAS in the rainforests of Borneo. The aim was to operate for long periods as isolated groups deep in the jungle. We'd learned how to move through the forest without leaving telltale signs; how to track an enemy, and how to lose one that was tracking you; how to engage in close-quarter battle in the thick bush; how to cache weapons and food supplies; and how to survive in the jungle.

As we contemplated the coming battle at Lungi Lol we realised there was one lesson from Borneo that we could well use here. The native tribes that live in the rainforests have a tradition of raiding each other's villages. As a defence against such attacks, they plant fields of sharpened bamboo stakes around their settlements – so-called 'punji sticks'. They're lengths of bamboo honed to a razor sharpness, and they are as lethal as a steel blade.

There are several variations on the basic punji theme. The stakes can be placed in the base and walls of a 'punji pit', so that when one of the enemy steps into it his leg is pierced in many places. They can be set in pits with their points facing downwards, so if he tries to pull his leg out the punjis will tear the trapped limb to pieces. They can even be arranged as a latticework of spikes and suspended from a tree, being triggered to drop on anyone passing below.

In terms of winning a battle, wounding the enemy is often more effective than killing them outright. Generally, wounding one opponent takes three out of the fight – because two are needed to evacuate the injured man. Punji sticks were the ideal means to wound, and there was no reason why what works for the natives of Borneo wouldn't work here. We were twenty-six facing 2000. We had very limited firepower. The rebels did not. Desperate straits called for desperate measures. The punji stick proposal got an enthusiastic response from all.

We sketched out the ideal areas in which to plant the punji fields. We'd need two work parties from the village: one cutting bamboo in the forest and shaping and sharpening it, another clearing vegetation and driving the sharpened stakes in. We needed the punji fields to be well-hidden, so as to ensnare the rebels. We didn't want twelve-foot-high monster spikes that were visible from a mile away. We wanted them hidden at around knee or thigh height, and maybe the odd punji pit dug as well, to really scare the shit out of the bad guys.

Third on our shopping list with chiefy went: 'Get villagers to make and plant punji fields.'

Finally, we needed trenches dug, to get the lads below ground. The rebels boasted vehicle-mounted heavy weapons – namely 12.7 mm DShKs, the Russian equivalent of the NATO .50-calibre heavy machine gun – plus belt-fed support weapons. That kind of firepower would chew through the vegetation and the built-up earth banks around our shell-scrapes. We needed proper battle trenches, two to each patrol, sited so they mutually supported each other, in case one was in danger of being overrun.

In addition to the two trenches per patrol – eight in all – we decided we needed one trench set forward on the main highway to control access into the village, and to ID any enemy forces massing to attack. We'd site that trench a hundred metres ahead of the village, and it would be manned by two guys on a 24/7 watch. It would also require some kind of cover constructed over it to provide shade, for it would be well out in the open.

We also figured we needed two further trenches set to either side of the road at the rear of the village. Presuming Mojo and his men agreed to play ball, those would be manned by the Nigerian peacekeepers – who we hoped had been persuaded of the urgent need to move onto a war-fighting footing.

Of course, if we sited the Nigerians in those trenches and we did have to fall back through the village, Mojo's men would likely be trigger happy and firing at shadows. They could end up killing some of us – that's as long as their rifles still worked. We decided the only way to prevent this was to ban Mojo and his men from firing back into the village. They would only be allowed to open fire towards the south and the west, so away from the centre of Lungi Lol.

Last on our shopping list with chiefy went: 'Get villagers to dig battle trenches.'

The reason why we needed the villagers to do this, as opposed to us, was simple: while they were building the defences, we'd be keeping watch for the rebels.

I figured now was also the time to radio in a request to The White Rabbit for trip flares and motion sensors. Those would be a total game-changer, in terms of stealing the enemy's element of surprise. The British military had them, that was for sure. We'd used them countless times on exercises. But whether they'd actually got any into theatre was a different matter entirely.

Priorities sorted, Wag and me went and fetched Mojo. We explained exactly what we needed the village chief to organise, plus we outlined the role we'd allocated to Mojo and his men.

'We need you to provide security to the rear of the village,' I told him. 'We'll need you to man one trench set to either side of the track. Your aim is to stop the rebels advancing from that direction. If the rebels attack you stay there and you do not leave and you hold that end of the village. Can you do that?'

Mojo nodded. 'Yes, okay. We can.'

I fixed Mojo with a very direct look. 'Right, so you are now involved in the active defence of this village, unless you tell us otherwise – at which stage you are on your own.'

'Right, okay, I understand,' Mojo confirmed. 'We are in.'

'What are the UN's Rules of Engagement?' I asked.

Mojo looked at me like he didn't understand the question. Our ROEs were tight: *do not engage the enemy unless fired upon; continue to fight until that threat is eliminated.* But ROEs seemed to be a totally alien concept to Mojo and his UNAMSIL force.

'Okay, breaking it down: at what stage are you as the UN allowed to open fire?'

Mojo glanced from me to Wag and back again. He shrugged. 'I don't know.'

'Right, our ROE is fire when fired upon; maybe you should do the same. But one thing: if you see battle being joined, you never fire up into the village, not under any circumstances. You only ever fire west and south – *away from the village*. You must brief your men never to fire into the village, okay?'

'Okay. But why?'

''Cause at the moment we have no way of ID-ing friend or foe and there could be villagers moving through. Secondly, our plan is that if we are overrun, then we withdraw from the village and we will be coming along the track passing by your positions. And we strongly recommend that you withdraw with us.'

From the look on his face I could tell that it was finally dawning on Mojo what a shitty situation we were all in.

'Our plan if we get overrun is we will be bugging out,' I reiterated.

'Okay, but we will need to stay,' Mojo remarked, quietly.

Wag and I exchanged glances. 'But Mojo, you'll be fucking massacred,' Wag objected. 'Mojo, mate, they will chop you up and eat you for breakfast.'

The Nigerian lieutenant's nickname had stuck so well that Wag had started calling him 'Mojo' to his face. I was slipping into the habit too, not that Mojo seemed to mind.

He remained inscrutable behind his massive Foster Grant shades. 'This is my post. Those are my orders.'

There appeared to be nothing we could do to persuade Mojo that staying put in the face of being overrun by the rebels would not be very good for the health or longevity of him and his men.

The British Army thrives on the concept of 'mission command': you are given an order and you do what is necessary to complete that order, but only up to the point when you realise that it needs to be adapted. Individual commanders of Mojo's rank and higher are given the freedom to make appropriate decisions on the ground. Most other militaries don't really have that concept, certainly not with their regular forces. As to the Nigerian military . . . Well, enough said.

Mojo only ever turned up to speak with us alone. His pride in his dress and appearance plus his educated English set him out as a man apart. The Nigerian military – as with most third world armies – was clearly rigidly hierarchical. In the British military you'd always have the 2iC, and maybe some patrol commanders, sitting in on the kind of briefings we were having. The ability of NCOs to provide ideas and input is unique to the British military, and especially to units like ours.

I figured we needed to shore Mojo up a little. 'Don't worry, mate, it'll never happen. We'll never get overrun. We've got a QRF on standby at Lungi Airport 24/7. People will be coming to our aid.'

Mojo forced a smile.

'Mojo, it's gonna take forty-five minutes for that QRF to get here,' Wag added. 'That is how long we need to make a stand.'

Mojo nodded. 'Okay, okay, I understand.'

'What kind of ammo do you have for your men?' I asked.

'Two magazines. Two magazines.'

Two FN mags should have meant forty rounds per man, but Wag had checked one of their mags and it contained six rounds. So, they'd most likely got a dozen rounds each. Even so, we couldn't afford to spare them any, for we didn't have enough ammo ourselves.

'So, if that's agreed we need to go ask the chief for some work parties,' I concluded. 'Lead on, Bonaparte ... Onwards and upwards, mate. Off we go.'

Mojo had woken up now to how much he'd been left to rot and stagnate, abandoned in his jungle outpost with no Intel updates or warning of what was coming. In the nick of time we'd pitched up and he'd learned just how dark and shitty his situation was. We were now talking about planting punji fields, siting Claymores, cutting the bush to clear kill zones and creating interlocking arcs of fire.

I could see this light in Mojo's eyes, a kind of realisation: *Oh my God, this is how you do it. This is how you fight the rebels.*

Maybe with these guys we just might get out of this alive.

He set off like the Pied Piper, taking us to see the village chief. It was pretty much the same routine as before – us standing off to one side not saying a word, while Mojo delivered the briefing. He must have done a great job describing what would happen to the village if we didn't get the assistance we'd requested, for within a matter of minutes the chief was in.

Mojo turned to us. 'Yes, he understands, and he will help you. He will gather the people you need. He will assign a head of the workforce, so you can show him what you want.'

'Top job,' Wag enthused.

'Mojo, get him to send the head of the workforce to us at the HQ ATAP,' I said. 'We'll brief him there on what we need. And Mojo, we need to start on this asap.'

We thanked the chief and walked away. It was now 1430 hours on day three of our mission in Lungi Lol, and with the chief's help we planned to turn this remote African village into Sierra Leone's version of the Alamo.

Within the hour this guy pitched up at the HQ ATAP. We were in the midst of having a brew and a snack, and in truth we hadn't expected chiefy to get his act together so quickly. The new arrival was this incredibly tall and lanky beanpole of a bloke who looked about nineteen or twenty years old. He was dressed in a green T-shirt over a green flower-pattern sarong, plus open-toed sandals, and he had a massive machete dangling from one hand.

'I am Ibrahim,' he announced. 'I have been sent by the chief to help the British. What you need?'

His English was pretty good, and this was clearly the chief's chosen foreman. Leading him off to Dolly's position on our left flank, we explained we'd start with vegetation clearance. We wanted the bush cleared back 200 yards to the edge of the jungle. We didn't need it cleared to ground level: just the taller foliage gone, so we could see the rebels as they advanced, to kill them.

Wag used a hand-cut gesture to show the kind of thick bush we needed cleared. 'Get this down. Get this down.'

Ibrahim nodded enthusiastically. 'I do! I do!' He motioned to a palm tree with his machete. 'And cut this too?'

'Yes, yes – shooting through there.' Wag made a rifle gesture with his hands, complete with pulling the trigger. 'Bang, bang. Kill the man through here. Need to see.'

Wag seemed to have struck up a real rapport with Ibrahim, just as he seemed able to do with any average working bloke from Burnley to Bombay. Next we showed Ibrahim the battle trenches we needed dug. Dolly had scratched out a shallow furrow in the ground using the blade of his machete, marking out two rectangular outlines.

'This wide and this long, and up to here,' Wag motioned at neck height. 'Dig 'em so deep.'

'I dig! I dig!' Ibrahim confirmed, mimicking Wag's up-to-the-neck height gesture. 'Up to here.'

'No, no,' Wag shook his head, laughing. 'Up to *my* neck height. Not yours. Ibrahim very tall. Otherwise, men cannot see over top to shoot!'

We did a repeat performance with Ibrahim all along our front, and we were back at the HQ ATAP by around 1600 hours. The sun was already low in the sky and in two hours it would be completely dark.

I glanced worriedly at the ragged line of jungle to our front. 'Nothing much is going to get done tonight, is it?' I remarked to Wag.

Wag shrugged. 'You never know with that Ibrahim bloke. The guy's a fucking human dynamo.'

A few minutes later Nathe came up on the radio. 'Guys, they're chopping. They're out front chopping.'

Grant, Wag and me hurried over to take a look. Out at the front of Nathe's position around thirty villagers had gathered. Mostly they were women and children. Ibrahim was striding about in their midst, shouting orders as they bent to their task. They wielded whatever tools they had – machetes, hoes and picks. Some were even using their bare hands to rip up the vegetation.

For several long minutes we stood there under the trees that shaded Nathe's position, watching in amazement.

Wag emitted this long, low whistle. 'Wow. Will you look at that? People power.'

'Take a look at Ibrahim,' I remarked. 'He's the foreman all right. There he goes – look at him chopping...'

Wag grunted in agreement. 'Yeah, no-nonsense – he's the big man now. About as good as it gets.'

Grant smiled. 'I guess that's what you get when you wield the authority of the chief...'

The villagers would be out there chopping until close to midnight, opening up our first field of fire. They'd clear from the left edge of Nathan's position – the highway – right across to the right edge of Ginge's arc of fire, then move on to the next position.

By the time they were done cutting, *33 Alpha*, *Bravo*, *Charlie* and *Delta* would be cleared to unleash hell.

10

While Ibrahim's army was busy clearing the bush, Wag and me did a walkabout, brainstorming every possible means of defence with the blokes. Nothing was beyond due consideration, but we were partly in reassurance mode as well.

'This is it, lads, we're in here for the duration,' I kept telling them. 'Everything you've ever trained for, every one of your skills that you've honed and honed – this is where they'll get put to the test.'

The attitude amongst the guys was fantastic. Feedback was great and the blokes were buzzing. Getting Ibrahim's army on the job seemed to have given them a real boost. The feeling seemed to be – *If the rebels are coming, let's get it on*.

Walkabout done, Wag and I launched the next stage of 'Operation Alamo' – as we'd nicknamed the defence of Lungi Lol: fashioning some DIY Claymores. When manufactured in an armaments factory the Claymore is a rectangular device about eight inches across and five inches deep, with a gentle curve in its face. The casing is packed with a mass of plastic explosive and ball-bearings. When triggered it fires horizontally in a solid wall of destruction, cutting down anything in its path.

Luckily, when Wag had blagged his pile of swag from Mick, back at the Lungi Airport ammo dump, he'd pulled together the basic raw materials to make some Claymores. First off he'd got the sticks of PE4. The plastic explosive is fairly inert. It can be moulded like Plasticine, and detonation cord – or detcord – is one of the few things that will set it off. Detcord explodes at a rate of 6000 metres a second: in other words, a length 6 kilometres long goes up in one second flat.

Detcord is highly volatile, and a length slung around a small tree will fell it. But it's PE4 that actually has the real killer punch behind it. It's a dynamic high explosive – the sheer magnitude of the blast and the shock wave so created will drive a scything wall of metallic death out of a device like a Claymore.

Wag had also scrounged ten mixed L1A2 and L2A2 electric detonators, to trigger the detcord, plus 100 metres of electronic firing cable. So all we were lacking were some containers to set the explosives in, plus some 'shipyard confetti' – any form of projectile to take the place of the standard ball-bearings.

Via the chief some empty cooking oil containers were scavenged from around the village. These were about the size of a five-litre fuel can, and made of thick tin-plated steel. They were the right dimensions for us to cut down and mould into shape. After doing so we ended up with a series of shallow tin trays, each eight inches long, six wide, and about two deep.

Perfect.

Next, we sent a couple of the blokes to scour the length and breadth of Lungi Lol, searching for shipyard confetti. Ably assisted by the village kids they came back with handfuls of old nails, bolts and screws, broken bits of machinery, old car parts, plus assorted other bits and pieces that could be used as improvised shrapnel. When the metal ran out we could even use shards of razor-sharp bamboo – the offcuts from the punji sticks.

Then we cut a small hole in the back of each tin tray, and moulded a slab of PE4 into a tennis ball shape. We placed the snowball of plastic explosive in the base of the tin tray over the hole, and kneaded it into a convex dish – so it would have a cone blast effect when detonated. A length of detcord – knotted twice to lend it extra umph – was pushed through the hole into the PE4. It was left hanging out of the rear of the device like a rat's tail.

Finally, the shipyard confetti was pressed into the convex face of the PE4. A length of cardboard cut to fit was laid over the front, and sealed in place with gaffer tape. We'd used the same weight of PE4 (about one and a half pounds) as a standard Claymore would be armed with – so we could pretty much rely on our DIY ones having the same kind of kill-range. At the apex of the blast – so fifty metres out from the device – the cone of destruction would be two metres high and fifty metres wide.

The next challenge was placing them. Claymores have a sixteen-metre back-blast. Anyone caught in that zone could be maimed or killed. We had a limited amount of firing cable, and we had to be able to see the enemy to be able to detonate. We were using Mini Shrikes to do so – a hand-held device about the size of an iPhone. Into that we'd plug the two leads – one black, one tan; a positive and a negative – which make up the firing cable.

We couldn't just blow the Claymores as soon as we detected voices or movement out there in the dark. If we triggered them blind we might kill innocent villagers, plus you needed to be sure the enemy would be caught right in the cone of the blast. The guy operating the Mini Shrike had to be able to see both the Claymore and the target, while not getting caught in the back-blast, or shot by the enemy.

We left it up to the patrol commanders exactly where to position their DIY Claymores. They would only be set in place after last light, so if there were any rebel spies in the village they wouldn't be able to see where we'd sited them.

That evening's Sched contained a crucial Intel update: the word was that the rebels had shifted their objective completely now. Rather than seizing Freetown and laying it waste, their main focus was on joining battle with the British military and capturing some British soldiers. Their push was to be wholly against Lungi Airport, where most of our forces were located.

Operation Kill British had truly come of age.

We called the patrol commanders together for prayers, and took a good long look at our situation. Priority one was to defend and hold this position. If we could hit the rebels hard enough and kill enough of them in the first contact, it might be possible to stop them. With the kind of defences the villagers were working on, we might hold out for long enough to turn the rebel tide.

But if they penetrated our perimeter then we were pretty much done for.

The feelings amongst the men cut both ways now. On the one hand Colonel Gibson and Brigadier Richards had shown absolute faith in our ability to make a stand here – and above any other force at their disposal. That alone was gratifying. But on the other hand it was becoming ever more clear what a massive barrel of shit we'd been dropped into. If we failed to stop the rebels and were forced to go on the run, the wounded would be piled onto the lone Pinzgauer, which would make a mad dash for Lungi Airport. The rest of us would attempt to E & E through the jungle on foot, but no one particularly rated our chances.

As if to reinforce the sense of impeding doom, the trickle of villagers who had started arriving the previous night had swollen into a veritable flood. We'd figured then that we had maybe two hundred sleeping on the square, ranged mostly around the edges. By midnight on our third day in Lungi Lol the open space was packed from end to end. Several hundred people, mainly women and children, were there – and all of them seeking the sanctuary provided by twenty-six Pathfinders.

With darkness the jungle came alive. There were sounds tonight that we didn't seem able to recognise. My mind was a swirl of thoughts. Were the rebels out there, lurking unseen in the fringes of the forest, getting eyes-on our positions and readying themselves to strike? Had they been in amongst us during the day, counting us and sketching out our whereabouts?

As the darkness thickened two blokes from each patrol crept forward of their positions, trailing out the electrical firing cable. On the far west of the village Dolly set one of his DIY Claymores to cover a V-shaped gully that ran from the dark fringe of jungle almost to the brink of his trenches. Thinking like the enemy, that was the point via which he would launch an attack, getting his men as close as possible before breaking cover.

To the front of H and Nathe's position, their target for the improvised Claymores was clear: it was the dirt track itself. Any rebel vehicles advancing on our position had to come that way. The Claymores were powerful enough to shred any soft-skinned trucks or pick-ups, but would have little effect against armour. If the rebels came forward in their captured United Nations APCs, we'd have to rely on our shoulder-launched LAW 94 mm rockets to smash them.

To the south lay perhaps our greatest threat after the dirt road – the railway track. Moving through thick jungle at night is noisy, slow work, even for those as highly trained as Pathfinders. That railroad offered a silent means of advance right up to the very edge of the village. Taff laid out his own roll of firing cable, setting his DIY Claymore to cover that point of silent ingress – the steel tracks.

The night passed. Long hours on sentry dragged by as tired eyes stared out into a dark, featureless mass of jungle. Sleep snatched here and there in two-hour chunks is never enough. The blokes were building up a sleep deficit, and fatigue was becoming a real issue. Crouched in the damp earth of the trenches, with every crawling-slithering-sliding thing dropping in on us, sentry duty was a shitty business – but that pretty much went with the territory.

But tonight was different. Every one of us could feel it in our bones: a hostile force was out there in the darkness, probing, watching and waiting to strike. The rebel commanders would know for sure there were just over two dozen British soldiers – plus a dodgy Nigerian UNAMSIL contingent – holding the village. With a couple of thousand rebel fighters under their command, their options in terms of how to launch the attack would be legion.

No matter how good we were, twenty-six blokes couldn't mow down hundreds of fast-moving targets at night, and the drugs and voodoo would drive their fighters forwards. But our real worry was that the rebel commanders would be far more capable than that. If they mounted a feint – a move to draw our fire, to mask the real thrust of their attack – we had no force in reserve to deal with it.

No rebel assault materialised during that dark night of tension, but none of us doubted that it was coming. It was only a matter of when the RUF commanders decided they were ready to smash us.

Just after first light the unmistakable figure of Ibrahim re-appeared. 'I am ready. We good? We start?'

'Ibrahim, you happy?' I asked.

'Yes, very happy.'

'Ibrahim, today we finish?'

'Yes, today we finish.'

'Ibrahim, very important we finish today cutting the bush and digging the trenches.'

'Yes. Today I do. I do.'

He was very enthusiastic and definite. I didn't doubt him for a moment, either.

'We've got one more thing on the to-do list, though,' I added.

'What is this?'

'Punji fields.'

Ibrahim looked confused. 'Poongy field? What is this?'

'We cut bamboo, Ibrahim, maybe five feet in length and this fat.' I used my forearm to indicate the width we wanted. 'One end we make a spike – very sharp, Ibrahim.' I grabbed my rifle to demonstrate the next bit. 'The blunt end we drive into the ground at a forty-five-degree angle, with the spike facing upwards. We need the spikes set this far apart, and not in lines or regular. Put them so a man cannot run or move through . . .'

Ibrahim's eyes had lit up. 'I know! I know!' he interjected. 'This is "poongy field"?'

'Yeah, punjis. When you're ready we'll show you where to place them, okay.'

Ibrahim nodded happily. 'I do! I do!' He was practically dancing from foot to foot with excitement. The idea of the punji fields clearly tickled his fancy. With that he turned and was gone.

Ibrahim set to work, and Wag and I wandered off on our early morning walkabout. As Pathfinders, we never move in less than a pair no matter where we might be going. Even if paying a visit to the shitters we still had to do so in twos. This is the buddy-buddy system, one that guarantees you'll never be jumped by the enemy without having a buddy to provide back-up. Hence Wag and me moved as a pair as we went to check in with Dolly's patrol.

We got there to find a couple of blokes on stag, one brewing up, and another sleeping.

'See anything last night?' I asked Dolly.

'Nope. Just all those weird noises all night long.'

'Yeah. We heard them too. Did you see all the civvies coming into the village?'

'Yeah. Sleeping in the square?'

'Yeah. It was chocker.'

I heard a light rustle of vegetation from behind me and three young lads emerged from the bush. One was a carrying a battered old axe, another a worn machete, the third a shovel with a broken stump for a handle.

The boys smiled nervously. 'We dig? We dig?'

Dolly returned the smile. 'Yeah, lads, go for it – dig.'

We watched for a while as the boys got to work. Clearly experts at this digging business, they had the vegetation cleared in an instant above the outline of the first trench. After a few seconds' work with the shovel they were through the thin, sandy surface and into a thicker, clay-like subsoil. It was criss-crossed with tree roots, and I could now understand the mix of tools the lads had brought with them. While shovel-boy lifted out the soil, axe-boy and machete-boy hacked out the roots.

We left the lads working away, and as we crossed over the road to check on Nathe's position we spotted the familiar figure of Ibrahim, surrounded by his army. The work party was out front of Ginge's patrol now – *33 Charlie* – clearing away the bush. Ibrahim was dressed exactly as he had been on day one – he was tall and green, like a willow tree. He was barking orders and leading by example and he'd got his workforce out real early.

We paused to have words with Nathe. 'How're the blokes getting on, mate? Bollocksed?'

'Yeah, mate, getting pretty knackered.'

'Right, make sure when the locals are out doing their stuff you get as much rest as you can. Make like a vampire, mate. Daylight's the time to catch up on the sleep. Keep two on stag and four off, and get as much kip as you can.'

We moved on to Ginge and Taff's positions, and all the time we could hear Ibrahim shouting his instructions, and the dull thud of trees and bushes getting the chop. It was around 1000 hours by the time we were done. Turning back towards the HQ ATAP, we saw a thin line of figures threading through the bush. We were on the alert for a surprise attack – always – so our first thought was: *rebel column*.

Then we noticed it was all women. They were making their way back into the village, and they had thick bundles of bamboo balanced on their heads.

There was a grove of bamboo to the west of Dolly's position, and that was where they'd chosen to cut the first of the raw materials to make the punjis. More groups of women started to appear from various directions. Two hundred metres to the west of Ginge's position there was a real boggy area, and it was from there that they seemed to be getting the peachiest lengths of bamboo. It was coming out in pieces as thick as your biceps, and in sections that were as long as your average scaffold pole.

All morning the work continued: kids digging trenches; women hauling bamboo; and all and sundry clearing the vegetation to

The Fan Dance. Pathfinder selection is a tough five-week trial, culminating in Endurance, a 64-kilometre forced march under extremely heavy loads over the notorious Pen-y-Fan, in the Brecon Beacons – terrain known to test many a man.

Pathfinders deploy deep behind enemy lines with the kind of specialist light weaponry – like sniper rifles – to take out strategic enemy targets.

Riding the tube. As one of the British military's most experienced Tandem Masters, I got to jump with a massive canister of heavy equipment strapped to my person. Landing it was spine-crushing work.

Once you pull the chute, your world goes from the adrenaline-pumping rush of the freefall to one of comparative silence and stillness, as you drift under silk towards the landing zone below.

Bergen first. Just prior to landing, you let your Bergen drop on the extension rope, so it lands ahead of you, taking the impact of its own weight and saving your legs.

Touchdown. Gathering in the silk after a monster freefall to earth, in a HALO – high-altitude low-opening – jump.

HALO. Diving off a Hercules ramp into the howling void as a four-man patrol, in a HALO parachute jump, with yours truly leading the stick.

In formation. Seconds later in the freefall on the same jump, myself in centre of photo. Note the M16s strapped to our left sides, in case the landing proves 'hot' – occupied by the enemy. You stick together close in the freefall, so that when you pull the chutes you can follow the lead jumper – me   into the drop zone.

Freefall. Same HALO jump as opposite, from above 25,000 feet, in full oxygen-breathing, parachute, survival and combat gear.

Solo. A different HALO jump, with yours truly flying high, with a General Purpose Machine Gun (GPMG) strapped to my left side, barrel downwards.

Desert rats. Pathfinders are tasked to go deep behind enemy lines in all kinds of terrain. On desert operations, shemaghs – traditional Arab headscarves – are vital for keeping sun and sand out of mouth, nose and hair. They're also great for anonymity. I'm in the vehicle commander's seat, so left of driver.

Sandy wanderers. Pathfinders in the North African desert, operating a mixed bag of Pinkies – desert-adapted, open-topped Land Rovers – and Armstrong 500cc motorbikes. I'm on the far right of the photo, leaning against the vehicle. All the others in this photo are now serving with Special Forces, hence faces being obscured.

Two wheels good. Yours truly, deep in the North African desert where we used Armstrong 500cc off-road motorbikes to act as an outrider force, scouting the route ahead and searching for the enemy.

The jungle is neutral. It's neither inherently hostile nor friendly, but only by becoming as one with it will you defeat an enemy. Wag is standing on the far left of photo, yours truly is far right, also standing.

Graham 'Wag' Wardle, trusty GPMG in hand, carrying a crushing load. We were best of mates: I was always twisting his arm about being the Brigade's ugliest man, while he would hit back about the size of my ears.

Captain Grant Harris, then second-in-command of the Pathfinders. A young but very capable officer, he did a sterling job when the shit hit the proverbial fan in Sierra Leone.

Jacko. In spite of not being able to get his swearing right, Jacko was a top operator, and there was no one better to take over command in Sierra Leone.

Nathe. He had somehow made it from turnip farming in Lincolnshire into the Pathfinders – and a better patrol commander I couldn't have wished for. He was also the king of bush tucker: if it moved Nathe would eat it.

the front of our positions. I didn't figure anyone was getting any work done in Lungi Lol, other than that connected with Operation Alamo. But the most amazing thing of all was this: *these people were singing as they worked*. This wasn't some dire dirge either: it was a rhythmic, lilting, soulful chant that sounded almost joyful. And whenever they took a break from the singing, this animated chat and laughter echoed back and forth through the trees.

We joked amongst ourselves about what we'd nicknamed 'Ibrahim's army', but in truth we were hugely impressed. This was hard, tough physical labour under a beating sun, but the villagers seemed to be driven and almost happy to be doing it. It was seriously impressive. I mean, in what village in Britain would you get young boys, girls and women clearing the bush, digging battle trenches or cutting bamboo punji fields, *and all voluntarily*? Forget it. They'd be too busy watching the Shopping Channel or gaming on their PlayStations.

We figured the people of Lungi Lol had to know what would happen if the rebels made it into their village. Everyone knew. In Freetown and neighbouring areas there were these so-called 'Amp Camps'. They'd been set up by the international aid agencies and charities, and they were peopled by the RUF's victims – from kids as young as toddlers to ancient grandmothers, and all with hands, arms or legs amputated.

So it was all hands to the pump here in Lungi Lol, because no one wanted to lose theirs to a drug-crazed rebel's machete. But that didn't make it any the less impressive.

I could hear the giggling of the kids who were digging the battle trenches, as they larked around with the blokes. It was a boiling hot day – the hottest yet in Lungi Lol – but those kids never once complained or flagged. And each time I heard it their laughter sent cold shivers up my spine – for I couldn't help thinking what would happen to those kids if we failed, and the rebels made it in here.

I'd had a tough childhood growing up in smoggy Middlesbrough, but compared to these kids it had been a party. School had never really worked out, and by the time I was in my early teens we'd had the police around the house numerous times. I was forever stealing milk floats and selling them as scrap to the gypsies, or climbing derelict buildings and ending up in hospital. I'd broken about every bone in my body and had got a reputation for scrapping.

There was no military tradition in my family – my dad was an electrician, my mum a barmaid – and we were seriously at loggerheads over my wayward ways. Then at the age of thirteen I happened to see a news report about the Parachute Regiment's famous stand in the Falkland Islands.

That changed everything.

Having seen the PARAs in action I knew what I wanted to be: I was going to win the right to wear that famous maroon beret. I was going to join the PARAs.

More or less everyone said I stood zero chance of making it. I was stringy and thin, with barely a muscle on me. But my dad stood by me. There was never a lot of money in the Heaney household, though what there was my parents spent on me and my younger brother, Neil. Dad took me to the local charity shop. He got me an old pair of Army boots and a pair of knackered combat trousers, plus he forked out for a brand spanking new bright orange rucksack from Millets. We nicknamed it 'the Satsuma'.

I started running for miles on end through the back streets of Middlesbrough. It was like a scene from *Rocky*, but with me a slim, wiry drink of piss with a giant satsuma strapped to my back. My schoolmates thought I was cracked, but my dad was rock solid. I started running the hills that ring the city. Dad would drive me out there and sit in the car reading the *Mirror*, while I tore up and down the slopes.

People still said that I'd never make it, but my reaction was – *sod them*. I *did* get accepted into the Junior PARA, which turned out to be like torture without the water-boarding. Most found it utter purgatory, but I loved it. I thrived on the physical challenges, and it quickly straightened me out. I even got selected for the Junior PARA's boxing team.

I'd just turned seventeen and Andy Gow – the guy who raised the 3 PARA flag over Port Stanley – was our CSM. He threatened to kill anyone who didn't win his bout. I put my opponent down in the third round, so Andy spared my life. I went on to the Parachute Regiment's P Company: six days of charging through woods and stagnant bogs, of log and stretcher races, the Trainasium (designed to test your fear of heights) and finally The Milling – where you stand face to face with another recruit and have to smash the fuck out of each other.

I passed P Company as the Champion Recruit, so I guess I did okay. Having joined 3 PARA in 1987 I got my first sight of the lads of the X Platoon. I was mesmerised: this was the mysterious unit I'd heard referred to as the Shadow Force. These were the guys who were always away overseas – whether on training or ops no one seemed to know. They wore their hair longer, showed no marks of unit or rank, and everyone – even the officers – addressed each other as 'boss' or 'mate'. I knew their role was supposedly to HALO behind enemy lines on clandestine taskings, but other than that I knew next to nothing about what they really got up to.

I was drawn to them like a moth to a candle flame.

But never once when I'd contemplated joining their number did I ever envisage being on a mission as out-there as this one – twenty-six blokes tasked with saving an African village from total mayhem and carnage . . . For that's what this mission had become to us. We'd been sent here to stop the RUF, but over the past few days we'd realised what the reality would be for the people who lived here if we failed.

The rebels would rape the women who were cutting the bamboo to make the punjis for us. They'd gun down Mojo and his men, or machete them to pieces. They'd murder Ibrahim and most likely the village chief too. They'd chop the hands off the kids who were digging our battle trenches, and doing cartwheels of joy over a packet of British Army boiled sweets. They'd take the survivors and drive them before their forces as human shields, as they advanced on Lungi Airport – to make Op Kill British a bloody reality.

And right now, for every one of us here failure to stop them was not an option.

11

It was late afternoon when Ibrahim turned up at the HQ ATAP once more. He didn't appear to be particularly tired, sweaty or dirty. In fact he looked full of beans and in the thick of it.

He approached Wag, whom he seemed to have identified as the guy in charge of the work gangs. 'Hey boss! Hey boss!'

Wag grinned a welcome. 'Ibrahim! Come on – take a load off. Take the weight off, mate. Sit down.'

Ibrahim folded up those long legs of his and sat cross-legged on the ground.

Tricky threw a packet of British Army ration biscuits at him. 'Here! Ibrahim, catch! Get those down you.'

Ibrahim didn't seem to want to drop the machete, so he could catch the biscuits more easily. Instead, he tried to catch them with the machete still gripped in his hands, and ended up slicing the packet in two in midair.

'Whoa ... Ibrahim, mate, watch it!' Tricky exclaimed. 'You'll have someone's eye out with that ...'

Ibrahim started to munch on the biscuits, but Tricky hadn't seen fit to warn him they were 'hard tack'. Hard tack biscuits taste pretty good, but they're impossible to eat without water – worse even than cream crackers. They're so bad we used to play a game: *bet you a tenner you can't eat six hard tacks without taking a drink of water.*

As Ibrahim munched away we started a wager on how many he'd manage before he was desperate for some fluid. There are six in a packet. He got one down him, then two. He was onto his third by the time his chewing got noticeably slower, as the hard tack glued his jaws together, drying up his saliva like a sponge. By now he was incapable of talking, but still he kept eating.

'That's his fourth,' Wag commented. 'Here goes . . .'

We'd been watching him for five minutes or so, and finally he'd got to the point where he could barely open his mouth any more. Being on his fourth hard tack – well, for a novice we figured he'd done pretty damn well.

Tricky waved his water bottle at him. 'Ibrahim, you want some water? Water?'

Ibrahim, nodding: 'Hmmm. Hmmmm.' He couldn't speak.

Tricky threw his water bottle over. Ibrahim didn't seem to want to let go of the killer biscuit packet, or the machete, so he tried to catch the water bottle in the crook of his arm. He got the water bottle wedged between his knees, and managed to lever it open with his elbows. He tipped it back, raising it to the vertical, and drained it in one.

Ibrahim threw the empty water bottle back to Tricky, picked up the two remaining biscuits and started eating again.

'He ain't getting any more bloody water,' Tricky muttered.

Unbelievably, we were still on the one-litre ration per man per day, and Ibrahim had just drained Tricky's dry.

We were all of us laughing now.

'Fucking hell, Ibrahim, nice one,' I remarked. 'So, are you finished? Not so much the biscuits, mate, but the work?'

In answer Ibrahim brandished his machete, and grabbed the one remaining hard tack biscuit: 'Yes, finished! Come check! You come check!'

He led off, Wag and me following after. Ninety per cent of the clearance was done. He still had people out chopping, and as we walked up and down the line of our positions we showed where we needed a bit more done.

'Little bit more here, Ibrahim,' Wag indicated. 'Cut a little here, okay.'

'Yes, yes, no problem!' He clicked his fingers, called some of his people over and they started to slash at the offending patches of vegetation.

That done he led us over to this massive pile of cut bamboo. 'This, now? This good?'

Wag picked up one of the lengths of bamboo. 'Make this end sharp; very sharp.'

Ibrahim: 'Yes, yes, yes! Very sharp!'

'This much,' Wag measured off a foot, 'into the ground.'

Ibrahim: 'Yes, yes! In the ground!'

Wag placed it at a forty-five-degree angle, pointing away from the village. 'Like this, Ibrahim. Not like this.' He placed it vertical. 'And not like this.' He placed it horizontal. He returned it to the forty-five-degree angle. 'So, it gets the man in here – it pierces his thigh . . .'

'Yes, yes, I do!'

'Wag, you mark out the one patch,' I told him, 'and I'll do the other.'

I headed down to where we wanted the southern punji field sited, while Wag dealt with the northern one. We each drew a furrow in the ground indicating the perimeter, marking out an area twenty metres deep by thirty-five metres long.

Punji fields mapped out, Wag explained exactly how we wanted them positioned. 'Not in straight line, Ibrahim. Random. Not in straight line.'

'Yes, yes, yes. Random. I do!'

Ibrahim had half his people busy putting the final touches to the cleared fields of fire. The other half were watching us.

'The man, he must run this way and this way,' Wag indicated, doing a little jinking dance with his feet. 'Back and forth. Back and forth.'

'Yes, yes. To and fro! I do!' Ibrahim turned to his people and beckoned them over. 'Come, come!'

He was now in the centre of his army, demonstrating with his monster machete how to fashion a punji stick, while talking his workers through how to plant them. It looked as if we'd left the building of the punji fields in very capable hands.

As we headed back through the trees that fringed the outskirts of the village, Wag and me chatted about the 'I-man' – Ibrahim. He had great man-management skills. Single-handedly he was overseeing half a dozen construction projects, with maybe a hundred villagers at work across them. No doubt about it, the I-man was a damn good bloke to have on our side.

We came up to Nathe's position, and we could see yet another work party at it – mattocks going up and down as a dozen boys cracked into their battle trenches. They were up to their shoulders in the dirt, six of them in each hole, *33 Alpha*'s trenches being a good halfway down.

We paused to have words. 'Nathe, how's it going, mate?'

Nathe shrugged. 'Nice to see someone else on the blister end of a shovel for a change.'

I tried not to laugh. 'Mate, they're kids.'

'Yeah, but look at 'em – they're loving it.'

Nathe did seem to have a point. As long as he and his men kept feeding them the boiled sweets, his trench gang seemed more than happy to keep shovelling.

We got back to our position, and the four of us took stock over a brew. We couldn't help but marvel at what the village chief, plus Ibrahim and the people of Lungi Lol, had got sorted over the last twenty-four hours. It was easy to see how these people were able to build their own houses, dig their own wells and carve out their very lives from the bush. They had nothing else, so they crafted their lives around what nature provided.

More to the point, they'd dropped everything to help us. The community spirit and cohesion here would put any English village to shame. We'd yet to hear a single gripe or complaint, yet back home we whinge and moan when our bins aren't emptied on time. The people of Lungi Lol were an example to the rest of us.

Being here had also given me a real insight into my fellow

operators. I'd always known Wag was a man of the people, but here it had truly come to the fore. Somehow, the stumpy Hobbit-man had really charmed the I-man, Mojo and the rest of 'em. I was more fiery and likely to flash than Wag was. If someone stepped out of line I'd be – *You fucking what?* Wag was far more of a mellow fellow: *Come on, lads, screw the nut.*

I guess that's why we made such a great team. Wag was the persuader, me the enforcer. Plus with Grant, we had a commander who truly got the ethos of our unit. He was the officer with the education and the gravitas, but it was the NCOs and patrol commanders who had the operational experience. Grant knew that. He got it and he was cool with it. The three of us together made a fine team, and that positive attitude was cascading down to the men on the guns.

Ibrahim's army were chopping away at vegetation, sharpening punji sticks and driving them into the ground well into the hours of darkness. Eventually, the patrol commanders had to ask the I-man to call off his work gangs, because the lads couldn't hear properly if the rebels were out there massing to attack.

By now Dolly's trenches were done, and the rest were at least usable, so we were in a good place. Confidence was growing that we could mount a blistering defence of the village. We hadn't asked for any trenches in the HQ position, for our fold in the ground was deep enough to lie flat in and avoid most of the fire, plus we were surrounded by thick vegetation and pretty much hidden from view.

We passed that night – the fourth of our mission – hunkered down behind our strengthened defences and watching for an attack. Still none came. But the stress of being always on the alert, plus the lack of sleep, fresh food or being able to wash was starting to take its toll.

The following morning the I-man had his people out as soon as it was light. The clearance out front was now so impressive you

could see all the way across from Nathe's position to the railway embankment, which lay a good three hundred metres to the
south of us.

As we admired the view, I noticed the flash of what had to be
lightning to the north of us. A roar of thunder rolled across the
village. Thick, boiling clouds piled up on the horizon, and when
the storm broke it proved to be a monster. The rain swept in like
a sheer wall of water, pounding across us in waves. I'd never seen
anything like it. It was so dense I couldn't see more than ten feet
in any direction, and even Ibrahim's army had ceased work under
the onslaught.

We sat there in the HQ ATAP almost feeling glad of the soaking. The rain was warm, and it was like being under the world's
biggest power shower. I could feel it washing the shit out of my
combats, and scouring some of the worst of the grime off my exposed skin. At the same time my SA80 was going rusty before
my very eyes, and the 319 radio would see the rain as the perfect
excuse to stop working. Thank God for the Thuraya satphone that
The White Rabbit had given us.

For the first time since we had got here the village was eerily
deserted and silent, apart from the pounding of the rain. It poured
off the main track in muddy orange torrents, and within minutes
the village square was flooded. But the storm was over as quickly
as it had begun: one hour after the first drops had started to fall it
abruptly ended. We were left with the pitter-patter of drops falling from the leaves of the trees, as the sun burst out from behind
the clouds and began to dry out the terrain.

The villagers emerged, and the I-man got his army out putting
the finishing touches to the punji fields. As the rainfall evap-
orated the humidity grew to unbearable levels. It felt as if we
were in one massive sauna, and I couldn't imagine what it was
like for those slaving away cutting and driving in the punjis.

Wag and I wandered down soggily to check on the patrols. We
figured the battle trenches had to be flooded, and sure enough

Dolly's had two feet of water standing in the bottom. It was half-way up to the knees of the guys on stag – like Glastonbury Festival in the African jungle. We just had to hope that by tonight the sun would have dried the trenches out enough for them to be good to fight from.

We headed for Nathe's position. 'All right, Nathe? How's it going? Survived the storm?'

'Wet.' He pointed to something on the ground nearby. 'You seen the fucking size of them?'

I looked where he was indicating, and to his right was the trunk of a massive forest giant, complete with buttress roots around four feet high. All around the base of the tree were these big holes like burrows. Above the nearest two I could see these enormous beasts glued to the tree bark, with their glistening heads poking out and antennae waving spookily.

I stared at them. 'What – the fuck – are they?'

Nathe shrugged. 'I dunno. Snails?'

'Well, you tell us,' said Wag. 'You're the fucking farmer.'

'Snails,' Nathe repeated. He pointed at a neighbouring tree. 'Yeah, and they're over there look and all.'

These things were like no snails I had ever seen. Their shells were dark brown, shiny and conical, spiralling up to a point at the back, and each was the size of a baby's head. We stood there for a good couple of minutes or more, wondering what planet we had landed upon.

Nathe voiced what had to be the obvious question to him. 'Reckon you can eat 'em?'

Wag glanced at him. 'Yeah, *you* probably could.'

I snorted with mirth. 'Ben would give you a run for your money, though, mate.'

My chocolate Labrador was infamous for eating everything and anything. He'd once broken into the Pathfinders' stores and got his teeth into the exercise mats we used to do our fitness. This wasn't just having a good chew: he'd devoured his third mat by the time someone managed to stop him. No doubt about it, Ben would have given Nathe a bit of competition on the scoffing-giant-African-beasts front.

The snails – if snails they were – must have been drawn out by the rain. All around us they were munching happily on vegetation and leaves, and they were clearly oblivious to Nathe's culinary intentions.

We got back to the HQ ATAP to find Tricky entertaining the I-man. He'd learned not to give Ibrahim anything that wasn't water-soluble. Each twenty-four-hour ration pack contained three sealed metallic bags – one with a breakfast like sausage and beans, the others containing main meals like meatballs and pasta, Lancashire hotpot, or beef stew and dumplings. In addition there was a tub of cheese spread, a small bar of chocolate, chewing gum, assorted drinks packs (tea, coffee, hot chocolate) and biscuits.

Sensibly, Tricky had opted to try Ibrahim on the Garibaldi-type fruit biscuits – ones that didn't require washing down with a litre of water. Just as soon as he spotted Wag and me the I-man jumped to his feet, cramming down the remainder of his Garibaldis.

'Come, come – come see! Finish! Finish!'

Tricky being the signaller, he was glued to the radio 24/7, so Wag, Grant and me followed the I-man down to the punji fields. Each contained around one hundred stakes honed to a dagger-like point.

The I-man waved his machete in the direction of the nearest punji field. 'You like? You like? Good?'

Under Ibrahim's instructions the villagers had done pretty much exactly as we'd asked.

Wag nodded enthusiastically. 'Yeah, fucking love it.' He bent low so he could get a good look across, checking for any potential routes through. 'But that one there – move it there, okay? And put another there, to even out the spread a little. Okay?'

'Okay, I do.'

'Then it'll be perfect, Ibrahim. Perfect.'

'I do! I Do!'

'Tell you what,' I observed to Wag, 'I wouldn't like to have to cut through that under fire.'

Wag smiled, evilly. 'Too right, mate.'

Ibrahim ordered us to follow him, as he set off towards the southern punji field. He was so proud of his work that he more or less force-marched us down there.

'Woah, Ibrahim, slow down a little, pal,' Wag remarked, as he struggled with his stumpy legs to keep up.

'No, no – come, come! You see!'

Punji field number two was pretty much a repeat of field number one. A bit of tweaking here and there, and Wag declared it to be a top job.

Ibrahim beamed. 'Is good, yes?'

'Ibrahim, mate, it's class,' Wag confirmed. 'Listen, we're going to speak to the village chief for you. Maybe for you a very big house now, very big house.'

Ibrahim's smile grew even broader. It was about to split his face in two. With that he tottered off into the tree line and was gone, leaving us in the midst of the punjis.

We made our way back via Nathe's position, pausing to check on their battle trenches. The blokes had topped them off with camouflage, spreading moss, dry leaves and other vegetation around the lip, rendering them practically invisible. You had to be standing right on top of one before you realised it was there.

To the rear of the trenches Nathe was hunched over a big black cooking pot. It was simply massive and it dwarfed the tiny, fold-up hexy stove that was heating whatever it contained. Nathe stirred away, like a wizard at his cauldron. Crouched next to him was one of his trench-digging gang. The boy had a snail gripped between his knees, and was levering out the flesh with a sharpened stick.

'All right?' Nathe grunted.

He was 100 per cent focused on the task in hand. The pot was bubbling away, and I could see the individual snails turning over and over as it boiled.

Nathe glanced at the boy and nodded to the pot. 'Go on, then, get another in.'

Beside me Grant's chin was practically on the floor. 'Nathe. What. The fuck. Is that?'

'Dinner,' Nathe replied, matter-of-factly. 'Mate, food is fuel. You don't eat, you die.'

Grant gave a snort of revulsion. 'Well, I won't be fucking eating with you, that's for sure.'

We were six days in now, and after that many days on British Army ration packs you did get a bit desperate for some 'fresh'.

Each day we'd had the village kids come and sit with us, throwing around a few words of English as we doled out the goodies. The relationship between them and us was becoming one of real camaraderie, and Nathe had clearly built up a friendship that was closer than most. The kid from Nathe's trench-digging crew seemed oblivious to Grant's obvious revulsion. He was totally focused on hooking out the next snail and adding it to whatever concoction Nathe was brewing up here.

'Tell you what,' I remarked to Grant and Wag, as we moved onwards. 'Let's give it twenty-four hours, and if Nathe's still alive we'll try some of the stew.'

Wag chortled. 'Aye, sounds good to me.'

Grant made a T-sign with his hands. 'Time out, lads. You're on your own. I'm strictly a boil-in-the-bag man.'

I figured Nathe's snail stew was going to prove the real man test here in Lungi Lol. Nathe wasn't the real wilderness man amongst us – he was just the hungriest. H was the hunter and survivalist par excellence. For sure, H would probably eat the snails raw, but only if he'd caught 'em with his bare hands. H's mantra was – *if it moves, kill it*. Once it was dead he could rely on Nathe to eat it, and that's why Nathe and H were such good mates.

Dolly and Ginge would force themselves to eat Nathe's snail hotpot, but only because of peer pressure. As for Taff, all we had to do was tell him they were from the Rhondda Valley. 'They're Welsh snails, mate.' Taff would be right into them. 'Oh, fuck-aye, bud, they'll be lovely, then.'

But there was also a serious side to Nathe's culinary experiments. Self-reliance is the mantra of the Pathfinders. There is no other way. Practically all of our kit was from non-British Army sources. The Army didn't provide a usable machete, so each of us had picked one up from a civvie store. We'd put together our own rifle-cleaning kits – crucial when using a temperamental piece of crap like the SA80. Our kits were waterproof, and had triple the capacity of cloth and gun oil – enough to last a long mission isolated in the jungle.

Likewise, there were no guarantees when our next resupply of rations would be flown in to Lungi Lol. We were running low already, and learning what local flora and fauna were good to eat was a sensible move – even more so if we were forced to go on the run. At that point we'd be living off the land, and Nathe's snail goulash might be all we could rustle up between us – boil-in-the-bag Grant included.

We'd spent just under a week in Lungi Lol by now, yet oddly it felt as if we'd been here forever. This mission was turning into one of those incredible, once-in-a-lifetime experiences – a view into a world and a way of life so different from our own as to be almost unrecognisable. As we worked with the villagers on Operation Alamo, and scavenged the local flora and fauna to supplement our rations, the mission was proving utterly unforgettable.

But nothing was to prove as unforgettable as the dark murder and mayhem that was coming.

12

In recognition of how we were now pulling together as one, in a united village defence force – Pathfinders, Mojo and his men, plus Ibrahim's army – I figured I'd get the blokes to set aside all the chocolate, sweets, biscuits and other goodies they could spare from the ration packs. Presented to the villagers, it would be our way of saying a heartfelt 'thank you'.

I called the patrol commanders in. 'Listen, lads, you need to get your blokes to surrender any scoff – anything you don't need – and bring it back to me. After what the villagers have done for us we need to repay the favour; so any goodies, hand 'em in.'

Nathe, Dolly, Ginge and Taff handed over stacks of biscuits, drink kits, boiled sweets and chocolate. I threw it all into a big box – one that had originally held ten of the twenty-four-hour ration packs. When I was done it was brimful with goodies, and Wag and me carried it over to the Kingdom of Mojo.

I showed him the box. 'Look, we want to give this out to the villagers, but we don't want to upset the chief. So what's the protocol? How do we best go about it?'

Mojo studied the box for a few seconds. 'Well, you must give it to the chief, and let him be seen to give it out.'

We headed over to the chief's place to do so. Wag and me placed the gift box reverentially at the foot of the wooden steps, as Mojo launched into one of his speeches, pointing at the box and miming eating and drinking. There was a bit of general chat, plus smiles all around, before Mojo turned to us.

'The chief, he says – thank you very much; this is very kind. This will be very good for him.'

'Please tell him thanks for all the work,' I said. 'Plus a special thank you for Ibrahim. They've done a fantastic job, all of them. The village is strong now, with good defences.'

Mojo translated what I'd said.

'Please also tell the chief this,' I added. 'We need to know if people come to the village and tell him anything about the rebels. Or if he sees people in the village he does not recognise – young men who may be rebels – then he must also tell us.'

Mojo related all of that, then translated the chief's response. 'Yes, he will tell you. They are watching very closely and they will see and warn about any rebels.'

We left the box lying at the foot of the stairs, suspecting that we'd pulled off some great hearts and minds work here. Sure enough, over the course of the next few hours we spotted villagers wandering around with stuff from the goody box, proving that the chief had been true to his word. And we passed our fifth night in Lungi Lol feeling a tad more secure behind our seriously beefed-up defences.

It was mid-morning the following day when the I-man rocked up at our position. He pointed at the ground where we'd been sleeping and started gabbling away.

'This here, you?' He made a load of snoring noises. 'You that here?' He made some digging and cutting motions, and repeated the snore noises again.

None of us had a clue what he was on about, but it had been all good so far with the I-man, so we figured we'd go with it.

'Yeah, Ibrahim, we kind of snore there, mate,' Wag confirmed, 'so crack on.'

With that Ibrahim was gone. He was back a few minutes later carrying an armful of cut branches. Having dumped them on the floor where he'd made the snore noises, he disappeared once more.

'What's he up to now?' I asked Wag. 'What d'you reckon they're for?'

Wag shook his head. 'No idea, mate, not a Scooby Doo.'

When Ibrahim returned he had a length of rattan – a strong jungle vine – coiled around his shoulder, like a cowboy with a lasso. He'd obviously been to different parts of the jungle cutting the bits and pieces for whatever he had in mind. Question was, what exactly was he building for us now? A garden bench? A gazebo? Toilet maybe? I hoped not, not with Wag's bowel movements being such as they were.

A few days back we'd asked Mojo the obvious – where did he and his guys go to answer the call of nature? Mojo had explained to us where the village shit-pit was situated, which appropriately enough was as near to Wales as you could get in Sierra Leone. It was just to the rear of Taff's battle trenches, on the edge of the trees that fringed the village.

'Go down to the end of the side track and turn right,' Mojo had explained. 'You will know where it is when you get near enough.'

He was damn right.

You could smell it from a good fifty metres away. It consisted of a hole in the ground four feet square and about fifteen feet deep, complete with a complimentary swarm of botflies – and it was filling up quickly. All around were these mounds of earth where other latrines had been dug, then filled in and topped over. This was truly shit city.

The only way to relieve yourself was to grab hold of a post planted for the purpose, and hang your ass out over the stinking hole. The first thing Wag and I did – we'd gone there buddy-buddy fashion, of course – was to test the pole for strength and stability. Wag promptly nicknamed the post 'the lean-tree'. British ration packs seem designed to make you constipated, which meant an age spent hanging onto the lean-tree. The only way to cut time at the pit was to get some fresh down you – hence the draw of Nathan's snail curries.

'How the hell d'you keep one hand on your weapon, one hand on the lean-tree, and wipe your ass at the same time?' Wag demanded.

It was a good question. I couldn't think of an answer. I was too busy trying not to laugh at the expression on Wag's face as he tried to go.

Ibrahim had dumped his building materials to the right-front of the crater-like depression that made up our HQ. No doubt about it, if Ibrahim was building us our own, private latrine here, it was going to be far too close for comfort.

We watched in fascination as the I-man proceeded to scoop out four narrow holes with his machete, each about twelve inches deep, so it swallowed the entire blade. Ibrahim was 100 per cent focused on his task, and we in turn were glued to whatever he was doing.

Next he took one of the long branches, stood it vertical and chopped it into four pieces, each two feet long. He slotted those pieces into the four holes he'd dug in the ground, then he took the soil he'd scooped out and tamped it around them, until he had four rock-solid posts arranged in a rectangle. He cut more lengths of wood, to make crosspieces at either end of the rectangle. Then he bent the rattan vine over the machete blade, sliced off a length, and lashed the two crosspieces to the uprights.

'Maybe it's some kind of evil trap to ensnare the rebels,' I suggested. 'One we haven't thought of.'

'Bollocks,' Wag snorted. 'But whatever it is, it sure beats going to Ikea.'

Next, the I-man took a long length of wood, stood it upright, marked where his shoulder came to with his fingers, and lopped off the excess. He then repeated the performance with another pole. That done, he knelt down and lashed the poles to the long side of the uprights, using the rattan to do so.

He now had about twenty feet of the vine remaining. After tying one end to the corner of the rectangular frame, he started to thread the rattan back and forth, looping it around the wood twice as he went. He worked his way from one end to the other. Once he was done he threw his machete down, point into the soil.

The whole process had taken about forty minutes, during which he'd never said a word to us – not even cracking a joke about what he might be up to.

With his back to us he sat on the rattan latticework, and took a bounce or two, clearly testing its strength. Maybe it was some kind of a garden bench? Then he swung his legs up and laid his whole body flat on the construction. He bounced and wriggled and shuffled about a bit and went: 'Hmmmmm ... Hmmmmm ... Hmmmmm ...'

With a seriously happy expression on his face he sat up and turned to us. 'Try! Try!' He made the snoring noises again. 'This very good here.'

Ah, so that's what it was – *a bed.*

I glanced at Wag. 'You're the heaviest – get on.'

He shrugged. 'Yeah. Fuck it. Why not?'

Wag got up, removed his belt kit and climbed on. He did a repeat of the I-man's performance. He rolled to the left and went: 'Hmmm ...' Rolled to the right: 'Hmmm ...' Rolled back again: 'Hmmm.' I was half expecting him to go crashing through, but the I-bed didn't shift an inch. Wag climbed off with a big smile and Ibrahim picked up his machete and started the whole process all over – making us bed number two.

Forty minutes later it was done, and there was a three-foot gap between the two of them. Ibrahim had never taken one proper measurement the entire time. No tape measure for the I-man. As Wag had said, it sure beat going to Ikea, where you'd spend an hour reading the instructions and then build it almost to completion before realising that some bits were missing and you'd fixed half of the others the wrong way round.

Ibrahim pointed at a clear patch of ground adjacent to the two I-beds: 'There? Another?'

Wag shook his head. 'No, no, no, mate, two is more than okay.'

Ibrahim, pointing at the four of us: 'No, no, no – *four.*'

Wag, pointing at the two beds already built: 'No, no, no – two Ibrahim is fine.'

There was a bit more toing and froing before Ibrahim finally seemed to get it that as two of us would be on stag, we didn't need any more I-beds. That understood, he collected his things and wandered off happily. It was early evening by now and we were all curious to have a proper go on the new furniture.

I tried one of them. 'Hmmmm ... Bit stringy on the back. I tell you what. We'll cut up the ration boxes, flatten them out and lay the cardboard ... Look, I'll show you ...'

The beaten flat ration boxes provided enough of a cardboard layer to cover the torso area of both beds, and the legs were fine anyway.

'Perfick,' I announced. 'The dog's nads mate.'

Wag's eyes glittered. 'Fucking 'ell, we've got two peachy beds. Wait 'til the blokes come for prayers and see 'em.'

The patrol commanders filtered in one by one. We gathered in a circle around the rim of the depression. We were waiting to see their reaction over the I-beds, but although Nathe, Dolly, Ginge and Taff were now all present not one of them had said even a word.

'They're just trying to ignore it ...' I mouthed at Wag. 'Fucking blokes.'

Wag decided to make a pre-emptive announcement. 'Look, before anyone says anything, yes we do have two very fucking nice beds, thank you.'

We were expecting a massive chorus of: *You wankers*!

Instead, Nathe just shrugged. 'So what? They're just like ours.'

'What, you've got beds as well?' I asked.

'Yeah.'

'What, like those?'

'Yep. The same.'

'Really?'

'Yeah.'

I turned to Dolly. 'Have you got two 'n all?'

'Yeah, two.'

'Ginge?'

'Yeah. Two as well.'

'Taff?'

'Two, bud.'

'How the fuck did you get beds? Ibrahim can't have been in five places all at once.'

'Nah, it was the kids,' said Nathe. 'We told 'em to build 'em set back from the trenches, in the shade of the canopy. Ibrahim turned up rattling his sabre and cracking a few heads and did an inspection. He found the beds fit for muster and left happy.'

Dolly nodded. 'Yeah, he turned up and did the same with us and all.'

Ginge and Taff had a similar tale.

The beds issue pretty much dominated that evening's prayers. Other than that, the patrol commanders reported that all the defences we'd asked for were present and correct – punji fields included. Now, it had become a waiting game to see who would be the first to blink and take a bullet: us or the rebels.

It was around seven that evening, so just getting properly dark, when Mojo pitched up unannounced. He was sporting shiny boots and a beret, and amazingly his Foster Grant shades were still in place. Balanced on his shoulder was a large cardboard box, like a fruit tray. He proceeded to deposit the box on the lip of our depression.

Inside it was a heap of fresh bread rolls. I could smell them from where I was sitting, and after a week of British Army rations the aroma was mouth-watering. I glanced at the others. This was way out left-field kind of shit. I mean Mojo wasn't exactly the Hovis boy on his bicycle, and this wasn't quite the cobbled streets of Shaftesbury's Gold Hill, in Dorset, where the Hovis ads were filmed.

'A gift from the chief,' Mojo announced. 'You will get one bread delivery every evening.'

For a moment we were speechless.

Then Wag posed the obvious question. 'Mojo, where the fuck did you get fresh bread?'

'They made it for you. The villagers. And also from tomorrow the ladies will fetch your water, as well.'

'What d'you mean – *the ladies will fetch us water*?'

'Every morning they will go to the water source and bring you drinking water.'

'Really?'

Mojo nodded. 'Yes. This also is from the chief.'

With that he about-turned and drifted into the shadows. We counted the bread rolls. There were twenty-six, one per man. We were flabbergasted. How the hell had they managed that? We removed our four, then Wag and me did a walkabout of the positions, starting with Dolly's.

'Here you go,' Wag announced, as he counted out six bread rolls from the tray under his arm. 'One, two, three ... that's six. One each.'

Dolly stared at the rolls in disbelief. 'What – the fuck – are those?'

'Bread rolls.'

Wag was being mega-straight-faced, which made it all the funnier. I was having to tighten my belt to stop myself from laughing. If I so much as sniggered the wind-up would be over.

'Where in God's name did you get those?' Dolly demanded.

'The shop,' said Wag.

Dolly stared at him. 'What shop?' The rest of his blokes were staring now too.

Wag jerked a thumb over his shoulder. 'On the corner. The baker's.'

Dolly had the hook deep in his mouth now. 'What baker's? I've been here seven days and ...'

'The corner shop at the end of the road,' Wag cut in.

Dolly shook his head. 'I haven't seen no baker's.'

Wag shook his head, in mock exasperation. 'Look, stop asking so many fucking questions. D'you want 'em or not?'

Wag was the past master at these kind of wind-ups. He was brilliant at acting as if all was completely normal. I was stood behind him desperately trying not to laugh.

'And if you're good lads you'll get the same again tomorrow,' Wag added. 'Plus I'll be sending someone in the morning to fill your water bottles.'

'Fuck off,' said Dolly.

But he still grabbed his ration of bread rolls.

The joke got repeated all down the line. It didn't get any less funny with each rendition. It took Wag and me an hour to get it done, for no one could quite get their heads around the bread delivery.

Like everything else we do, we also eat in pairs. Most blokes were having one major meal in the evening and making it an 'all-in'. You'd save up your boil-in-the-bag meals and mix in your hard tack biscuits, making one big gloppy stew. A little bit of fresh like those bread rolls provided a massive boost to morale. They were a little taste of home, of family, of the familiar – and maybe even of safety.

By the time we got back to the HQ position it was fully dark. Tricky had just got an Intel update via the Thuraya satphone, for the 319 radio was still kaput after the rainstorm. He'd taken the radio set to pieces, removed the batteries and left it all to dry in the sun, but still it wasn't playing ball.

The Intel update was as follows: 'Be aware the rebels are coming. All Intel suggests two thousand plus. All comms intercepts suggest they will come through your position. Repeat: they will be coming through your position.'

That night was one of sleeplessness and high tension, in spite of the luxury of having the I-beds. Something was different about the jungle. The noises had changed, and we were becoming increasingly convinced it wasn't animals making most of them any more. We figured the rebels were using the hours of darkness to do their close-target recces – so scoping out our defences and the best potential routes of attack – and were signalling to each other via their spooky 'animal' cries.

Just after stand-to the following morning two women appeared at our position. They wore bright scarves tied around their heads, and multicoloured wrap-around sarongs knotted over one shoulder. Each had a five-gallon cooking-oil container perched on her head – the clear plastic ones. They were using them to carry water. Each must have weighed a good forty pounds and God only knows where they'd had to go to fill them – most likely the wetland area from where they'd cut the best of the bamboo.

They plonked their burdens down on the lip of the depression, gave a shy kind of a smile, then turned and wandered off. As promised, this was our early morning water delivery.

Amazing.

I didn't doubt that all the patrols were getting their water delivery – and so it proved. Once it was put through the Millbank bags to rid it of any sediment, and treated with Steritabs – a sterilising tablet that kills most nasties – it would be good enough to drink. Until now we'd been on seriously tight water discipline. We'd been rationed to seventeen one-litre bottles per six-man patrol, to last three days – so slightly less than one litre per man per day.

It was nowhere near enough in the gruelling heat and with guys on stag or out doing their foot patrols. We were getting seriously dehydrated – suffering lethargy, exhaustion and pounding headaches. This early morning water delivery was going to be a lifesaver. With two jerry cans per patrol, we now had an extra sixteen litres a day – or four litres each, which was more like the kind of amount we needed to be drinking.

But equally importantly, this was classic hearts and minds stuff. Somehow, we'd really started to win the battle on that front, and there were few militaries in the world that could have done this.

The villagers had taken us into their hearts, built the defences we needed, started a regular water and bread delivery and shown us how to harvest and cook the local fauna. They had their eyes and ears out scanning for the enemy, and the best Intel you can ever get is good local humint.

Nathe's snail baltis were part and parcel of the whole hearts and minds process. The most insulting thing you can ever do is refuse to eat the locals' food, or turn your nose up at it. We'd achieved all of this while looking and smelling ever more like a bunch of street hobos. In spite of our rain-shower, we were grimy as hell. During the heat of the day we were attracting swarms of flies. They'd settle on our sweat-soaked shirts in voracious clouds, eating us alive.

It would have been impossible for us to dig the battle trenches, clear the vegetation, and make and plant the punji fields on one litre of water per man per day. We'd managed to make the villagers feel as if we were here to protect them, and that if we worked as a united team we could win this thing – because if we didn't we were all getting slaughtered anyway. If we had for one moment appeared like a force of occupation, we'd have lost the battle before we even got started.

More rain fell that morning, and this time it just kept coming. Pathways turned to raging torrents, and within seconds just about every piece of kit we possessed was soaked. In addition to the dodgy Clansman 319 HF radio, we also had Clansman 349 VHF radios for short-range communications between patrols. The 349s consisted of an earpiece, plus a throat-mic to speak into and send. But they were almost as vulnerable to moisture as was the 319. Much more of this kind of rain and it'd put an end to them as well. This was a real issue, for we had decided upon a single code-word to be given over the radios if the rebels were spotted: *maximise*.

If *maximise* was given, all would know we were about to be hit and to stand-to in our fighting positions.

13

The formal role of the Pathfinders is to 'cue the deep battle'. In theory, we go forward into enemy territory to guide in the main force, and bring in battle assets: fixed-wing warplanes, helicopters, mortars, artillery, rocket fire. We also act to sabotage and divert enemy forces, by hitting their command nodes and key personnel – using sniper rifles and other precision weaponry.

Accordingly, Pathfinders have to be mentally and physically tough enough to operate as small teams in isolation over protracted periods of time. The twenty-six of us positioned in Lungi Lol were capable of doing all of this and more – if only we had the kit to enable us to do so. But right now, with our main radio kaput and our personal radios on the blink, that was looking decidedly doubtful. The call to *maximise* might well never be heard.

With only the one set of clothes we sat there soaked to the skin after the cloudburst, and set about stripping down and cleaning our SA80 rifles. We did so two on and two off, so those on sentry were always ready to fight should the rebels appear. As the sun dried the clothes to our bodies, so the danger of 'prickly heat' intensified – whereby dirt and shit blocks up the pores, causing unbearable rashes and itching. With the lack of hygiene, boils were starting to form on our skin, and our feet were rotting in our warm and damp socks.

A week in by now, part of the danger had become the routine: sentry, sleep, eat; sentry, sleep, eat. Routine leads to boredom and in a situation like this boredom can prove lethal. Now we had a reliable supply of drinking water I figured we could do more. I decided to push out the foot patrols beyond the village clearing.

They'd search for signs of the enemy that we figured were out there in the forest fringes, scoping our positions.

I told the patrol commanders to take time to sit at the edge of the jungle looking back into the village, assessing where and how they would launch an attack.

'You've got to think like the enemy,' I told them. 'Think like the enemy and pay them the respect they deserve.'

H came in from one such patrol having spotted a route through the punji fields. New bamboo stakes were planted to block it. Taff came in from another patrol suggesting we thread a running track around the village perimeter, so we could start 'running the fence' again. It was partly in jest, but the point was well made. With all the lack of physical exercise blokes were losing their edge – and so was planted the idea of building some makeshift gyms.

That morning Wag made the announcement: 'Right, I'm gonna see if I can make some weights.'

He vanished into the small patch of woodland that lay adjacent to our position, and I could hear him chopping away with his machete. After five minutes or so curiosity got the better of me. I found him hacking up various lengths of wood, trying to fashion some makeshift dumbbells.

Halfway through the chopping he paused: 'Fuck it – I need a weights bench.'

In a brazen attempt to copy the I-beds, Wag started to try to build an exact reproduction – but one set within the shade of the woods. He began by planting a couple of uprights, each branching into a V-shape at the high end, forming the rest to lay the weight bars on. Then he started work on the weight bench itself. He got about halfway when he realised he had a problem.

'Fuck it – I've run out of rattan!'

By now Wag was a man on a mission. He went and fetched a length of paracord, one that was rolled up into a dog's-bone shape, like you buy washing line in a hardware store. He switched to using that to lash the framework together. I was assisting as best

I could, cutting down branches here and there, and two hours in the bench was done.

Next, Wag set about hacking out some massive blocks of wood, to make the weights on the end of the bar. But now he faced a problem. He rubbed his hand across his shaven head, glancing from the bar to the weights and back again. The problem was how to attach one to the other.

'Fuck it – what now?' he kept muttering. He paused for a second, then looked at me. 'Right, you seen the fucking I-man anywhere?'

'Nah, mate, I've not seen him. But he'll be about, won't he?'

'Come on, let's go find him.'

Wag shrugged on his belt kit and off we went. Generally, if you walked up and down Lungi Lol's main drag a couple of times you'd find just about anyone. Sure enough we spotted Ibrahim, still in his green shirt and flowery sarong, pottering about on one of the pathways just off the track.

Wag marched over. 'Ibrahim, mate, we need a hammer and nails. Bash, bash. Nails. Pointy object.'

For a few moments Ibrahim stared at Wag uncomprehendingly, before he finally seemed to get the idea. 'I fetch! I fetch!' With that he was gone.

We returned to the HQ ATAP and a few minutes later Ibrahim appeared. In one hand was a rusty-headed hammer with a wooden handle and in the other was an assortment of fifty different bent and blunted nails.

'I have! I have!' he announced, excitedly.

Wag held out his hands. 'Right, okay, give us them here then.'

Wag hurried off towards his woodland gym, tools in hand. I followed, telling Ibrahim that he'd better come with us.

We found Wag surveying his enterprise. He bent to pick up the bar, with the weights, hammer and nails balanced in his free hand.

From behind me Ibrahim came barging through. 'You want this fix here?'

'Yeah,' Wag nodded. 'Yeah, yeah.'

Ibrahim gestured at the hammer and nails. 'Give me, give me.'

A little reluctantly Wag handed them over. Ibrahim hammered away for a few seconds and the lump of wood was attached to the bar. Wag told him we needed another lump on the far end the same size. Within minutes Ibrahim had found one, made a few alterations with his trusted machete, and hammered it on. We now had a bar with a lump of wood nailed to each end, ready for use.

We hefted it between us. I figured it had to weigh a good forty pounds. It was clear the I-man didn't have the slightest idea what we were up to here. He most likely figured we were building some kind of cunning trap akin to the punjis.

'You want me to give it a try?' I asked Wag.

'Yeah. Go on. Go on.'

I took off my webbing, laid my weapon on top to keep it out of the dirt, then lay on the bench. I could hear it creaking and groaning horribly under my weight. No doubt about it – this was not a genuine Ibrahim. It was a cheap Western copy. Wag was stood over me staring into my face, the weights bar between us.

I reached up for the bar. 'Fuck it – in for a penny, in for a pound.'

I was looking up Wag's nostrils as he leant over, preparing to help me lift it.

My fingers closed around the bar. 'Mate, you'd better get ready to catch it if it snaps.'

'Fucking get on with it.'

I eased it off, so I had it held above my head, and started to bench press. After half a dozen pushes, I said: 'Here, mate, grab a hold.'

Wag took the weight and put it back on the rests.

I sat up facing Ibrahim. He had his machete dangling from his hand and was staring at us in total disbelief. He started doing these slow, silent shakes of his head. They just kept coming. He did one final shake – *the white men have finally lost it!* – then turned around and left.

From behind me Wag said: 'Here, let's have a go.'

We reversed the procedure, the bench creaking and grinding but somehow holding fast under Wag's bulk, and that was it – gym sorted. We returned to the HQ ATAP, got a brew on and told Tricky and Grant all about what had happened.

Wag's gym had to be worth it just for the laughs we got out of it. It was impossible to remain laser sharp and focused if all you ever did was stare down the barrel of an SA80 into a wall of jungle. After a while you'd go stir crazy. I added to the list of desirables that we'd radio through to The White Rabbit some alternative fresh food – as opposed to giant African snails – so Nathe and the other masterchefs amongst us could keep themselves busy.

A local cycled through the village with one bloke perched on his battered handlebars and another on the seat behind him, while he himself was standing on the pedals. Three on a bike – it was like Billy Smart's Circus. A call was made for everyone to be eyes-left and have a good laugh. Anything to break the routine. And as it happened, our biggest ever routine-breaker was just about to emerge from the jungle to the south of the village.

It was around lunchtime when a white Lada taxi puttered into Lungi Lol from the direction of Freetown. We were sat in our depression finishing off our brews, and Tricky was the first to spot it.

'What – the fuck – is that?'

Wag glanced over. 'It's a white Lada taxi.'

We stared at it. We'd had practically no vehicular traffic through Lungi Lol, and certainly no taxis pottering out from the nation's capital. It came crawling along the road towards us, as if the driver was highly unsure of where he was going. Once opposite the chief's place it slowed to a snail's pace, then pulled to a halt beside our Pinzgauer.

The back door swung open. I watched in disbelief as a tall, sandy-haired fellow emerged from the rear. He was dressed in neat chinos and a crisp white shirt, and he had a camera slung around his neck.

He stood by the Lada and practically sniffed the air – as if he was saying; *I say, anyone here speak the Queen's English*? He held onto the car door with one hand and peered all about. Unless you knew exactly where we were positioned you'd never be able to see us.

'Better go see who it is,' I announced. 'Grant, you coming?'

We rose as one and went to investigate. The moment the stranger spotted us emerging from the bush, his face broke into an expression of sheer unadulterated joy. It was like all his Christmases had come at once: *the taxi driver hasn't screwed me; I am not about to get kidnapped, tortured, buggered . . . and ransomed for a million dollars.*

He bent down, reached inside the Lada, pulled out a daysack and slung it over his shoulder. By the time he'd done that we were pretty much on him. Neither of us had the slightest idea who this might be, except for one thing: he was a prize-winning A1 lunatic.

'Ah, I am in the right place then!' he announced, as an opener.

I stared at him. 'That depends what you're looking for.'

He shut the door, stepped towards us with real purpose and introduced himself as a reporter for a major newspaper.

I put out my hand. 'Steve. And this is Grant.'

'Ah. Steve and Grant. So, are you guys 1 PARA?'

'No.'

'Are you SAS?'

'No.'

'So who are you?'

'We're Pathfinders.'

'Great,' he enthused. 'Great. Great. Pathfinders.'

We were stood at the front of the Lada taxi, and we were still none the wiser as to who this guy was or what he was doing here.

'Sorry, but you do know where you are, don't you? Where you're coming from ... Where you're going to ... What planet you're on ...'

'Ah, erm, I was trying to find the furthermost British position, actually.'

I shook my head in disbelief. 'Well, mate, you're standing on it.'

'Great. Great. Am I? Superb.'

When anyone has done anything completely and utterly insane, a phrase comes into my head: *When God gave out heads, you thought he said 'beds' and said I'll have a big soft one . . .* That was exactly what I was thinking now. What on earth was this crazed loon doing here, alone and unarmed and riding in a Lada taxi cab?

'Oh, erm, it would be great to get an interview with you guys and some pictures.'

Grant and I exchanged glances. 'Okay, you'd best come with us.'

We led him in silence down the track and through the bush towards the HQ ATAP. We threaded between some trees, to where Wag and Tricky were draining the last of their brews. Our surprise guest laid eyes on them, kind of jumped backwards a step and stared.

'Urgh . . . Ah! There are more of you!'

Tricky being the brewmaster had a giant metal mug perched on the hexy stove between his legs. Both he and Wag were a week into Lungi Lol, and neither had had a wash or a shave in that time. They – like Grant and me – were stinking. Our mystery guest stared at them for a long second, before running his eyes around the position. His gaze came to rest on the I-beds.

He glanced up at Grant and me in disbelief. 'Erm . . . How long . . . How long have you guys been here?'

'A week.'

'Really?'

'Yep. Really.'

'So, how many of you are there?'

Grant gave me this look: *Mate, time to read him the riot act.*

'Look, we cannot stop you from having access to this village,' I told him. 'You are free to walk around. In fact, I'll take you around.

But we're going to have to place some restrictions on you, and agree some ground rules, okay?'

'Right. Right. Okay, fine.'

'Okay, so, we'll let you speak to people and show you around the village. But no photos of the blokes, and especially no facial shots. No photos of defensive positions, and no talk about our strengths, weaponry or numbers. Agreed?'

'Yep. Fine. Understood. Got it.'

Tricky had finished brewing up. He held out the battered, dirty, gungy mug to our visitor. 'Brew?'

The journalist stared at it. 'No, erm, thanks – I'm fine.'

He removed his daysack from his shoulders, bent down, unzipped it and pulled out a ring-bound reporter's notebook. As he did so I spotted what looked like a satphone in the depths of his pack.

'Is that a satphone?' I asked.

He nodded. 'It is.'

I smiled. 'I do for you, you do for me.'

He looked a bit confused. 'Sorry?'

'We'll give you full access to the village bar the restrictions already stated, if you let me have use of that phone while you're here. You know – calls home.'

'Calls home?'

'Yeah – let the married guys have five mins each to speak to their wives. They've not spoken to them for nigh-on ten days.'

'Oh, yes, I see.' He smiled. 'Deal.'

I turned to Tricky. 'Mate, take the satphone, cut around the married guys, five mins each on the blower. Do it.'

Tricky grabbed the phone and set off towards Dolly's position going like the clappers.

'Wag, go lend Tricky a hand, will you?' I added.

Wag grunted an acknowledgement and set off after him. I figured it made sense to keep Gimli the Dwarf and the press as far apart as possible.

We had our own satphone, of course, courtesy of The White Rabbit, but its purpose was strictly military.

I gestured towards the patch of trees to our front right. 'Okay, let's start the tour.'

He set off after me, daypack on his back and notebook in hand, with Grant bringing up the rear. We threaded through the trees, Wag's gym lying ten feet off our line of march. I pressed on, but behind me I sensed our guest come to an abrupt halt. He was staring at the makeshift weight bench and dumbbells.

He pointed. 'Erm . . . what's that?'

'Oh, yeah, we've just finished it. It's a gym.'

'Sorry?'

'Yeah, it's a gym.'

'A gym?' Pause. 'You've *made* a gym.'

'Yeah, Wag and me made it this morning.'

He kept glancing at the gym, back at me, then back at the gym again, as if waiting for some kind of a sensible, credible explanation.

'Well, we've been here a week and we were getting lazy . . .'

He shook his head in disbelief.

'You know, big arms for the summer, mate.'

'Big arms for the summer,' he muttered under his breath. 'Oh yeah . . . Working out. Ho, ho.'

I waved him on. 'Come on, come on. Lots to see.'

I walked on, glancing behind me to check on him. He wasn't looking where he was going any more. Instead, he was sketching out Wag's gym in his notebook. From there to Nathe's position was sixty-odd metres, and the journalist was busy drawing and scribbling away the entire distance.

I spotted Nathe up ahead of us. He was in his regular pose – seated, with his arms resting on his knees and bent over the dirty cauldron, which was three feet in front of him, steaming away. Gripped between his knees he had a tree stump, and in his hands he had a big, very sharp-looking knife.

'All right, Nathe?' I called out.

He glanced up. 'Yeah, all right, mate.'

Then he was back to his chopping.

On the block he had a new one on me – a massive, black-topped mushroom. The rain had brought the fungi out big time, but I hadn't quite realised that Nathe had moved on to snail and mushroom baltis by now. He sliced the stem off, leaving a cap about the size of his hand. It was spongy underneath, not gilled, and glistening like a fresh cowpat. Nathe started slicing chunks off it and tossing them into the pot.

Presumably, snails alone had proved a tad too bland, so Nathe had decided to add some local flora. This didn't surprise me in the least: this was Nathe. Likely as not the boy from his trench gang had suggested that the giant black fungi with fluffy white edges were particularly tasty, so in the pot they went.

I figured Nathe would have done all the usual edibility tests. The first is the allergic reaction test. You rub the fungi or flora on an exposed part of your skin – say the back of your hand. Then you wait fifteen minutes to see if you get any kind of adverse reaction – like a rash, lumpiness, redness or itching – which might indicate it was toxic. No reaction seen, you break off a small piece and place it on your tongue, then spit it out. You wait fifteen minutes and if you experience no bad reaction you move on to stage three: breaking off another piece and eating it. You'd have to wait a full hour to see if you had any stomach pains, cramps or vomiting. If you had none of those, you could be pretty sure it was safe to eat, and cooking it would generally add another layer of safety.

I came to a halt beside Nathe, quietly relishing what was coming. The journalist was closing fast, head down writing. Nathe finished the mushroom, grabbed himself a freshly deshelled snail, and nailed it on the chopping block. He was living the village good life, and it was close to his lunchtime.

I spoke to the top of his head. 'Nathe, there's this British journalist who has pitched up. He wants to talk to the blokes.'

Nathe didn't even pause the slicing. 'Yeah, all right, mate.'

The reporter walked in still scribbling away, and an instant later he'd all but kicked over Nathe's cooking pot. He dragged his notebook to one side, finally got a look at what was in front of him, and jumped backwards.

'Fuck!'

Nathe glanced up at him. 'Hey, mind the pot.'

The journalist shook his head in consternation. 'Sorry, sorry.'

He took a couple more steps backwards. He stared at the concoction that he'd very nearly kicked over. It was bubbling away and hissing like the world's most evil brew. Nathe meanwhile was back to his task, tossing glistening chunks of sliced mollusc into the cauldron.

'What – is – that?' he finally managed to choke out, his voice like a strangled whisper.

I guessed to him deshelled giant African snail probably looked a bit like sliced child's brain . . .

Nathe didn't miss a beat. 'Lunch. D'you want some?'

He visibly blanched. 'Erm . . . Erm . . . Erm . . . I think I'll pass.'

I was massively intrigued about what exactly Nathe had in there. 'Let's have a try, then, Nathe.'

I retrieved my spoon from the side pouch of my webbing. It was a massive metal one – a classic 'yaffling iron' as we call them. Normally, you cook in pairs, so the bigger the spoon the more you're able to get down you. I bent, scooped, and managed to land a lump of glistening flesh, a chunk of brown stuff that looked like . . . tree bark, plus a slice of what I figured was fungus, all of which swimming around in a thick black gravy. I raised the yaffling iron and in it went.

It tasted particularly salty.

I smacked my lips. 'Mate, well done. A bit chewy. A bit too much seasoning. But not bad.'

The journalist was rooted to the spot. I could hear him almost retching, as he stared at Nathan and me in revulsion and horror.

I replaced my yaffling iron. 'Okay, if you're not feeling hungry best go speak to the blokes.'

'Great . . . The blokes,' he mumbled. 'Not particularly peckish . . . Great, great, thank you.'

I backed off to let him through, without him having to pass too close to the cauldron, and he hurried off in the direction of the battle trenches.

He passed by *33 Alpha*'s I-beds as he went, giving them a good long stare. By now he was convinced we had gone 100 per cent native – Nathe's Lungi Lol balti being the *coup de grâce*. I presumed he'd been flown in by 1 PARA to report on the conflict, so he would have come through Lungi Airport – which would be a place of shower blocks, mess tents, and clean-shaven smart young soldiers by now. From there he'd arrived at . . . this. We were like Kurtz and his band of renegades in *Apocalypse Now* – eating whatever we could scavenge in the jungle . . . Clearly, if we hadn't already started, cannibalism was only a short step away.

We left him free to chat to the blokes. He asked them all the usual kinds of question: What's life like here? How are you coping? What have you seen of rebel activity? How are the villagers? When do you expect an attack? He was very respectful of the reporting restrictions I'd placed upon him. I guessed he feared he might be for the cooking pot himself if he stepped out of line.

It was in Kosovo that I'd first come across the media and begun to appreciate their hunger for the story. I'd also witnessed the insane risks individual journalists took to get it. They'd push themselves into situations of enormous danger. But this guy – he was out on a limb as never before. If he hadn't spotted the Pinz, God knows where he would have ended up, or in whose hands. We were twenty-six elite operators trained to survive in the jungle, and packing some real firepower: he was one guy with a camera in a white Lada taxi cab.

We bounced him around the patrols, but we didn't show him the punjis or the Claymores or any of our other less orthodox Op

Alamo defences. Meanwhile, Tricky and Wag were buzzing about with his satphone, getting around the married guys. They didn't manage much in the time allotted to them: *Yeah, I'm all right, love; don't believe all you see on the news; love to the kids and I'll see you soon.* But even that was pretty special.

I didn't bother to call home, because the only one I had to speak to was Ben, and I figured he'd get a right arse-on when he heard about all the lovely scoff he was missing out on here in Lungi Lol.

We managed to spin the journalist's tour out to a good two hours, by which time Tricky gave me the thumbs-up that all the lads had got to make a call. I reminded the reporter he was at the furthest forward position of any British forces in Sierra Leone, and that he'd best be getting back to Freetown. Otherwise, we'd invite him to stay for dinner, and no guessing what was on the menu.

At that he reclaimed his satphone, we walked him to his taxi and he got the hell out of Lungi Lol.

14

Bang on schedule that evening Mojo turned up with our bread delivery. He had some worrying news for us. 'You need to come and speak to the chief. He has something important to tell you about the rebels.'

Mojo led the way, as Grant and me went to have our audience. Just as we'd hoped, the chief had got his people out watching and listening, and he'd secured some peachy humint as a result.

'People arrived here today who come from a village five kilometres northeast along the main track,' Mojo translated. 'They saw the rebels coming to attack their village and they ran for their lives. They came here for safety and asked for the chief's permission to stay.'

We asked about rebel numbers, weaponry and the like, but the answers we got were pretty sketchy. Hardly surprising, considering the villagers had been running for their lives. But at least now we knew: the rebels were 5 klicks away and closing.

'Tell the chief to get as many people as he can inside the village tonight,' I advised. 'Spread the word that if the rebels come there will be fighting. No matter what happens he must make sure the villagers stay in their homes or under cover. If they are seen running around they could get mistaken for the bad guys and we do not want to end up shooting them by mistake.'

Mojo translated and the chief confirmed that he understood.

I fixed Mojo with a look. 'We hope we can count on you and your men, mate, to respond as we've asked.'

Mojo nodded. 'Okay, yes, yes – I understand. We will help. We will help.'

We thanked the chief, hurried back to the HQ ATAP and briefed Wag and Tricky. Tricky had just received that afternoon's Sched, with an Intel brief that pretty much confirmed what the chief had told us: 'Highly likely your position will face a rebel attack tonight. The force is 2000 strong.'

Tricky called the patrol commanders in. H had been put in charge of the lone battle trench situated on the main highway, so he would be joining us. We gathered in a circle and Grant set about the briefing.

'There is a very strong indication the rebels are as close as five ks out. If they are that close they may be making a move on us tonight. Priorities: ID your targets, maintain battle discipline; fire control; management of ammo. And remember, keep us informed of all that's going on at all times, if you can.'

'Right, guys, remember what we decided,' I added. 'The fallback plan has not changed. If you're overrun make your way back to the fallback point. And remember, if you're coming in – clear and loud: "We're coming in! We're coming in!" The radios are shite and we can't rely on them in a firefight: I will not be listening to them. So, shout like fuck. Make doubly sure weapons are prepped and ready.'

I finished with this. 'Right – this is it. *Showtime*.'

'Fucking let 'em come,' Nathe grunted. 'About time.'

H: 'Yeah. Pissed off waiting.'

Dolly: 'Yep, no problem – let 'em come.'

Ginge and Taff confirmed they were likewise ready.

To our left we were aware of this massive influx of people. As we'd talked, silent crowds of mainly women and children had been moving in towards the village square. Somehow, their silence was oppressive. It spoke volumes. They were clearly shit-scared. Petrified.

Our chief worry was that rebels were mingling amongst them, weapons hidden under their clothing. It would only require half a dozen to do so, and start firing from inside the village as the main force attacked, to really mess us up. We'd be facing an attack from without and within, which would not be a top fluffy feeling. But there was fuck-all we could do about that right now.

As dusk faded into full-on darkness we were on an absolute knife-edge. No one would be getting any sleep tonight. The quiet in the village only served to accentuate the increase in noises from the jungle. There were more weird animal-like yells and shrieks, and here and there the snap of a branch rang out like a pistol shot. Plus there were the low murmurs coming from those villagers still making their way in to join the hundreds gathered on the square, huddled together for safety.

We spent our time with safety catches off and fingers on the trigger, waiting for what was coming. We could sense that the jungle was alive in a way it hadn't been before. It felt thick with malice. It was watching and it was hostile. I could sense the enemy presence, and feel the threat hanging heavy in the air.

By first light we'd still not been hit, though I didn't doubt the rebels had mapped our positions comprehensively. As the early rays of sunlight streamed through the uppermost branches, I felt a wave of relief wash over me. We had fourteen hours of daylight ahead of us, and if they hit us during that time the advantage switched to us. We'd be able to see clearly, and we'd be fighting over ground we'd prepared exhaustively. The chances of scoring a first-round kill were greatly increased, which meant ammo became less of an issue.

If they wanted to hit us during the hours of daylight – *bring it on*.

'The following stuff's just come in,' Tricky announced, once he'd scribbled down that morning's Sched. After he'd read it out he'd destroy it, so nothing useful could ever be captured by the enemy.

'The Amphibious Readiness Group has moved into a position where 42 Commando can be put ashore. The intention is that 1 PARA will be withdrawn and the Royal Marines will RIP those positions held by 1 PARA, and by us. Be prepared for an RM delegation to come in by helo to your resupply LZ, to scope out your positions.'

'RIP' stands for relief in place – when one unit comes in to relieve another in their positions. It stood to reason we'd get relieved at some point, but as of yet we'd been given no timescale to expect the Royal Marines (RM) to fly in and check out our positions. In any case, our mindset remained this: *the rebel attack is imminent; they're five klicks or less away; they had eyes-on us last night; they'll hit us within the next twenty-four hours, which means it ain't gonna happen on the Marines' watch.*

Wag and me did our morning walkabout. Doubtless the blokes hadn't slept during the night, so we needed to reiterate the need to get some rest during the daylight hours.

'We need the same level of alertness as ever,' I told Dolly, 'but those not on stag need to get as much sleep as possible, plus get some food in your stomachs. If we end up on the run we won't be stopping to eat, so get as much scoff as you can on board.'

We repeated the message with all the patrols, and the chat and the banter was all good. Morale seemed amazingly high in the face of a force that outnumbered us pretty much a hundred to one. As we moved through the positions, we'd seen the odd villager going about their business, smiling and waving. By now they were utterly convinced that the twenty-six of us were their saviours: *The British are here; God's on our side* ... That in turn served to strengthen our resolve and the sense that we were all in this together.

As we returned to the HQ ATAP, I made a comment to Wag. 'Mate, the blokes are holding up well. We're as prepared as we'll ever be. If it's going to come let's just get in amongst it.'

'Aye.' Wag nodded. 'It's time.'

We got back to the HQ position, only to have another vehicle roll in from the same direction as Mr Butcher had come. But this time it was very different from a lone Lada taxi cab. It was some of the SAS from Lungi Airport, driving their open-topped Pinkies. There were eight Regiment lads in two wagons. We invited them to partake of whatever hospitality we could offer. Oddly, they didn't seem too partial to a Lungi Lol balti, but they were happy to share a brew.

For some reason they had no weapon mounts on their wagons, so they could carry no machine guns. All they had were their personal weapons, but those we eyed with great envy. Being official UK Special Forces they had all the usual Gucci kit. Six of the blokes had the lightweight M16 variant with M203 40 mm underslung grenade launchers attached. The other two hefted Minimi SAW (squad automatic weapon) light machine guns, a beautiful little drum-fed LMG perfect for fighting in close jungle.

What we wouldn't have given to have been equipped with Minimi SAWs and lightweight M16s.

We did loads of joint training with the SAS. Right now, I was involved in several cutting-edge equipment development programmes with the Hereford boys, HAPLSS being one such enterprise. Now they'd pitched up in Lungi Lol with their top-notch weaponry, while most of us were holding the line with precious little ammo and the cursed SA80.

Because we did training and ops together, we had loads of friends in common. Blokes migrated from the Pathfinders to the SAS for the extra pay, the kit and the career stability. In UKSF you got a better pension, better chances of promotion, plus job security. None of that was available in a black outfit like ours. We exchanged news over a brew, swapped stories, and then the SAS lads told us they were moving ahead to get 'eyes-on' the bad guys.

We warned them the rebels were less than five klicks away. Having agreed to keep in touch via the radios – that was when they were working – the SAS guys mounted their Pinkies and set off on the highway heading out of the village. It was day nine of our mission by now, and still we'd not taken one round of fire from the enemy. But the SAS lads had reiterated what every man and his dog was telling us – that the rebels were preparing to steam-roller through Lungi Lol and surge south to take the airport.

Around lunchtime we got a warning via the Thuraya that the Royal Marines were on their way to scope out our positions. Grant and I headed down to the LZ. By now the Chinook pilots knew what they were flying into here, but the RM guys would be coming direct from their ship. Most likely, all the RM pilot would have been given was a grid in the midst of the jungle. From his perspective he was flying into a gap in the canopy, so it made sense to help guide him in.

I stood with my back to the wind holding up an orange air marker panel (AMP) to my front. Every Pathfinder carries an AMP: it's a foldable piece of fluorescent vinyl that collapses to the size of a deck of cards. I could hear the distinctive beat of the rotor blades already, though this sounded like a Sea King, as opposed to a twin-rotor Chinook.

The helo appeared over the ragged fringe of the jungle. I saw the pilot spot me and my AMP and adjust his line of approach, and then he was flaring out to land. He came down nose-onto me, fifteen metres in front. I gave him the thumbs-up, signalling they were down safely, and got the same in return.

I moved around to the side door, knelt down with Grant, and waited for the RM advance party to disgorge. We were expecting several marines, but when the door swung open just the one figure dismounted. He jumped down and ran in a crouch to join us, the Sea King already winding up for takeoff. Because I'd air-marked the LZ I was slightly closer, which meant that the RM bloke greeted me first.

He thrust out a hand. 'Captain Richard Cantrill, 42 Commando.'

'Steve Heaney, Pathfinders.'

Grant joined us and shook hands. 'Grant Harris, Pathfinders.'

Neither of us had given our rank, and I could see the guy searching our uniforms for any rank slides. The Sea King was now at treetop height and pretty much gone.

'Just the one?' Grant asked.

'I'm OC 42 Recce Platoon. Been sent in to get a feel for the lie of the land and your positions. Intention is Recce Platoon will come into here to relieve you guys.'

The RM captain's accent was southern English and well-bred, with a bit of a lisp thrown in for good measure. He looked to be in his mid-twenties and was around six-foot-one, with close-cropped hair. His uniform was spotless, his boots were gleaming, and he seemed fit, athletic and purposeful, not to mention scrupulously clean.

His visit was scheduled to be a short one, and he was carrying nothing but his SA80 and his webbing. I figured he was doing his best to ignore our ten days of facial growth, mixed with sweat, shit, piss and general grime. But still there was the hint of a look that he flashed at Grant and me: *You've let yourself go there a bit, haven't you, lads?*

If Mojo was up there with Guardsman standards of parade-ground smartness, Captain Richard Cantrill was immaculate. He'd out-Mojo Mojo. I could smell the soap and the aftershave, and his Combat Soldier 95 (CS95) uniform had knife-edge creases ironed into it. Combat 95 was notorious. It was made from a thin and flimsy nylon in Disruptive Pattern Material (DPM), which cuts into you and doesn't breathe. We might wear it around camp in the UK, but as soon as we deployed anywhere we'd ditch it for some cotton jungle fatigues – just like we were wearing now.

They were durable, reasonably breathable, and nice and baggy. By contrast, Captain Cantrill's Combat 95s were bordering on the figure hugging, if not skintight. He was wearing standard British Army boots, ones that would be next to useless in this kind of environment. They were rubber-soled, with leather uppers, and great for yomping across the rain-and-wind-swept Brecons – but in this kind of heat and humidity your feet would roast, sweat and rot to pieces in them.

The American military made the perfect jungle boot – one with a hardened sole, sporting a metal spline that would stop punjis from piercing it. The bottom half of the boot was made of leather, but with drainage holes in it, complete with perforated metal covers like mini-grills. They allowed the boot to breathe and drain when filled with stagnant water, after wading through swamps. Above the leather was canvas that came up high around the ankle, and it was dryable and easy to move in. They were designed for the jungle, and each of us had managed to get our hands on a pair.

The nearest the Royal Marines have to a unit like the Path-finders is their Brigade Patrol Troop (BPT). The BPT boys are a pre-assault force, consisting of Mountain Leaders trained to scale cliffs and fix lines, to enable the main force to come behind them and assault a coastal position. They're superlative at what they do, but their specialism is vertical assaults up rock faces – not going beyond an enemy's front line as a deep battle asset, or oper-ating in isolated jungle.

We had two Pathfinders that had qualified as Mountain Lead-ers. It stood to reason that scaling cliffs and mountains had to be a part of your skill-set if you were operating deep inside enemy territory. In 1994 a British military expedition had gone missing in Lowe's Gully, a notorious jungle chasm in Malaysia. A mixed force of SAS, SBS and Pathfinders were sent in to find them. The only way in was to rope down a one-thousand-foot waterfall at the head of the gully. It was two Pathfinders who led the way, for our blokes had the greatest capability and experience.

Royal Marine Captain Cantrill had flown in to get a sense of what exactly they were about to take on here in Lungi Lol. To be fair, he'd come direct off a ship, and hygiene is such a key part of living in the close confines of a Royal Navy vessel – hence his squeaky clean appearance. But I wondered what he'd make of things here. As we walked him up to the HQ ATAP, Grant pointed out our various positions, explaining how long we'd been on the ground and describing the integration of the locals into the village defences.

'Recently, there's been a significant increase in the threat level,' he explained. 'We thought we were going to get hit last night, so it will more than likely be tonight. Intel says it's a force of some 2000 RUF rebels, so those are the numbers.'

As Grant spoke I was monitoring the captain's facial expressions. I'd noticed a distinct change come over him. He'd gone from this smart, shiny, über-confident, thrusting figure to something very different. He looked visibly shocked by what we were facing here, and what he was supposed to be flying his men into in due course. It was clear that no one had briefed him on the isolation of our position, the threat level, or the unorthodox measures we'd adopted to defend this place.

Captain Cantrill seemed particularly taken by the punji fields. I couldn't wait to offer him my yaffling iron, so he could have a go at Nathe's snail-and-fungi balti.

We reached the HQ ATAP and introduced him to Tricky and Wag. He took a seat on the edge of the depression in between Grant and me. Tricky passed a brew over, and it did the rounds clockwise, everyone taking a sip. When it got to Cantrill, I could see him having to force some of it down him. Sharing a brew with a bunch of evil scumbags like us was clearly not to the captain's liking.

'So, explain to us what's happening with the Marines and the 1 PARA RIP,' I prompted. 'What's the timeline for the handover and is it the same for us getting RIP'd here?'

'All I've been briefed is that 1 PARA will leave and 42 will come in and take up the mantle of those positions. I'm here to scope out RIP'ing you guys from here.'

We spent fifteen minutes sketching out the village on a hand-drawn map, and explaining all the nuances of the village defensive system that we had set in place, and the chief's pivotal role. We briefed him on Mojo and his men and the role they'd play as a back-stop force, and then we took him on a walkabout.

We ended up at Dolly's position, across the highway and out on our left flank. In the interim, Cantrill had got to see the punji fields, the DIY Claymores, the cleared arcs of fire, the battle trenches, the works. Plus he'd got a good eyeful of how the men had adapted to village life. He was scheduled to leave on a helo at 1630, so it was a whistle-stop tour, but even so he appeared somewhat disturbed.

What really seemed to have got to him was how the blokes had settled in to living under such conditions, and yet how upbeat and positive they remained. The highlight had been Nathe waxing lyrical about the joys of jungle cuisine, as he crouched over his bubbling cauldron. We got back to the HQ ATAP shortly before his helo pick-up was due, only to learn from Tricky that it was all-change for Captain Cantrill.

'We've had a message in from Lungi ref "our guest",' Tricky announced. With nearly all comms being done via Thuraya by now, The White Rabbit had adopted a kind of coded way of speaking. The Thuraya was 'insecure means' – unencoded and vulnerable to intercepts – and in theory anyone might be listening in. Tricky eyed Cantrill. 'I guess "our guest" has to mean you. Message is there will be no pick-up today: earliest 0800 tomorrow.'

Cantrill nearly coughed up a lung. He had absolutely nothing with him for overnighting with us lot: all he had were his personal weapon and his belt kit, two water bottles and zero food. Glancing around, he practically begged if he could have one of the I-beds. I did a long intake of breath, commented on how good he smelled with all the aftershave, and said he was welcome to share mine . . .

The slagging really started now. We slipped into Navy-speak, just to really twist him.

'So, it's turning out to be a nice run ashore for you, eh?' I needled. 'Don't worry, we've got a wide and varied menu on offer in the galley.'

'Can you imagine how smelly you'll be, after a night with us lot?' Wag gloated. 'Got your toothbrush?'

'Want us to have words with the village chief, to see if he can set some showers up?' Tricky threw in. 'You got your foo-foo powder? You do know it's hands-to-bathe, don't you?'

Hands-to-bathe is Navy-speak for when a vessel gets into port and all aboard are permitted to dive off the ship for a mass swim. Foo-foo powder is talcum.

'Fuck off, fucking pongos,' Cantrill muttered. 'The fucking Army.'

He was sat there eyeing the four of us like he was surrounded on all sides by pure evil . . . and we hadn't even got to show him the village shit-pit yet. It struck me that he had an expression on his face similar to the one the newspaper reporter had worn, when I'd given him the village tour.

'D'you want me to get a wet on – cheer you up a bit?' Tricky added. 'Sippers?'

A 'wet' is Navy-speak for a brew. Sippers means sharing between all. We always did that – passing the one massive mug between us. Navy types never did.

'Like I said, you can sleep next to me tonight,' I added. 'You fucking smell lovely.'

That was it. Cantrill was staring at me like I was the Antichrist. Sharing an I-bed with me was clearly his worst ever nightmare.

The torturing only really stopped when the SAS lads came beetling back through the village. They pulled over in their Land Rovers to share their news over a brew – sippers, naturally. From all that they'd been able to glean, the rebels were massing some serious firepower just to the north of us. They asked us what our drills were if we got overrun. I joked that we were going to hand over the lone Royal Marine as a sacrificial peace offering.

Joking aside, I told them that our plan was to hold firm at all costs, or at least until our meagre supplies of ammo ran out. But if the rebels got around the back of us and hit us from the south and the west, we'd have problems. If that happened, we'd try to fight through their number and E & E through the jungle.

At that the SAS lads wished us luck, then set off en route to Lungi Airport.

15

That evening Mojo pitched up with the bread delivery, and now there were twenty-seven rolls, one extra for Cantrill. The Marine captain's eyes were out on stalks. Suffice to say the poor bloke didn't know what to make of it, particularly when we invited him to sit down and dunk his roll in one of Nathan's balti specials.

In fact this one was *really* special. Today, Nathe had somehow managed to get his hands on a giant African pouched rat – a rodent about the size of a small dog. Nathe argued that the locals ate this kind of shit so why shouldn't we? *A lovely bit of fresh.* But strangely, Captain Cantrill didn't seem to be hungry.

I asked him what he had with him ammo wise. He had two mags, so sixty rounds for his SA80. It was approaching stand-to and time to slip into night routine. We called prayers and briefed the patrol commanders that we were shortly to be RIP'd by Captain Cantrill's boys from 42 Commando, but to remain eyes-peeled while we still held the village.

That done, I said to Cantrill: 'No point you stagging-on or being on the comms, mate, 'cause you don't know the routine. May as well get your head down.'

With our levels of fatigue – not to mention malnutrition; in spite of Nathan's curries, the weight was dropping off us – a fresh pair of eyes might well have been very useful tonight. But we were so into our stag rosters by now that it was too much hassle to slot Cantrill into the rotation of sentry duties. The Royal Marine captain bedded down on some cardboard left over from the ration boxes, as the rest of us settled into dark routine.

My first stint on stag was tense, but relatively uneventful.

My second sentry duty was scheduled to last from 0100 to 0230 hours, when I would go to wake the next man. I joined Grant on watch and asked him what he'd seen. He told me nothing as such. But there were loads of those weird animal-like noises echoing through the jungle, and tonight he was 100 per cent convinced they were human. He did some whispered impressions. I ripped the piss a bit, but we both knew exactly what it might mean.

Not only did the RUF use those chilling 'animal cries' to signal to each other as they moved through the bush – they also made them to terrify those they were about to attack. Their targets were almost invariably villages full of women and children. Well, if they were out there massing to hit us right now, they were going up against a very different adversary to their normal fare of defenceless civilians.

I gazed into the darkness, straining my ears for any weird or unusual sounds. Sure enough I detected these odd, inhuman, piercing shrieks and wails coming from out of the distant tree line. A lot of jungle animals make calls like that – troops of monkeys in particular. But somehow I didn't figure this was any group of primates moving through the darkness. These weren't like any normal cries of nature that I'd ever heard.

Instinct told me these were the bad guys.

Their unearthly cries sent these icy chills up my spine.

At 0230 hours I woke Tricky so he could take my place on stag, then returned to my watch for a further thirty minutes, while he got himself ready. We staggered the changeovers, so you never had two blokes going off sentry at once and a position left unmanned.

By now I was really struggling to keep awake and remain alert. Pathfinder Selection needs to be as rigorous and brutal as it is – failure rates are normally in excess of 90 per cent; on one recent Selection we had thirty-five start and only three make it through – because these were the sort of operating conditions blokes had to be able to handle day after day after day.

When Tricky was ready to take over I went to get some shut-eye.

Wag had already replaced Grant, and he'd brief Tricky on whatever we had seen or heard. I collapsed onto the I-bed, and swung my legs onto the rope mattress with my boots still on, lay back and closed my eyes.

I was looking forward to getting a good few hours' kip before stand-to. Mine was the second bed out from the depression, with Cantrill on the floor next to me, and Grant on the I-bed beyond. I lay there for a while trying to get comfortable, before gradually drifting into semi-consciousness.

The next thing I knew I had Tricky kneeling beside me, shaking me violently awake.

'STEVE! MAXIMISE! MAXIMISE! MAXIMISE!'

Instantly I was up on the bed, feet swung down. I elbowed Cantrill in the ribs. 'Get up! Get up! Get up and get your kit on!'

Cantrill was wide-eyed awake now. He shrugged his webbing on, and joined Grant and me in the depression, facing east towards the silent threat. I had no idea what time it was exactly, but the absence of any noise felt all wrong. The jungle had gone unerringly quiet.

The stillness felt crushing.

Claustrophobic.

Suffocating.

The intense, eerie quiet was broken by a single shot. It had the unmistakable dull thud that a low-velocity round makes. It was one single low pop – the signature noise of anything above 7.62 mm in calibre, and more than likely the sound of a pistol being fired.

It had come from the front and slightly to my left, so from the direction of the track leading into the village. There was just the vaguest possibility that someone might have had an ND – a negligent discharge (firing their weapon accidentally). It was extremely unlikely with one of us, but quite possible with Mojo and his men. Still, the way things were feeling right now I really didn't think so.

The next instant the darkness to our front was torn apart by a long, punching burst of fire. I caught the instantly recognisable hammering crack of the GPMG, as it unleashed a savage volley of rounds. It was a ten- to fifteen-round burst – *zzzzzzzzzttttttttt* – and it was pretty obvious it had come from the single battle trench to our front, the one manned by H. It could only be H letting rip with his favourite weapon – the Gimpy.

We weren't using tracer, so it wasn't as if I could follow H's rounds into target. All I could see was the flash of his muzzle, as he unleashed hell. Tracer rounds have the advantage of pointing out the enemy's position. All a soldier has to do is follow his own side's tracer to the target, but likewise the enemy can also follow the tracer back to find and target you (unless you're using modern delayed action rounds).

The roar of the GPMG was answered almost instantly by return fire. It wasn't automatic shots at first, but very repetitive single shots and lots of them: *crack, crack-crack-crack, crack-crack*. It sounded like bigger calibre weaponry than 5.56 mm, so it had to be AK47s as opposed to our own SA80s – and that had to mean the rebels.

Maybe twenty seconds had passed since that first single low pop, and it was now that all hell was let loose. There was a massive eruption of fire from the jungle. The entire forest seemed alive with it, muzzle flashes lighting up the ragged fringe of trees in all directions. We knew in that instant that this was it: the rebels had launched a human wave assault from all along our front.

I could feel the rounds tearing through the branches above us, and I could see the tracer streaking through the night sky like swarms of giant, supercharged fireflies on acid. With the fire came a roaring wave of sound that washed over us, as if one long continuous tsunami had us gripped in its depths.

The nearest rounds went buzzing past my head like angry wasps – *bzzzt-bzzzt-bzzzt-bzzzt-bzzzt* – barely inches away. The next instant the roof of the ATAP above us was ripped apart, as a barrage of incoming tore through it, scattering wooden splinters and shredded leaves across the lot of us.

I saw Tricky's radio shack disintegrate under a murderous blast of fire. Then I saw trees to either side of us juddering under the impact of rounds, trunks blasted asunder with the sheer volume of leaden death that was pounding into them. I shuddered to think how many rebels were out there.

I'd never known a rate of fire like this. There is one particular exercise that involves crawling on all fours, with scores of machine guns zeroed in and firing above your heads. We had Overhead Fire and Flanking Fire guns zoomed in on us, and it was designed to make us get used to being under murderous levels of fire.

This was far worse.

NATO 5.56 mm rounds make a distinctive *pop-pop-pop* sound as they scoot past your head. This was very different. Much of the fire coming our way was 7.62 mm short – the calibre of bullet fired by the AK47. It makes a much heavier *chthud-chthud-chthud* as it rips by. And from the rate of fire the rebels were unleashing it was clear that they suffered none of the shortages of ammo that we did.

Amongst the AK47 fire I could make out the heavier crack and thump of bigger calibre weapons opening up now, as the rebels' machine guns kicked into action. Just as we'd feared – they out-gunned us as well. This was sheer fucking murder. Either we started to get the fire down and kill them, or they'd be on top of our positions, swamping us.

Right at this moment they'd have their fighters surging forwards, using the cover of the hail of fire to rush us. I figured I could hear rebel voices screaming out of the darkness, plus more and more of those weird, animal-like cries – although now there was no doubt who was making them. The savagery and blood lust embodied in those ghostly howls was spine chilling. I knew now what the rebels were trying to do: *they were baiting us.*

In theory, this was an Operation Other Than War (OOTW) that we were on, and under the rules of engagement we could only open fire in response to being fired upon. Well, we'd just been given every excuse possible to let rip, if only we had the ammo to do so. Instead, our priority was going to have to be to *conserve* our ammo, but still kill a shedload of the bad guys.

That first, single, low-velocity pop had sounded like a rebel opening fire, but getting an immediate stoppage. The instant reaction from H suggested he'd had the guy in his sights and was just waiting for an excuse to open up on him. But almost immediately H's GPMG had been drowned out by the sheer volume of return fire.

In fact, several minutes back H had spotted two columns of figures creeping down either side of the main highway, sticking to the drainage ditches for cover. H had given *maximise* as soon as he'd identified them as rebels, so dragging those of us asleep to instant attention. That done, he'd continued to watch the rebels as they'd drawn closer, keeping them nailed in the stark metal sights of his machine gun.

The lead rebel figure had raised himself into a crouch, and opened fire with his AK47 – the signal for the rest to launch the attack. He was the one who'd had the stoppage – so firing off the single shot. The fact that his gun had jammed had enabled H to get the drop on them, and open up with the GPMG, mowing down that first rank of RUF fighters. But the advantage had lasted barely moments. Hordes of rebels had crowded in from behind and let rip.

During the hours since last light the rebels must have filtered into the jungle all around us. They'd sited their machine guns all across the forest to our front. In every direction I looked I could see muzzle flashes sparking under the canopy, and I could feel the rounds tearing past just a couple of feet above the HQ depression, the trees and vegetation getting torn to shreds.

I glanced behind me at Tricky and Wag. Tricky was crawling

towards the 319 radio, trying to reach it before it got shot to pieces. Wag was on his hands and knees and had somehow managed to grab the Thuraya, which was a massive fucking relief. I knew he'd get a contact report away – format: what had happened, where and when, and get the QRF scrambled.

Behind us the village was utterly deserted. The noise was enough to wake the dead, but the villagers had clearly decided to stay put and hunker down, which was exactly what we'd told them to do should the rebels attack. Any shadowy figures moving through the open we'd treat as hostile, and they'd very likely get gunned down.

I turned back to the front. Time seemed to have slowed into an agonising stillness. I had Grant kneeling to one side of me, Captain Cantrill to the other, his eyes like bloody saucers. I guessed this wasn't quite what he'd bargained for. He'd flown in for a short recce in his nicely-pressed uniform, only to have to bed down in the dirt, and get woken to seven bales of shit breaking loose all around him.

The rebels were unleashing with tracer rounds and where they were firing high their trails were arcing into the heavens way beyond the village. Tracer takes a good kilometre or more to burn out fully, and the night sky over Lungi Lol had erupted into Sierra Leone's most fearsome ever firework display.

The number of weapons hammering rounds into us was unbelievable. Terrifying.

As our fire rose in volume to meet theirs I could hear the popgun bark of our SA80s, as the blokes out front gave their all. They were letting rip with four- to six-round bursts – aimed deliberate shots – mixed in with longer eruptions from the GPMGs. Trouble was, at this rate of fire we'd soon be out of ammo, let alone keeping a third in reserve so we could make a fighting withdrawal.

I couldn't let that happen. I needed to take immediate action. I needed to take control of the battle, or we were done for. As platoon sergeant my place was forward with the guys. I had to get there and I had to make the move now.

I heard Wag's voice screaming from behind me: 'Steve! I've got the Thuraya! Sending contact report now!'

I yelled a reply. 'Got it! Wag! Wag! I'm going forward!'

Every night I'd slept with my weapons beside me: my SA80, my Browning pistol, the 51 mm mortar, plus the bag of mortar rounds that Wag and me had scrounged off Mick, back at Lungi Airport. My plan if we were hit during the hours of darkness was to use the 51 mm to put up illume, so as to light up the battlefield. I'd expose the rebels in the kill zones – the areas where the villagers had cleared the vegetation – so the lads could see to shoot them. Plus I'd make them visible at a far greater range, so we could kill them before they overran us.

Putting up the illume was crucial to our defence of the village. The lads would all be expecting it. It was part of our game plan for a night attack. But to get the mortar rounds up I had to move forward, and that meant into the teeth of the enemy fire.

I reached for the 51 mm mortar, then glanced to my immediate front, checking the route via which I needed to crawl. I could see a line of muzzle flashes sparking out of the dark jungle to either side of the track. I counted a good dozen, and each had the fast, rhythmical *fzzzt-fzzzt-fzzzt-fzzzt-fzzzt* of a belt-fed 7.62 mm machine gun.

I yelled at Grant to stay put and keep a grip on things from here. I grabbed my SA80 with my other hand, but I needed someone to bring the mortar rounds and act as my loader. Wag was busy sending the contact report, Tricky needed to stay on the comms, and Grant was here to make command decisions.

That left only one possible candidate.

I locked eyes with Captain Cantrill.

He was lying on the ground, mouth hanging open. His expression said it all: *I didn't expect this when I came ashore!*

I tossed the daysack of mortars across to him. 'Here you go, mate! Grab that and follow me!'

I got into a belly-crawl and prepared to move. At night an attacking force tends to aim high, for they can't see where the ground starts. Right now rounds were hammering past maybe four or five feet above us, for the rebels had yet to adjust their fire to ground. Cantrill and me had to remain below that level if we were to stand any chance of making it forward without being hit.

I had the pistol-grip of the SA80 grasped in my right hand, the butt resting on my right forearm. The barrel of the 51 mm was gripped in my left hand, the base plate resting on my left forearm. Plus I had a bandolier of 150 extra rounds for the SA80 slung around my neck.

I started the crawl – right arm forward, left leg up, and vice versa. I was on my belt buckle as I inched over the lip of the depression and into the more open, bullet-blasted terrain beyond.

I glanced behind me for Cantrill. Sure enough he was on it. He was a foot away from my right boot. His SA80 was gripped in his right hand, plus the bag of mortars in his left, so he could drag its 40-pound weight behind him.

I turned back to the front. My eyes traced the route ahead of us, but the trees and thick vegetation to either side were rocking and rattling with the weight of fire tearing into them. I found myself thinking: *Fuck me, that's accurate and sustained fire . . .*

Having crawled out of the cover of the depression the sound of battle came to me much more clearly now. I could hear H in his fire-rhythm, squirting out eight- to ten-round bursts. He was unleashing a volley, breaking fire, then letting rip with another. The barrel of the GPMG tends to climb to the left the more rounds that are fired, so after each burst he was bringing it back onto target.

They didn't call H the 'Death Dealer' for nothing.

No doubt Tackleberry was in the zone right now, and his withering fire would be hammering into the waves of rebel fighters.

All to his front they would be dropping like flies, but it didn't seem to be having the slightest effect on their rate of fire.

Beyond H's trench I could hear blood-curdling screaming and shouting – but not the screams of agony that I'd been hoping for. This was very much yelling – in drugged-up, bulletproof, voodoo-frenzied attack mode. Long banshee howls echoed from the forest, as if we had the devil and all his minions at our front.

I could hear this weird, wild chanting in the background, interspersed with what sounded like jungle drums. It sounded utterly crazed and fucked up.

The rebels had a motto that they'd shout before battle.

'What makes the grass grow?' one would shout.

'Blood! Blood! Blood!' would come the answering chant.

What makes the grass grow?

Blood! Blood! Blood!

What makes the grass grow?

Blood! Blood! Blood!

What makes the grass grow?

Blood! Blood! Blood!

By the time they'd got into their stride, most sane people would have fled in terror – those who could run. If the rebels had got a village surrounded, those trapped would have nowhere to flee, and they'd be imprisoned in their fear. Imagine that happening. Imagine if you were a mother or a father with children trapped in such a village. And that's what the rebels had come to Lungi Lol aiming to do – spread sheer terror and savagery.

Instead, they'd run smack bang into H on the Gimpy.

As I listened to the light *pop-pop-pop* of our SA80s answering the rebel war cries, I cursed the fact that most of the blokes were using 5.56 mm. The British military had switched from 7.62 mm to 5.56 in 1987, when it became standard across all NATO forces. The Yanks had used 5.56 mm in Vietnam, and they were sold on the smaller calibre. The upside was that a man could afford to carry far more of the lighter ammo, but the downside was the sheer size and velocity of the round.

We'd learned all about the lack of stopping power of 5.56 mm in Northern Ireland and Iraq. It fires with a greater muzzle velocity and has less drag. It hits a target with such speed that it punches through tissue pretty cleanly. As a result it can take two or three rounds to stop a man, and especially one high on drugs and voodoo gibberish. By contrast, one round of 7.62 mm drops a man pretty much instantly, wherever he's hit. With its lower velocity and larger head it rips flesh and shatters bone.

With 5.56 mm you needed to score a head shot or hit a vital organ to be sure to stop a man. Facing 2000 drug-and-adrenaline-fuelled RUF rebels, how many bullets could we afford to waste trying to put each of them down?

I forced myself onwards, getting into the rhythm of the crawl. Arms and legs were pumping. I bulldozed over tree stumps and whatever unidentified crap was jabbing into me and tearing at my combats. After all the torrential rain of recent days I could feel thick soggy dirt and shit under me. I tried to concentrate on keeping the barrels of the mortar and the SA80 out of the worst of it. With both weapons resting on my forearms, my points of contact were elbow, stomach and knees.

Cantrill and me had made about twenty yards when I stopped dead. I'd sensed the fiery *pshusshshh* of an incoming projectile. Only one weapon makes such a distinctive sound – the rocket-propelled grenade (RPG) – and we were well within the RPG's maximum 500-yard range.

I saw the projectile come flaming out of the darkness – like a road-cone laid on its side and trailing fire, but one packed with high explosives and wrapped in razor-sharp steel. It was flying high, but if it hit the branches above us it would detonate, peppering the ground below with a lethal spray of shrapnel and splintered wood – which would be me and Cantrill pretty much done for.

I dropped my head as it tore past six feet to the right of us with a deafening *whooooosh*. Miraculously, it went roaring through the tree branches and on into the night *without exploding*. It continued across the village and didn't appear to hit a thing. I figured it must have buried itself in the jungle somewhere out the back, where Mojo and his men would be positioned. *That's if they had got into their positions* . . . But no point worrying about that now.

I set off at a crawl again, eyes scanning the darkness for further RPGs. How that one hadn't detonated I just didn't know. The RPG-7 is designed with a 'graze mode', so that the minute the warhead touches anything it explodes. It doesn't require full impact to do so. I glanced back at Cantrill, fearing that the Marine captain might have gone to ground. But he was right on my heels, God bless him, dragging the mortar pack behind him.

So far, he was doing a sterling job.

Rounds snickered off the vegetation to the left and right of me, as a rebel gunner hammered in a horribly accurate burst. Not for the first time I cursed the fact that none of us had body armour. It existed. The Yanks had the best body armour money could buy, plus the SAS lads had it. Just someone somewhere within the MOD had decided that the X Platoon could do without. In this kind of climate you'd never wear it all day long, but once the fire started you'd want to have it on.

Cantrill and me had to push right forward if I was to get a grip on this battle. As the adrenaline pumped through the system, young lads not long into the Pathfinders would be tempted to let loose with the ammo, or even to break cover to try to better target the enemy. If we allowed ourselves to get carried away in the rush, we'd start running out of rounds and we'd get blokes killed.

Cantrill and me needed to move as far and fast as we could, to have any chance of winning this one.

16

I belly-crawled ahead, arms scrabbling amidst the filthy under-growth and the squelching dirt. My mind was a whirl of thoughts. *What if this was just a probe, one designed to sacrifice a few hundred rebel fighters for the bigger prize? What if they'd sent hundreds more to one or both flanks, to encircle the village?* They had enough men to do it, and it's what I would have done if I'd been their force commander.

I was trying to second-guess what was happening. Was this really only a tidal wave onslaught – hitting us with a human wave directly to our front? Or were they smart enough to use the railway track – this being a feint while they hit us from the side?

Right now all I could be sure of was that it was dark, with bugger all ambient light, and it had to be tough as hell for the lads to ID their targets. I needed to get the illume rounds up, but I was still under the canopy of trees that surrounded the village. I figured I needed to push on for another thirty yards or so, at which point I'd hit open terrain.

Every ten or twelve pumps of my elbows and knees I paused to check on Cantrill. No point reaching a position from where I could fire if I was minus a loader and rounds. He wasn't breathing a word but he was right behind me, glued to my heels. I could hear the spud-gun *pop-pop-pop* of SA80s directly to my right now, which had to mean I was drawing level with Nathan's battle trenches.

I flicked my gaze in their direction, and I could see the blokes of *33 Alpha* hunched over their weapons, pouring fire back at the enemy. I just knew for sure we were burning through the ammo,

Taff Saunders. Like many a Welshman, Taff believed that England was a carbuncle attached to Mother Wales. But never a better bloke in a punch-up. Here he is flanked by two of the Nigerian United Nations troops, who joined forces with us in Sierra Leone.

Tricky. In action on the ranges putting down intense fire during live contact drills training.

The architect of evil. Foday Sankoh, a former sergeant from the Sierra Leone Army turned founder and guru of the Revolutionary United Front (RUF) rebels – known as 'Africa's Khmer Rouge'. By the time our operation was finished, Sankoh had been captured and the rebel resistance broken. Sadly, he died in custody before he could stand trial for mass war crimes.

The bad guys. Rebel fighters of the Revolutionary United Front – those who had declared they were launching 'Operation Kill British', to force us out of the country. We were outnumbered 100 1 and heavily outgunned.

A pair of CH47 Chinooks from the RAF heading low and fast over the Sierra Leone capital, Freetown – the means via which we would deploy on operations deep into the jungle.

Going in. You could cut the atmosphere with a knife as 26 Pathfinders flew into the teeth of the rebel advance, and with no idea what we'd meet on the ground in the jungle.

Long-sleeve style. The rebels' speciality was lopping off the hands of women and children, using axes or machetes, to spread a dark reign of terror. They gave their victims the choice of long- or short-sleeve style – amputation above or below the elbow. How could we do anything else but fight to the last man to stop them?

Mango, anyone? Barefoot angels – that's how the kids in the village of Lungi Lol struck us. No rebels were kidnapping them, lopping off their hands, or forcing them to be child soldiers – not on our watch.

The kids are all right. We were 26 Pathfinders facing 2,000 rebels. But with smiles like these from the local kids, how could we do anything other than smash the rebel advance and stop them butchering the village?

Having decided we were their heaven-sent saviours, the locals scavenged food from the jungle for us and fetched our daily water – as we waited in our trenches, poised to kick seven bales of shit out of the rebels.

Bush tucker. When it rained in the jungle, snails as big as your fist came slurping out of their tunnels to munch on the wet vegetation. Nathe being Nathe, he decided they were for the pot, and so his legendary Lungi Lol Snail *baltis* were born.

Village people. This is why it mattered. We flew into the jungle to smash the rebel advance, and stop them wreaking carnage in the capital city and at the airport. We ended up in the fight of our lives to save an entire village.

The bunker. The forward battle trench manned by 'H' – 'The Death Dealer' – with his tried and trusted GPMG. No rebels were sneaking past when 'H' was on duty.

Brigadier Richards, our overall force commander, sent us in to stop the rebels in their tracks. This we had done. Here villagers gather up the rebel dead, after the first night's combat.

Ready for anything. 1 PARA mortar crews load up the 81mm rounds, to beat back the rebel forces massing in the jungle.

Fire! Once we got the 1 PARA mortar teams in, with their 81mm mortar tubes, we could really take the fight to the rebels.

Hunter-killer. After the initial massive firefight, we knew we'd given the rebels a bloody nose. Next we did the utterly unexpected: we left our battle trenches and went into the jungle on a hot pursuit to track them down.

X Platoon at the end of the Lungi Lol Op: The A-team. The 26 Pathfinders at Lungi Lol, plus 5 support staff from Lungi Airport. Rear row, from left: 4th, Taff Saunders (*33 Delta*); 9th, Ginge Wilson (*33 Charlie*). Middle row, from left: 4th, Eddie 'The White Rabbit' Newell; 5th, Grant Harris (*Sunray*); 6th, Mark 'Jacko' Jackson; 7th, Graham 'Wag' Wardle; 8th, Neil 'Tricky' Dick; 9th, Nathan 'Nathe' Bell (*33 Alpha*); 10th, Sam 'Dolly' Parton (*33 Delta*). Front row, from left: 5th, yours truly; 6th, Joe 'H' Harrison; 10th, Bryan 'Brl' Budd VC.

and I hoped Nathe could keep a grip on the fire discipline. There was no shouting or cries of alarm yet, and there was no panic in the air – which was reassuring. But I could tell the lads were waiting for me to put up the light, and I knew I had to cover more ground more quickly.

I had to get further forward. I needed to be somewhere where I could see the enemy and use the mortar to best effect, but most importantly where the lads could see and hear me, so as to take my lead. I needed them to slow the rate of fire, get one shot to equal one kill, and get the fire discipline tight. But I was tiring under the exertion. The sweat was pouring off me in bucket-loads. I was soaked with it, and my arms and shoulder were sore and burning with agony, my breath coming in sharp gasps.

I paused to wipe the slick of sweat from my eyes. It was half blinding me. I glanced forward and I could just make out a glint where the darkness of the foliage was broken by moonlight filtering through. That was where I had to get to. Once I was out from under the trees I'd be in the clear to send up the mortars. But it didn't escape me that once I left the cover of the foliage I'd be completely exposed: the rebels would be able to see me, and target me with fire.

There was bugger all I could do about that. You can't put mortars up when you're under tree cover, or they'll very likely burst in the branches above you – end of story.

There was a solid stream of bullets hammering past just inches above me now, and I could feel the pressure waves thrown off by the rounds thumping into the back of my head. The rebels were bloody good: they were adjusting their fire, dropping it to meet ground level, leaving Cantrill and me less and less of a margin for error.

No ifs or buts, I was fucking terrified, but adrenaline was driving me forwards. More to the point, I'd been here for days readying myself for just such a battle. Poor bloody Cantrill had flown in on a short recce jolly, and now this. He had to be totally shitting himself. I knew I was basically pulling him forward with the sheer effort of my concentration and my force of will.

I crawled on for another ten yards, dragging Cantrill with me. I was 60 yards to the south of the track, with H's trench lying to my front left. We had to be on our own front line now, and this was as good a place as any to set up the mortar. But as I glanced upwards I cursed. Above me there was still thick vegetation – the spreading canopy of a grove of fruit trees – and that meant I couldn't use the mortar.

If I sent up rounds here they'd detonate in the branches, which would be no good to anyone but the enemy. I steeled myself. Gritted my teeth. We needed twenty more yards, maybe thirty, and we'd be out from under the branches . . . and right under the enemy guns.

I paused for an instant longer. I needed to gather my thoughts, get a sense of the battle space, and orientate myself to make sure we didn't crawl off at a tangent. We'd come forward maybe sixty-five yards. I knew Wag would be back there with Tricky and Grant, getting the message through to headquarters. Already the gears would be turning at Lungi Airport to rack up the QRF. The 1 PARA duty signaller would be waking Gibbo, so he could issue the order for them to launch. In my mind's eye I could see a platoon of paratroopers gathering their weapons, the fire in their eyes. *Fuck it, let's go!*

We just had to hold out for long enough to get the QRF in. We'd then be sixty-odd blokes facing a couple of thousand rebels – so odds down to 33–1 – which was much more like it.

To my left I heard H screaming out targets. 'Right of bent tree, two o'clock, a hundred and fifty yards!'

To my right Nathe was yelling out similar fire orders to his blokes, and Cantrill and me were sandwiched in between. I couldn't hear Dolly, Ginge or Taff, but their voices were very likely drowned out by the horrendous rate of fire going in both directions.

Then I heard the cry: 'CHANGING BELT!'

H was yelling out a warning, so the lads could keep the fire going with the SA80s as he changed a belt on the GPMG. That meant he was 200 rounds – or a third of his ammo – already gone.

Nathe and the lads from *33 Alpha* opened up with long bursts from their SA80s. And then I heard that worst of cries: 'STOPPAGE!'

There was the stark steel-on-steel *clatch-clatch* as whoever it was tried to clear their weapon. I just hoped to fuck another of our SA80s didn't go down. We'd kept the assault rifles scrupulously clean and rust free. We'd never stopped polishing and oiling the fucking things. But the SA80 was just a heap of shit whichever way you treated it.

An instant later H had sparked up the GPMG again, which meant the worst of the moment was over. He'd have one further belt of ammo laid out next to his weapon, on a waterproof poncho to keep it off the dirt. As he fired he'd keep one eye on the ammo level, to check how close he was to needing to do another belt change. But all we needed was H's GPMG to run out of rounds and we were going to be seriously buggered.

H was pushing the weapon to the very limits. The normal rate of battle fire on the GPMG is twenty-five rounds a minute in short, three-round bursts. The rapid rate of fire is a hundred rounds a minute, in four- to five-round bursts. H was unleashing in eight- to ten-round bursts, so he'd upped the fire to cover the mass of rebels he was facing. The GPMG pumps out rounds in a cone-like spray, and is ideal against bunched-up targets at shorter ranges. H had to have the enemy charging down his very barrel right now, with the rate of fire he was unleashing.

Trouble was, under heavy fire you are supposed to change the barrel of the GPMG, or it gets red-hot and you get a cock-off, or breech explosion. The working parts get so hot that when you feed a round into the breech it ignites with the heat, exploding in your face. With the rate of fire H was putting down he knew what he was risking – but no way could he afford a barrel change any time soon.

If H tried that, he'd be overrun.

Likewise, if he ran out of rounds.

Right now the blokes were targeting whatever they could see: muzzle flashes, the glint of moonlight on gunmetal; movement; rebel war cries. It was far from being the best way to use up our limited supplies of ammo.

We needed the light.

I forced myself to cat-crawl onwards into the face of the enemy. Above the gunfire, I could hear blood-chilling rebel yells coming from all directions. It was as if they were getting us surrounded and deliberately *taunting us*.

I was thrusting forward with my elbows when all of a sudden I sensed the ground in front of me give way. I half-tumbled into a stinking, muddy ditch. For an instant I feared I'd fallen into one of our own punji pits. Those fields of sharpened bamboo spikes were just forward of our front positions. I'd figured the nearest one lay off to my right, but maybe I'd miscalculated.

Fuck, the punji fields are just around here.

Fuck, I've drifted too far right into the punjis.

I felt around myself gingerly, but no spikes had pierced my combats or torn into my flesh, so I figured the punjis had to be a fraction further forward and off my line of march. Rolling half around, I checked on the canopy of vegetation above me. As I did so I realised I was lying in twelve inches of stagnant, shitty, putrid water that filled the bottom of the ditch. Doubtless, it was infested with every kind of sucking, biting, slithering thing the jungle had to offer, and right now they were having a good feed.

I cursed. We were still under the bloody trees.

There was no option but to push on.

I elbowed ahead through the dark and fetid water.

I must have cat-crawled a good thirty yards beyond our line of battle trenches when I finally emerged from under the trees.

Glancing behind, I saw Captain Cantrill was still with me, though he was hanging back a good few feet, the poor bastard.

Directly to our front lay the enemy.

The ragged fringe of jungle was dead ahead, and I didn't doubt that the rebels were getting right in amongst us. Just to my right lay this dark, shadowed mass – the sweep of the nearest punji field. It was good to know that it was there. To my left I could just make out H's silhouette, crouched in his lone battle trench adjacent to the main highway – which showed as a barely-visible yellow slash cutting through the darkness.

From where I was lying I could hear figures thrashing about in the bush ahead of me, and blood-curdling cries. All around there were the flashes of weapons firing, as unearthly shadows and shapes flitted through the darkened terrain.

I heard cries from behind me, voices tinged with panic. 'STOP-PAGE! STOPPAGE!'

They were coming from Nathe's position. Like H's, it was right in the line of the rebels' mass attack, and it had to be in danger of being overrun. The priority was to get the light up now, but that meant raising myself into the level of the rebels' fire.

I could hear the bullets scything through the vegetation a foot or more above where Cantrill and I hugged the earth. I could fire the 51 mm from the prone position, that I knew. I could slam the base plate down, level it with the spirit level built into the tube, grab a round from Cantrill, reach forward and drop it down. It was all doable lying prone as I was, and I'd be far safer that way. But like this I couldn't see properly to target the enemy with the light.

If you can't see you can't fire accurately, I told myself. *Get on your knees, Heaney.*

Decision made, I laid my SA80 on the dirt – no other place to put it – and levered myself up into a kneeling position, all the while trying to blank out the hiss and crack of rounds tearing past to either side of my head and shoulders. I cursed again the lack of any body armour. Right now if an accurate round came my way I was taking it with no protection, and it would likely kill me outright.

I stole a glance around me to sight my targets. We were right in the heart of the battlefield – the no man's land between the two sides. It was carnage. Streams of tracer fire were pouring out from the jungle, from where the rebels had sited a good dozen or more machine guns. To either side of me I could see scores of AK47s spitting flame, as rebel fighters probed forward, unleashing long, savage bursts.

To the southeast of the village I caught a momentary glimpse of distant moonlight glinting on a pair of linear objects – the railway tracks. *Fuck me.* I was so far forward I could actually *see* them, despite the darkness. On the opposite side of me and just to my rear I had the reassuring sight and sound of H's lone GPMG pounding out the rounds.

I heard H yelling out target instructions: 'Sixty yards! Dead ground exit *Lowe*!'

Sure enough the rebels were closing in for the final push, and they were doing so via the dead ground – where we couldn't see clearly to shoot them. If they were at dead ground exit *Lowe*, that meant they were just dozens of yards away from Nathe's battle trench. For an instant I wondered how the other patrols were faring, and if any of those had yet been overrun.

I told myself to keep one hand on my SA80, in case the rebels swarmed us. They would know where our main positions were by now: our muzzle flashes would have given us away. But we couldn't know where they were unless we saw them firing or moving – and for that we sure as hell could do with some flare rounds.

Siting the mortar base plate was key to accuracy, so the first thing I did was swipe the ground with my hands, to clear it of any rocks, roots or other obstructions. That done, I placed both hands on the tube and drove it down as hard as I could, slamming the solid base plate into the earth to anchor it. The kickback from the first round would really bed it in, and stop it skidding around or jumping.

I moved my right knee back, in case the tube jumped with the first round, smashing the base plate into my kneecap, which could easily break it. With my left hand on the heavy mortar sleeve – a tough canvas shield that protects the operator's hand from getting scorched – I glanced behind for Cantrill. He was flat on his belly, bang on my right heel. Good positioning. His rifle lay to one side of him, the daysack full of rounds right next to him. I reached out with my right hand palm upwards, feeling for the mortar that I needed him to deliver, like a relay baton.

'Round!'

He flipped open the top of the pack, reached in, dragged out the first mortar and slapped it into my hand. As it went past my face towards the mouth of the tube I did a quick visual inspection, just to check that it hadn't been damaged during the long crawl forward. Last thing we needed now was a dud round getting stuck down the tube.

I raised myself on my haunches, reached forward and dropped it down the tube, tail-first. I heard it slide down the barrel and make a hollow thunk as it hit bottom, coming to rest on the firing pin plate. I aimed by sight and feel. The 51 mm has a sighting mechanism, but I had neither the time nor the light to use it. Instead, I was aiming by intuition. The higher you angle the tube, the higher the round goes, but the shorter the trajectory.

From long practice I knew that at a 45-degree angle the round would burst 500 to 600 metres in front of me, which was just where I wanted it. I needed the light behind the enemy, throwing them into silhouette against its glare but leaving us cloaked in darkness. I needed the rebels smack bang under its 200-metre cone of light, and us well out of it. That way, we would be invisible, and they'd be pinned under the blinding glare.

Being this far forward I needed to let the lads know it was

Cantrill and me opening fire, otherwise they might mistake us for the enemy and slot us.

'STEVE HEANEY – PUTTING UP ILLUME!'

I repeated the yell in both directions, to our right and left front. I saw the silhouettes of two heads nodding their acknowledgement from H's trench, so at least those guys had heard. I was also giving the lads a warning: *Prepare for the rebels to be lit up, and be ready to put down aimed shots to smash 'em.*

I left a second for the lads to prepare, checked the orientation of the barrel one last time, grabbed the dick-like handle to the front and slammed it down, hammering the firing pin into the rear of the mortar. It emitted a loud *phuuttt* as it fired, the flash of the thing throwing Cantrill and me into sharp relief. If the enemy hadn't known we were here they sure as hell would now. They could range in on us, using the noise and the thick plume of smoke hanging in the air to target us.

I blanked my mind to the threat and gazed skywards, following the trajectory that the mortar would have taken. The fire from the rebels was as intense and murderous as it had been from the start. A great deal of it was zipping past to either side of my head now – so I guessed they'd seen the telltale signs of the 51 mm firing.

Everyone on our side knew a mortar was in the air. They were poised for the burst and what it would reveal. But the level of fire from the enemy and their wild shouts and screams continued unabated, so hopefully they hadn't a clue what was coming.

The 51 mm illume fires to a height of 250 metres. It detonates to leave a flare drifting beneath a parachute – one that looks like a giant roman candle. It burns with a 350,000 candle-light power – illumination by which the lads could see and kill. But it would also signal that I was here, taking charge of the battle.

If we'd had HE rounds I'd have got an illume up, nailed the enemy positions, then hammered them with HE to tear them to pieces. On a good day I could put down six to eight HE in sixty seconds.

But right now we didn't have any HE. We didn't even have 40 mm grenade launchers to mallet the rebels, putting ten rounds into them on the back of the illume. All we could do was get the light up so we could better call down the GPMG and SA80 fire.

I waited the last few seconds it took for the round to reach height, and then *pop!* – it hung there like a tiny sun burning in the heavens. It had burst just where I wanted it: bang above the line of the jungle, throwing light over all the ground to the front of it. Just for an instant I sensed the enemy fire falter, the pounding percussions from their machine guns seeming to stall in mid-fire.

They hadn't been expecting that – not to be pinned under the fierce, fluorescent daylight of the illume. For an instant we had them foxed. We had to seize the advantage. A sense of euphoria swept over me that maybe this was all doable – *we still could win this one.*

'PICK YOUR TARGETS!' I yelled. 'PICK YOUR TARGETS! PICK YOUR TARGETS!'

In spite of having rebel gunmen charging down their very throats, the guys had refrained from using rapid fire. They'd been aiming at shadows. Now they had the light, all of that had changed. All to our front rebel fighters were frozen under the glare, and trying to find some cover to go to ground. Thanks to the villagers cutting the vegetation, they had precious little foliage in which to take refuge.

I glanced behind me for an instant, and in an arc bending around to my right I could see a solid line of muzzle flashes, as our guys opened up. In an instant the goading, animal cries from the enemy died. Instead, I could hear screams of agony as rebels went down. Voices started yelling out what had to be orders, as their fighters scrabbled to get out of our line of fire. But the ground from the dirt highway across one hundred yards or more to our front was lit up like a football stadium under floodlights.

For the rebels, there was nowhere much left to run or to hide.

17

I straightened up, so more of the lads could see me: 'USE THE LIGHT! USE THE LIGHT! DELIBERATE FIRE! DELIBERATE FIRE! PICK YOUR TARGETS! PICK YOUR TARGETS!'

A rapid rate of fire with the SA80 – when it doesn't jam – is thirty rounds a minute. Ten minutes and you'd be 300 rounds down – which was all each of us had. That's why I'd called for 'deliberate fire'. With deliberate fire the lads would put down controlled, aimed single shots – so around ten a minute. Even so, some of the lads were very likely pushing 150 rounds down already.

I remained on one knee as that first illume round drifted to earth, long bursts of machine gun fire kicking up mud and shit all around me. I was spotting for rebel movement in the light, and yelling out the fire instructions like a madman.

We also needed the illume so badly because most of the blokes didn't actually have workable night vision equipment, or at least not gear you could rely on. Each patrol had been issued with one common weapon sight (CWS) – a long, black night vision unit that screws onto the SA80. Trouble was, here in the soaking wet and humid tropics it would rapidly steam up, which made it unusable.

All across our patrols I could hear more of the lads having problems with their SA80s. 'STOPPAGE! STOPPAGE! STOPPAGE!'

Those with a stoppage they couldn't immediately clear would try to use the CWS sight to help direct the GPMG fire – yet there were no guarantees that the CWS would be working properly. Without the light from the illume, any number of us were going to be left fighting blind.

I went down on my belt buckle again. Illume round up and

targets spotted – I could afford to hit the dirt for a good few seconds. Rounds were coming in thick and fast, so the rebels must have switched on to where Cantrill and I were positioned and what we were up to. To my left H was hammering away like a good one, slamming fire into the bunched-up fighters caught under the harsh glare on the main highway. The rebels were being cut down as the Death Dealer got to work.

But then I heard him screaming out a warning: 'MOVEMENT! By the railway track! By the railroad!'

Pinned under the illume to our front, the rebels were desperately trying to get away from its murderous glare. But just as I'd feared, they were also trying to hit us from over on our right flank, and that's where the Death Dealer had spotted them.

That's where they needed the light.

I forced myself into the kneeling position again, getting my head and shoulders up above the surrounding foliage and fully into the enemy's line of fire. No other way to do it. I swivelled my body through 90 degrees, until I was facing southeast. I dragged the tube around with me and slammed the base plate down again. The 51 mm tube is fixed to the base in such a way that you can only adjust elevation – hence the need to haul it around every time you seek a new target bearing.

My arm shot back towards Cantrill: 'Round!'

The guy had anticipated the move, and the cold steel of the mortar slapped into my open palm almost before I'd asked. Good lad. The railway line was 450 yards away, but I needed the illume a good 100 yards beyond that, so we were talking a 550-yard shot. Working on muscle memory and instinct alone, I lowered the barrel to the 35-degree angle, dropped the round in and checked the alignment one last time.

I hit the firing lever. *Phuuttt – the second mortar was away.* It left Cantrill and me enshrouded in the telltale pall of smoke billowing out of the muzzle. I hit the deck again, and lay there tracing the mortar's trajectory, staring into the dark night and trying to ignore the bullets zipping past to the left and right of us. We now had one mortar shell to our front, hanging under its chute and gently oscillating as it drifted towards the forest canopy, and another about to burst over the railroad.

The second illume popped a good 150 metres beyond the railroad, casting a cone of brightnes like daylight across the ground a hundred metres to either side. It hung lower in the sky than the first – I'd had to fire it on a shallower trajectory, to achieve the range – so it would have less than the optimum burn time, but there was nothing I could do about that.

I yelled out the fire instructions, screaming at the top of my lungs to try to get heard by Ginge and Taff's patrol. 'PICK YOUR TARGETS! PICK YOUR TARGETS! PICK YOUR TARGETS!'

Almost before I'd finished I heard Ginge's distinctive Mancunian accent cutting through the night: 'Two hundred metres, half right railway track – rapid fire!'

In the light of the illume they'd nailed the rebel figures advancing stealthily along the steel tracks. Patrol *33 Charlie*'s GPMG spat fire, a long burst hosing down the new rebel target. I saw figures diving for cover, as the GPMG rounds tore into them. Once hit by a GPMG's 7.62 mm bullet you weren't getting up again, no matter where it tore into you.

Or at least normally you weren't . . .

Here in Lungi Lol things were a little different.

We were facing hordes of drugged-up fighters who truly believed they were invincible in battle. The rebels gave themselves *noms de guerre* – war names – like Baby Killer, Belly Slasher, Colonel Savage and the Born Naked Squad (those who stripped their victims naked before abusing and killing them). They were infamous for 'playing' the Sex The Child 'game'. A pregnant woman would be captured, and her belly slashed open with a machete – the rebels placing bets beforehand on the sex of the unborn child.

'Bathed' in their voodoo 'medicine' prior to going into battle, they truly believed they were bulletproof. The voodoo priestess would promise them: 'With this I make you invincible in battle! The bullets will flow off you like water!' Doubtless they'd have done just that in preparation for the first major battle of Operation Kill British, and in part it seemed to be working.

I saw rebel fighters get slammed to the ground by a round from one of the guns, then clamber to their feet and start charging forward again, screaming maniacally. Some took three or four rounds from the SA80s before they finally went down and stayed down.

Not good for conserving limited supplies of ammo.

Right now the main thrust of the assault seemed to have shifted to the railroad. But no matter how much light I put up the rebels just seemed to keep coming. It was sheer suicide to charge ahead when the cover of darkness was ripped away, but I guessed the rebel commanders could afford to sacrifice any number of fighters ... and over on our right flank serious battle had now been joined.

The battle trenches of *33 Delta* lay some three hundred and fifty yards away, and I could see the long tongues of fire spitting out of them towards the enemy massing along the railroad. I could barely hear Taff's dulcet Welsh tones – he was too far away for his voice to carry properly above the deafening noise of battle – but I presumed he was calling out the targets to his blokes.

For an instant my mind flashed to fears of the rebels totally outflanking us and getting round our rear. That must be what the move down the railroad was meant to achieve. Just as I would have done it, they'd sent in one force on a full-frontal assault, while filtering their main body of fighters silently past our right flank. It was only getting the light up over the railroad that had blown their cover, and I didn't figure any of the rebel commanders had been expecting us to have flare rounds.

Right at this moment we'd seized a slight advantage. But I was certain of one thing now, more than ever before: the RUF commanders were no slouches. In fact, for all the voodoo crap and the taunting animal cries they'd launched a textbook attack. If I was in command of their forces I knew what I'd try next: I'd go for an outflanking manoeuvre further to our left or right flanks, one that would get my forces in to our rear. Then I'd hit us from behind.

All we had to hold them off with were sixteen Nigerian peace-keepers with very likely a dozen rounds per man.

That's if Mojo and his men had even got into their positions.

Wag was back in the HQ ATAP, so hopefully he'd overseen the Nigerians rallying under Mojo and getting into their battle trenches. *Hopefully.* But right now I had no guarantees that Mojo and his merry band were in position and every man ready to fight, and no way of knowing. Our rear could be wide open. Unwatched and undefended. That's just how it was.

The rebel commanders were moving to outflank us, that much I was sure of. Plus they had the numbers to do so on *both sides*. That meant Dolly's patrol – *33 Bravo* – could well be in their line of march. Dolly's lot were way out on our left flank on the far side of the highway. Were they in action too? If so we were getting hit all along the 600 yards of our front, meaning they were coming at us from all sides.

Risking a peek, I levered myself up into the kneeling position. I glanced over the top of H's trench, and sure enough I could see the guns at Dolly's trenches spitting fire.

Fuck me, that was everyone in action.

The entire platoon was sparking.

The highway effectively split the rebel formation, for H had that nailed as a kill zone. I'd seen him blast apart any number of rebel fighters as they'd tried to move across that open patch of dirt. Ginge and Taff's patrols had the railroad similarly covered. So, in effect, the rebels were split into three units: those north of the highway facing *33 Bravo*; those sandwiched between the highway and the railroad, facing H and *33 Alpha*; and those south of the railroad, facing *33 Delta* and *33 Charlie*.

We could kill them in their droves as they tried to cross those open areas under the light.

But if they filtered through the thick jungle to one or the other side of us, we were going to have problems.

The first flare was about to fizzle out, going dark as it hit the jungle. I figured Dolly's was the patrol most in need of light right now. The vegetation was closer and thicker around *33 Bravo*'s trenches, the terrain being wetter and more swampy, which had made it harder for the villagers to fully clear *their* arcs of fire. Plus there were folds in the ground – ditches and hidden gullies – for the enemy to use to mask their advance.

I felt it in my bones: *Dolly was the one who most needed the light.*

I took hold of the 51 mm, hefted it up and swung it through 180 degrees, pivoting on my right knee. I got it in position and drove it down again, base plate smacking into the earth with a heavy thud. It was now orientated towards the north, with *33 Bravo* being some three hundred yards away from me. I angled it at 45 degrees, to get the range, and reached behind me.

Cantrill was still lying prone on the deck and I didn't blame him. With all the fire we were taking, it made sense to keep lower than a snake's belly. The air was thick with the peppery, firework smell of cordite, and a haze from all the gunfire lay low across the village. But still he had a fresh mortar round ready and waiting, and he slapped it into my hand. The Royal Marine captain was doing me proud.

I yelled like a madman. 'DOLLY! YOU'RE GONNA GET ILLUME! PICK YOUR TARGETS!'

With Dolly being so isolated out on our left flank, I wanted him and his boys to have plenty of prior warning. I let the mortar fly. It flew on its silent trajectory, before bursting to the front of *33 Bravo*'s trenches, throwing the ragged jungle into stark relief.

I straightened up: 'USE THE LIGHT! PICK YOUR TARGETS! PICK YOUR TARGETS!'

The moment I'd finished yelling I heard a massive upsurge in

fire from Dolly's battle line. There was the *pop-pop-pop* of controlled SA80 fire, plus long, punching bursts from *33 Bravo*'s
Gimpy.

To my immediate left a second GPMG joined in the fire, hosing
down the rebel fighters massing at Dolly's position. It was H. Due
to the fact that all the other friendly positions were behind him,
H could cover a 180-degree arc from due south to due north. Or
at least, all friendly positions *should* have been well behind him.
Right now he had us two lunatics bang out in the open on his right
and with not even a shell-scrape to hunker down in.

H kept ramping the Gimpy to left and right. He was dropping
rebel fighters as they tried to sneak along the drainage ditches
to either side of the main highway, then pivoting left to give Dolly
supporting fire, hammering rounds into those trying to rush *33
Bravo*'s trenches. On H's right shoulder he had James 'Bucks' Roebuck, the second guy manning that lone trench, and I could see
Bucks likewise blasting away with his SA80. That was one assault
rifle we didn't want having any stoppages.

Their position had borne the brunt of the battle since the opening shots had been fired. I'd heard H make the one ammo belt
change already on the GPMG. He had to be burning through his
second belt. Firing ten-round bursts, it only took twenty pulls on
the trigger and that was a belt of 200 rounds of link exhausted.
With sixty bursts, that would be all his ammo finished – and then
H and his wingman were either going to get overrun, or they'd
have to bug out and abandon their position.

'H! Watch your ammo!' I yelled across to him. 'WATCH YOUR
FUCKING AMMO! WATCH YOUR AMMO!'

I turned in the direction of Nathe's trenches. After H, they'd
taken the next greatest volume of enemy fire, and they had returned it with good measure.

'Nathe! Watch your ammo! WATCH YOUR FUCKING AMMO!
WATCH YOUR AMMO!'

I'd fired three of the illume rounds now, meaning I had fifteen remaining. With the light up our fire was fearsome and precise, if only we could keep a careful watch on the ammo. But when you could see your targets under the light, the temptation was to let rip on auto. What I wouldn't give now for some HE rounds for the 51 mm. In the time it took one illume to drift to earth I'd get four to five HE mortars launched in quick succession, smashing the enemy apart.

I'd be calling out to Cantrill: 'Illume! HE! HE! HE! HE! HE! Illume!' And so on and so forth.

But even without HE, the 51 mm was still proving a game-changer. Getting the light up had tilted the balance of things maybe just in our favour. The battle was balanced on a knife-edge still, but at least we had deliberate aimed shots going down, and we were getting pretty damn close to where we needed to be: *one shot = one kill*.

The first illume round went down and out now, fizzling to darkness in the jungle. Round two was only seconds away from plunging into the forest to the far side of the railroad. Round three was halfway to earth above Dolly's position. It was time to light them up again.

I swung right 90 degrees, hefting the mortar with me, so I was facing to my front. The extreme exertion of the long crawl, followed by the sheer physical effort of ramping the 51 mm tube around was half-killing me. I felt as if I'd been sitting under one of Lungi Lol's drenching tropical rainstorms, my combats were that soaked with sweat. I was literally steaming with it – clouds of water vapour evaporating from my body into the cool night air.

The fourth illume went up without a word having been spoken between Cantrill and me, other than: *Round!* I sensed it was a nice, long, deep shot, one that would burst a good two hundred yards beyond the fringe of jungle. The moment it ignited my eyes were drawn to flashes of movement out on the main highway.

In the few short moments of darkness since that first illume to our front had died, the rebel commander had got his men on the move. Scores of heavily armed figures were darting across the dirt track, heading in the direction of Dolly's position. Being the man furthest forward, there wasn't anyone better placed to spot the rebels, or to call down the fire.

I could see fighters armed with AK47s, plus others hefting RPGs and belt-fed RPK light machine guns, the Russian equivalent of the GPMG. H had his focus on targets to the front of Dolly's trenches, which he was blasting apart with his gun. His wingman, Bucks, was likewise smashing fire into them with his SA80. I needed them to swing right ninety and mallet the rebels surging across the highway.

'H! Bucks! Target movement on track four hundred metres! Bend in track! Bend in track! RAPID FIRE!'

H tensed his shoulders and swung his gun east. The muzzle spat out a long burst of flame, as he hammered out the first burst. It tore into the ditch to one side of the track, where the rebels were mustering to make the dash across the open road. We weren't using tracer. We had none. We'd have used it if Mick had had any – packing each 200-round belt with four normal ball rounds to a fifth of tracer. At night, the first tracer round gives you your line to aim for: *fuck, I'm high, drop down three.* The second confirms you're on target.

In daylight you can see the strike of bullets on the ground. You can gauge from that the need to adjust fire: *drop ten and come right five.* Fighting in the dark and with no tracer, the only indication we had whether our rounds were on target was seeing people get hit and fall. The way the rebels on the roadside were going down, H had to be hammering in the rounds bang on the bull's-eye.

I saw figures get smashed to the ground and struggle to get up again, but before they were halfway to their feet the Death Dealer had cut them down once more.

Some three hundred yards out from the village the main highway kinked north, beyond which it lay out of our line of sight. The rebels were surging across it at the bend in the track. I figured they had to be planning to move to our far left flank and advance on Dolly's position from there. At 300 yards' distance from us, it was well within range for engaging with the GPMG, which is accurate up to 1000 yards or more.

With the SA80, 300 yards was about the limit of its accurate range, even if every weapon had been fitted with a night optic sight. As it was we were using the basic iron sights – the metal V at the rear of the carry handle, which you line up with the nipple on the muzzle-end – which meant Bucks was having to operate at the very limit of his marksman's skills.

I remained in the kneeling position, scanning the terrain 180 degrees to our front and trying to get a sense of what the rebel commanders were going to try next. The light over Taff's position spluttered out, throwing the railroad back into shadows and darkness. I checked the one above Dolly's patrol, where I figured the rebels had shifted the present thrust of their attack. Their fighters had got well malleted to our front and on our right flank, so it made sense to shift well left.

I figured the railroad had to be littered with bodies – rebel dead and injured – as was the highway. I could see the corpses littering the dirt road ahead of us. Any rebel commander worth his salt would have learned a vital lesson by now: Operation Kill British was going to be no pushover. Wherever he got his men moving out in the open we were getting the light above them and they were getting smashed. Hence the need to stick to the cover of the jungle and the darkness, and to try to hit us from fronts we least expected.

Hence the need on our part for maximum vigilance.

As I knelt there eyeing the distant fringe of jungle, I was scanning for any close movement as well. Surely the rebel commander would have sent some of his fighters forward to take out Cantrill and me. With the state of mind his fighters were in, he was sure to have no shortage of volunteers. *Oh, take me, me, me! Take me! I'm bulletproof!*

If he managed to take us out – by either killing us or worse still capturing us – in one fell swoop he'd have half of his problems sorted: *no more light*. With the threat from the rear as well, I felt like I needed eyes in the back of my bloody head.

But as luck would have it, the rebels were about to hit Cantrill and me right from our very front.

18

I caught the flash of fiery movement even as the noise washed over me: *pshshuuusshshh!*

RPG launch.

From somewhere to the southeast of us the fiery trail of an RPG cut through the blinding darkness. The high-explosive projectile came barrelling towards us, with me and the 51 mm tube bang in its line of fire. Time seemed to freeze. I hit the deck in slow motion, even as the express-train *whoooooooossh* of the thing drilled into my head.

At the very last instant the increasing velocity of the RPG round must have forced it to climb a fraction higher, and it tore over the top of my head, missing me, the mortar tube and Marine Captain Richard Cantrill by bare inches. I was left enveloped in the back-blast of its rocket motor, fumes billowing around my ears and a choking, burning smell hanging in my nostrils.

It screamed onwards. I figured it would smash into the trees around the HQ ATAP, which lay next in its line of fire, I tensed for the blast, but none came. I didn't hear any explosion at all – fuck knows why. All I did know was this: *that had been no lucky shot*. It had been targeted directly at Cantrill and me. The rebel commander knew where the battle was being orchestrated from, and killing us had to be his number one priority now.

'What – the – fuck!' I exclaimed.

Cantrill was lying face down in the dirt. He didn't so much as raise his head to acknowledge me.

For a good thirty seconds the fire from the enemy side slackened, as if upon orders to do so. From the positions to our front I figured that as few as three belt-fed machine guns were lancing in the tracer now. The rest had ceased firing. Then even those few remaining guns fell silent.

All quiet on the Lungi Lol front.

What the fuck were the rebels up to now?

In the eeriness of the comparative silence I heard cries of 'MAG CHANGE!' Blokes to either side of us were shoving fresh magazines onto their SA8os.

The loud click and slide of a fresh bullet being rammed up the barrel was followed by a tense, expectant stillness, as we waited for whatever the rebels were going to try next. I figured we'd just survived their first two major pushes – one a feint to our front, the other along our right flank on the railroad. I didn't think for one moment the rebels were done with us. Without doubt they'd be regrouping in the jungle for a third try.

I flicked my eyes back to Cantrill. We hadn't spoken a single word since the RPG had torn across us. Apart from the fact that we were still alive, the amazing thing was how we'd somehow been working faultlessly as a team. He hadn't fumbled even one of the mortar rounds; each had been ready and waiting where and when I needed it. I gave him the faintest of nods. He forced a smile in return.

We had to win this thing in the time the light would buy us, for sooner or later we were going to start running out of illume. Somehow, I needed to keep the light up, while rationing the mortar rounds. I'd dived onto my front to avoid the RPG, which meant I was pretty much unsighted right now. I risked bobbing up again to get eyes-on the silent battlefield.

I got on one knee, glanced north and I could see the flare round drifting earthwards over Dolly's position. Bare seconds now and the light over *33 Bravo* would go dark. Directly to my front, the most recently-fired illume round was still riding high above the main highway, oscillating gently from side to side. But over Taff's position on the right flank all was very dark.

I grabbed the 51 mm tube, twisted 90 degrees right, planted the base plate, took a baton from Cantrill and fired. Even before the round had burst over Taff's position I swivelled through 180 degrees, sighted over Dolly's patrol and got a second round airborne. They burst in quick succession, throwing a burning halo across the sky to either of our flanks, Cantrill and me sandwiched in the centre of the glare.

We were six illume rounds down now. Twelve remaining. Or four more blasts of three across our front.

My gut instinct was telling me that the bad guys were heading for Dolly's position, way out on our left. I'd spotted the rebels surging across the main highway in that direction. At the distance they were out from the village, I figured they had to be heading for a distinctive feature that we'd already scoped out as a major threat. The blokes had discovered it via the probing patrols that we'd pushed out from the village, and they'd given it the nickname Fern Gully.

Fern Gully was a knife-cut ravine some seven to eight feet deep. It ran from the fringes of the main highway out towards *33 Bravo*'s front. Come one of the torrential rainstorms we'd been having, the gully would fill with water, draining off the road and the surrounding terrain. But right now it was comparatively dry. Fringed with thick bush, it provided great cover to mask the movement of a large body of men at arms.

It was the perfect feature via which to advance on *33 Bravo*'s battle trenches unseen, and get in amongst Dolly and his blokes. I risked raising myself still higher, getting into a half-crouch so I could check for any enemy movement through Fern Gully itself. It was only the fact that I was fractionally higher than I'd been before which alerted me to the threat to Cantrill and me: the rebels were danger-close, creeping through the bush to overwhelm us.

From the corner of the punji field nearest to us I heard a distinctive *crack* – dry vegetation crunching under the weight of a human footfall. My head darted around, my eyes flicking towards the noise, my ears straining. I figured I could detect rustling in the low undergrowth now – all that had been left standing by the villagers who'd cleared out the arcs of fire. We hadn't got them to cut to ground level: we'd only asked them to clear anything that might hide a man from our fire.

Then I heard an unmistakable sound: the hard clink of metal on metal. It rang out through the silent darkness like a gunshot. It was the kind of noise a spare magazine makes when banging against a rifle, or a grenade against a steel webbing buckle.

Either Nathe's blokes had moved far forward of their trenches without giving warning to anyone, or we had rebels between Nathe's position and ours. I spotted a shadow creeping forwards. This wasn't fucking Nathe's lot. It couldn't be. If they were coming in the least they'd have done is yell out a warning: *Steve! Steve! Nathe plus one coming in!*

The rebels were there – right fucking on top of us.

They were so far forward that they were well out of the cones of light cast by the illume rounds. Now I understood the silence: the rebel commander must have sent a hunter unit forward to nail Cantrill and me. Smash the guys putting up the light, so he could launch his next offensive in total darkness.

I let the mortar tube fall from my grip, and in one smooth movement I grabbed the SA80 in my right hand, lifted it from the dirt and brought it into my shoulder.

Bang-bang-bang-bang-bang-bang-bang-bang-bang-bang!

I let rip with a savage ten-round burst, aiming at the movement and the flitting shadows. Thank fuck that even after laying my SA80 in the dirt for so long I hadn't had a stoppage. I paused for a second, watching like a hawk. Cantrill was down on his belly and I'd not breathed a word to him of the threat. I figured he had to be wondering who the hell I was shooting at, though surely he could hear them.

More movement.

Hordes of shadowy figures rushing us.

Bang-bang-bang-bang-bang-bang-bang-bang-bang-bang!

Shifting my aim left and right, I hammered rounds into them. I heard the hollow, soggy *thuttd-thuttd* that 5.56 mm rounds make when they tear into human flesh at very close range. Any nearer and we'd be poking the fuckers with bayonets. They were so close I didn't need the SA80's metal sights: I was scanning the darkness with the weapon in my shoulder, sighting down the length of the barrel.

I heard screams now, agonised screams.

I realised how dark it was.

It was pitch black.

Dark, dark, dark.

More movement. *How many of the fuckers were there*? I saw figures rear up from the bush in front of me, eyes white in the darkness and wide with ... what? Adrenaline? Drugs? Voodoo-bulletproof-madness?

Muzzles sparked from barely a few dozen yards away.

I answered fire with fire: *Bang-bang-bang-bang!* Four more rounds.

Bang-bang-bang-bang! Another four.

More screaming.

Deafeningly close.

I was dripping in sweat, my heart was going like a jackhammer, and I was high as a kite on the adrenaline.

I heard these spine-chilling cries of agony rend the darkness, this time a little further to my right. It had to be from where the rebel fighters had blundered into the punji fields. My fire must have driven them back that way, the injured and the survivors fleeing into the safety of the open darkness, only to get stuck with bamboo spikes honed to a razor sharpness.

For an instant I wondered what it had to be like stumbling through the darkness, only to get stuck by those bamboo staves. I figured I could almost smell the rebels' confusion and fear. They were in amongst the punjis – I was sure of it now. And once you've stumbled into punjis in the pitch darkness, your greatest fear is you don't have a clue where to go next. *They could be anywhere all around you.*

Generally, if you've fired more than six to ten rounds you slot on a new magazine, grabbing any spare moment in which to do so. That way you always have a full mag on your weapon. I'd fired off far more than that by now, more like close to a full mag, so I used the momentary lull in close-quarter battle to do a lightning-fast change.

I made a mental note to try to grab a few seconds to recharge my mag from the bandolier of ammo that I had slung around my torso. That way, I'd have as many mags as possible fully bombed up and good to go. But right now I didn't have a spare moment, for the battle was balanced on the very brink.

I could sense it. *Feel it.*

Right now, in the next few minutes, we would either win or lose this thing – Operation Kill British vs. Operation Alamo.

Or at least we'd win or lose the first battle in what promised to be a far longer, wider and bloodier war.

All to our front I heard probing bursts of fire, signalling the rebels were back on the offensive again. I had to get my focus off the enemy, danger-close to Cantrill and me, and back on the wider battle and the light. But I felt frozen by indecision: *If I put the fucking rifle down, to fire the mortar, I'll be defenceless – and they're fucking right on top of us. But if I don't get the light up, they could creep through our positions unseen and get in amongst the lads, not to mention the village.*

For several long moments I kept the SA80 hard in my shoulder, my focus on the rebels barely spitting-distance away. Time seemed to have slowed to an agonising, slowmo loop. A second seemed to last a lifetime, as I scanned the spectral battleground. The night was thick with the scent of adrenaline, blood, hatred, pain, aggression and fear.

If I dropped my weapon and they rushed Cantrill and me, we

were done for. But to my left I could hear H rattling through the ammo big time. Beyond him, I could hear Dolly yelling out urgent fire instructions from the direction of his trenches. I figured the rebels were in amongst Fern Gully in serious numbers now. At the same time they'd sent a force forward to hit Cantrill and me and keep us from putting up the illume rounds. The fuckers.

What the hell was I to do? Get up the light? Help the lads conserve the ammo? But I had enemy engaging us in close-quarter-battle. Ammo? Light? CQB? Which was the fucking priority? And where the fuck had the rebels gone to who were right on top of us?

Should I get Cantrill to cover me? Get him under orders. *Get your SA80 going and cover me, as I use the mortar.*

I was so focused on my weapon I'd almost forgotten he was there. Then I remembered his pitiful lack of ammo. He only had the two mags. That's what he'd flown in with. *No way could I rely on him alone to cover us.*

The illume round to our front – the fourth that I'd fired – drifted silently into the trees and went dark. The darkness became thicker, as illume rounds five and six floated earthwards. Soon they would be snuffed out in the thick jungle. *Decision time.* Either I discarded the SA80, took up the mortar tube and fired more illume, or all along the battlefront it was going very, very dark.

I heard Dolly's voice screaming fire control orders, his words laced with desperation.

'Fern Gully! FERN GULLY! FIRE! FIRE! FIRE!'

Fuck it, the lads needed the light.

I dropped my rifle, grabbed the mortar tube, brought it up in the aim and punched a hand back to Cantrill.

'Fucking round!'

He slapped it hard into my palm. With my SA80 resting on my jungle boot I shifted 90 degrees to my left and launched the illume. I was aiming up and out beyond the gully, over the terrain that Dolly's blokes were hammering the rounds into. That was where they most needed the light.

As the mortar flew to height my mind flashed to the HQ ATAP, and what Tricky, Wag and Grant would have been doing while we were having the fight of our lives out here. I'd left Wag on the Thuraya, so I figured he'd have got a contact report through, while Tricky would have been trying to work his magic on the 319 radio. So even now the QRF should be riding to our rescue in a Chinook.

It was a fine feeling: *the cavalry are on their way*.

We just had to hold on.

The illume burst blinding-white over Dolly's position.

Almost simultaneously, the enemy redoubled their fire from the jungle directly to the front of us, just to remind H, Nathe, Cantrill and me that they hadn't gone away. The deafening eruption of violence underlined just how much we needed the QRF. The rounds screamed in, and the night sky above me was rendered into a blinding latticework of tracer.

If they were firing one tracer per five – 'four bit'; four ball rounds to one tracer, as we would – that meant there was practically a solid wall of bullets whipping past across us. The upsurge of fire was met with an instant response from our side – blokes hammering in short, aimed bursts. Seconds later the fire to our front petered out. I heard the odd *pop-pop-pop* of an SA80 from our side, before it went completely quiet again, the fire dying down over at Dolly's position as well.

The eerie silence drew out: ten seconds became twenty ... There was the odd single shot from out of the tree line, but not a sniff of return fire from our lads. They were holding their fire, which meant they were keeping great discipline with the ammo.

Eventually, the rebel fire petered out completely.

Silence.

Nothing moving.

Stillness like the grave.

I grabbed the opportunity to yell around for any casualty stats. I figured we had to have injured, but with all the chaos and the deafening noise of the firefight no one had been able to report in via the Clansman 349 radios. If anyone had called 'Man down!' on the net, I wouldn't have had the slightest chance of hearing them.

Nathe yelled across confirmation that all were okay in his trench, but I couldn't get a sniff of a response from the others.

The seconds dragged into minutes, as the tense silence settled heavy and ominous all around us. The rebels weren't even making their evil animal cries any more.

Where were they?

And what in hell were they up to?

The silence was deafening. Eerie. Spooky. Unsettling. In a weird way I'd felt happier when we were under fire: at least then we could see the enemy and know where they were trying to hit us.

One minute stretched into two, and still the empty, ringing quiet. For a moment I wondered if that was it: *battle over*. Maybe we'd given them the shock of their lives, and they'd withdrawn to lick their wounds and count their dead. But something – that fail-safe soldier's sixth sense – told me that wasn't so. The night was rippling with menace. It pulsed back and forth through the trees, like a palpable evil.

Two minutes became five. Still nothing. For a moment I wondered whether Cantrill and me should pull back, getting ourselves into a position of relative safety. We'd had the enemy charging down our gun barrels. There was nothing to stop them doing so again. Out here we were prime targets for Op Kill British – or rather for getting bound, gagged and dragged off into our worst ever nightmare.

But if we pulled back and my sixth sense was right, the lads would have no light for when the rebels hit again. *No: we had to stay put.*

I wondered if the rebel commander might have sent his men in covertly, which might account for the quiet. Were they even now belly-crawling through the bush to get right in amongst us? In which case, did I put up some more light? But I only had a limited amount of mortar rounds remaining – and my priority, as with all of the blokes, had to be to conserve our precious supplies of ammo.

Five minutes became ten, or at least it felt that long, what with the weird, otherworldly slowing down of time that comes with ferocious battle and the adrenaline rush of combat. I'd reclaimed my SA80 and I was scanning my arcs all around me, but each second staring down the gun barrel into the silent night felt like an hour.

For a moment I heard this faint rustling and scrabbling in the bush just to my front. My rifle barrel nailed it, finger bone-white on the trigger. *Come on – fucking show yourselves.* I tensed to unleash hell. Then a centipede the size of a prize-winning Lincolnshire carrot came wriggling out of the vegetation, crossed the dirt in front of me, and slithered away on the far side, moving in the direction of the punjis.

What the hell was that doing scuttling about in the midst of a firefight like this?

As with their snails, they built their insects big here. The giant centipedes came complete with a nasty, venomous bite. They were one of the few species of wildlife Nathe hadn't got into his cooking pot. Apparently, they were crunchy as hell and the venom wasn't good for the digestion, or so his trench-digging lads had told him.

I went back to scanning the empty darkness. For a moment my mind drifted. During a lifetime spent soldiering the only time I'd ever remotely felt as on-the-edge as this was on a previous jungle operation – one of my first ever with the Pathfinders. I was a twenty-three-year-old lance corporal, with three years' experience in the PF, and I was the lead scout of a four-man patrol. We'd been sent to Rideau Camp, in the Belize jungle, to run six weeks' training for the Gurkhas.

The CO of the Gurkha unit was ex-SAS, and one morning he'd called us in to tell us we were getting retasked. On the remote border with Guatemala a lawless rebel drugs gang was preparing to ship a consignment of heroin from one of their refineries to the US. Our mission was to get inserted by Puma helicopter into the jungle, then trek to a ridge overlooking the drug gang's operation, where we'd set up an OP. We were to go in with five days' food, ammo and kit, to get eyes-on the bad guys.

We were issued with live ammo – as opposed to the blanks with which we'd been training – for our M16s, food rations, thermal imaging optics, the works. Our patrol commander was a very capable bloke called Andy Parsons, plus there was a signaller called Bill Basha Barnes and a medic, Johno Smith. Having studied the maps, we chose a clearing for the helo insertion 5 klicks from our intended OP. We got dropped by the Puma, and then began the killer trek through the jungle.

It was typical 'egg box' terrain: thick forest and vines cloaking a series of egg box-shaped ridges and gullies. The loads were crushing. As well as oxygen bottles, we had eighteen batteries for the thermal imaging kit, each battery weighing a pound. We couldn't guarantee there would be any water on the ridge, so we were carrying all of that, plus food, ammo and survival gear. We'd been warned that a Gurkha patrol had been ambushed here by the rebels just a few weeks earlier. They'd got badly shot up and had been forced to go on the run.

The rebels funded their insurgency via drugs, and they didn't want any pesky British soldiers poking their noses in. It could easily take a whole day to cover 5 klicks moving tactically through such appalling terrain, and we only made the high point – our intended OP – at last light. We prepared to hunker down for the next five days, with the rebel drug-runners' den in clear sight below us.

Carved out of the forest was this deep-jungle clearing. It contained a dirt street lined with gambling dens and whorehouses, with some massive, warehouse-like buildings that had to be the drugs refineries. Badly distorted Mexican-style music drifted up to us, and with darkness the boozed and drugged-up partying began. Gunshots rang out every few minutes, blending in with the Mex-beat and the *put-put* of the generators. This was a lawless Wild West Dodge City, financed by a rebel mafia drug-running operation, and we really did not want to be discovered spying on this little operation.

From here mule trains carried the white powder out via the Belize jungle, and then by boat to Miami and the wider USA. We set up the OP, then got to study the place via a tripod-mounted Swift scope. Our first task was to log key points of interest: guards' posts and numbers; mule-train routes in and out; locations of refineries; vehicles on the move. We were on strict hard routine – so bedded down on the rock, with no washing or hot food or drink allowed. To avoid detection, we were shitting in cling film and pissing in coke bottles, so we could carry it all out with us.

One thing struck us immediately: the place was much bigger than our maps and satphotos indicated. We sketched it out in more detail: it had expanded massively since it was originally mapped, and it was creeping towards the Belizean border. Dodge appeared to be booming, and due to its enlarged size we couldn't see enough from our elevated position. Andy knew we couldn't complete the task as given from here. We'd do a 70 per cent job, and 70 per cent wasn't good enough. He figured we needed to move closer, but that would mean crossing the border into Guatemala.

The CO hadn't told us explicitly to 'do whatever it takes', but that is what lies behind every Pathfinder tasking. This being a very sensitive op, if we did get scarfed up in Guatemala our own people would very likely deny those were our orders, for it would cause a massive political shit storm if they didn't. No one underestimated the dangers of what Andy was proposing.

We were a four-man patrol, and our heaviest firepower were the 40 mm grenade launchers slung beneath our M16s. Ranged against us were several hundred drug-running rebels, and if they got wise to us we were not trained to wound. The ensuing firefight would be fast and brutal, and for us capture would lead to torture, abuse, death or worse.

Andy wasn't about to order us to go in, especially as Basha was totally against it. He reckoned the risks were too great. I said I'd back Andy, and Johno went with the flow. It was three against one, and so the decision was made. We stashed our gear, and at last light we headed down through the jungle, crossing into another sovereign nation's territory and past the point of no return. Johno remained behind as our backstop, 100 metres into the forest, and we laid a string from there to the edge of the canopy, where we left Basha as our fire support.

Andy and I headed out into Dodge, under the glare of the floodlights that ringed the place. Every inch of our exposed flesh was blacked-up, so as not to catch the light. The only way to penetrate further unseen was by the cover of these drainage ditches that ran around the base. We slid into the first: it was three-foot deep and full of stinking, stagnant water. I was on point. As I belly-crawled in, unidentified slithering and sliding things went 'plop' and 'sploosh' all around us.

We crawled onwards for three nightmarish hours, covering a good five hundred yards. Dodging guards by keeping submerged in the festering water, we got to a point where we could see and hear just about everything. Andy opted to take the people as his targets, me the buildings. Wriggling forward, we did our close-target recces, our faces barely peeping from the stinking swamp water. We were trying to imprint everything on our minds, for we couldn't write anything down.

We were right in the chaotic heart of the place: gunshots kept ringing out on all sides and there were open street brawls. I could see the front gate that led into Dodge, and the path heading off into the jungle, which had to be the mule-train route. I counted the big, metal-roofed structures that had to be the refineries. The drug-runners were dressed in a mixture of combats and local dress. They were armed with AR15 assault rifles – the predecessor of the M16 that the Americans used in Vietnam – and they looked serious and businesslike enough.

We'd reached Dodge Central around midnight. By now we'd discovered just how many leeches had got into our combats and were feasting away on our blood. Scores had worked their way into my groin area. They'd got lock-on and were making themselves very comfortable. But there was nothing we could do to fend them off: one false move and we'd be spotted.

We lay in the fetid murk getting drained of our blood, trying to keep bodies and minds sharp as a razor blade, as we waited for the rebels to show us what we really needed to see: a mule train laden with bales of drugs, revealing just what kind of gear they were refining, and smuggling out of here.

We'd lain unmoving in the swamp in the very heart of Dodge and we'd waited to get the killer shot . . . For how long were the rebels going to make us wait here in Lungi Lol, I wondered? How long before they showed themselves? How long before they made their killer move?

I flicked my eyes away from the stark metal sights of my SA80 to the horizon towards the east. Was I just imagining it, or did I detect the faintest skein of light – just the barest hint of the coming dawn? First light was what – maybe sixty minutes away? A lot could happen in that time, but come sunup the advantage shifted to our side – to the village defenders.

I got my answer about the rebels' intentions pretty quickly now. As if on one word of command from their leader, the enemy just seemed to open up on us with everything they'd got. After the long and deafening silence, the sudden eruption of violence was stunning in its intensity. The incoming fire was fearsome, yet now it was coming from one main direction and was concentrated pretty much on one single target.

Our far left flank.

Dolly's position.

33 Bravo.

To the north of us, the lads at *33 Bravo*'s trenches were taking a massive pounding. Dolly's lot were getting totally smashed, tracer like a solid stream of flame scorching into them. It was like a dragon was perched at the jungle fringe due east of *33 Bravo*, mouth open and streaming fire into their battle trenches. During the long minutes of silence the rebel commander must have shifted hundreds of his fighters that way, in preparation for his final big killer push.

I dropped the rifle and rose on one knee, mortar gripped in hand. But I didn't need to yell out any fire instructions any more. Instead, the response from the lads was instantaneous. I saw this sustained volume of rounds smashing back from our side and tearing into the enemy. But our rate of fire was really scaring me now: *it was too much, too fast*. Keep this up and pretty soon we'd be down to fighting them with our pistols, machetes and bare hands.

I reached behind me: 'ROUND!'

Cantrill scrabbled forward and thrust the mortar at me. I dropped it down the tube, fired it, and seconds later I'd got light bursting over the far side of Dolly's position.

I started screaming: 'WATCH AND SHOOT! WATCH AND SHOOT! PICK YOUR TARGETS! WATCH YOUR AMMO! WATCH YOUR AMMO! WATCH YOUR FUCKING AMMO!'

As I yelled out instructions I spotted scores of figures sprinting across the dirt highway at the fringes of the jungle. More and more of the rebel fighters were pouring north to join the killer thrust of the assault, which had turned against *33 Bravo* big time.

I screamed out a warning: 'REF TRACK TWELVE O'CLOCK AT TREE LINE ENEMY – RAPID FIRE!'

An instant later the guns in H's trenches swivelled around and unleashed hell, scything down figures on the highway. I grabbed my SA80 from where I'd laid it on my boot and joined them. As I opened up I could see rebel fighters taking hits, getting smashed and stumbling to the ground. I was halfway through my thirty-round mag within seconds.

As I fired I started yelling at Nathe's position to my right: 'NATHE! CAN YOU SEE THEM? CAN YOU SEE THEM?"

'YEAH! ON! ON! ON! ON!'

The lads at *33 Alpha* opened up on the rebel targets, adding their firepower to mine and H's. I was firing by 'battle-sighting' now – looking over the top of my sights and sighting down the barrel alone – so as to allow me to maintain my peripheral vision. The last thing I needed was to get tunnel vision, and miss some rebel fighters creeping up to hit Cantrill and me.

From my vantage point I spotted a new threat now: hordes of shadowy figures surging through Fern Gully to swarm Dolly's trenches.

I screamed out a further warning. *'33 BRAVO* DUE EAST – WATCH AND SHOOT! WATCH AND SHOOT! NEAR END OF FERN GULLY!'

Barely had I finished yelling when a savage burst of rounds sparked out from Dolly's position. It was their GPMG tearing the night apart, signalling that their gunner had spotted the enemy fighters all but on top of their positions. This was it now: this was where the rebel commander had chosen to make his die-hard push. This was where they would overrun our first positions, or die trying.

Then I heard it. Desperate cries of: 'STOPPAGE! STOPPAGE! STOPPAGE!'

More SA80 bullshit, but this time from over at Dolly's trenches, and with the rebels surging out of Fern Gully and spitting-distance close.

Then, even worse from H: 'CHANGING BELT! CHANGING BELT!'

An instant later H's Gimpy ceased fire, the solid stream of rounds that he'd been hammering into Fern Gully coming to an abrupt end.

For a long-drawn-out moment Dolly's lot were on their own, guns malfunctioning and the enemy right on top of them. H must have done the fastest GPMG belt change in history. Barely seconds later he had the weapon up and into action again. He hammered in the rounds up and down the length of the target, saturating Fern Gully with leaden death: from his position he could pretty much fire into the entire length of it.

But H was on his last belt of 200 rounds of link now, and if Dolly's lot lost H's fire support, they were pretty much finished.

'H – FUCKING WATCH YOUR AMMO!' I yelled. 'WATCH YOUR FUCKING AMMO!'

By rights H was now eating into his escape and evasion (E & E) rounds. We'd agreed that when we got down to the last third of our ammo it was time to get the hell out of Dodge. I didn't doubt that there were a whole lot more blokes who'd passed the same point – but now was hardly the time to turn and run. If we tried to bug out right now, Dolly's lot were going to get slaughtered.

The illume over Dolly's position was drifting low towards the trees. It'd soon be gone. I reached for another, then hesitated. By firing this one, I was about to eat into our E & E ammo for the mortar. We'd fired twelve: we had six remaining. I was about to cross the same line as H, and any number of the other lads.

Over the raging din of the firefight I could hear Dolly yelling desperate fire orders at his blokes. Though I couldn't make out the words, right at this moment I knew how much he needed accurate supporting fire, and for that he needed light.

I said a quick prayer, gave Cantrill the nod, then dropped the round down the tube.

19

There was a pop in the sky as the illume burst right over the top of the deep, V-shaped gully, throwing the length of it into this harsh, phosphorescent glare. I yelled out the fire instructions, but there was almost no need: from every position that could get eyes-on Fern Gully the lads were smashing in the rounds. It was getting hosed down by a murderous barrage of fire.

Fuck rainwater: right now the Gully had to be churning with rebel blood.

All of a sudden a voice rang out from behind me, tearing my mind away from the brute savagery of the fight.

'STEVE! STEVE! STEEEEEVE!'

I glanced over my right shoulder, thinking it had to be Cantrill. Maybe he was warning me that the rebels were rushing our position again. The Royal Marine captain was lying there staring up at me, next round held at the ready, and it clearly wasn't him doing the yelling. I glanced over my other shoulder and there was Grant. He was a few feet back from Cantrill, lying prone on the man's heels.

'STEVE! RIGHT – LET'S GO!' he yelled. He jerked a thumb over his shoulder. 'MATE, LET'S GO! COME ON! LET'S GO!'

I stared at him, caught in a moment of confusion. *What was he saying? Who should go? Just me and him, or all of us?*

'Mate, let's withdraw!' Grant yelled. 'We need to withdraw!'

It suddenly dawned on me what he was saying: *Time to get the hell out of Lungi Lol.*

I didn't know how long we'd been fighting for now, but it felt as if we'd been battling for a lifetime. I figured Grant's rationale for withdrawing had to be this: me, Dolly, H, Nathe and the others were so far forward and absorbed in the firefight that we'd lost any perspective. We'd passed the one-third of our ammo limit, the trigger to bug out and start the E & E; we'd been hit all along our front line positions, so very likely we were getting surrounded. I could understand how Grant had made the judgement call that now was the time to go.

'Mate, withdraw!' he yelled again. 'Mate, let's withdraw! Let's go! Bug out!'

But I hadn't been expecting this. A chaotic jumble of thoughts crashed through my head. I figured I had a better sense of the battle, being so hands-on as I was. I figured we could still win this, that we had the measure of the rebels now. If we could hold on for just a few minutes more we'd get the QRF in, and sooner or later we'd start to get a little light. Come first light we could see the rebels properly to kill them, and we wouldn't need any more illume.

Sure, we were well down on the ammo. I figured H, Nathe and Dolly's lot were well past the one-third mark. I was taking a wild stab in the dark, but maybe Taff and Ginge would be better off on the ammo front. I didn't know what casualties we'd taken, but I hadn't heard a single cry of 'man down' – the call for a wounded man needing urgent evacuation and treatment. We still held our defensive positions, and we'd be more exposed if we abandoned those and went on the run. Who knew what we'd stumble into if we tried to E & E through the jungle?

Those thoughts flashed through my mind in microseconds. If we pushed the rebels back from Dolly's position they'd be forced to regroup, having taken scores of casualties. That meant we could get the QRF inserted into our battle trenches, which meant thirty fresh blokes from 1 PARA plus shedloads of ammo. Time becomes hugely warped and confused when drugged out of your mind on adrenaline, but either way the QRF could only be minutes away now.

If we tried to withdraw right now, we'd be doing so with Dolly's lot still under a murderous siege. If we ceased firing and pulled back we'd be leaving them to face the brunt of the rebel assault, and I didn't figure they'd make it. Plus we still had a village to protect here. The villagers of Lungi Lol fucking needed us.

Decision made.

I shook my head violently. 'NO, MATE! No fucking way! We're staying! We stay! We're staying!'

I didn't have the time to give Grant a detailed heads-up as to my reasons why. But Grant and me had such a relationship that I figured he'd trust my call on this one. He could rest assured that I'd considered all the options and made my decision accordingly. Grant would trust my call, I was sure of it.

'Mate, we're staying!' I repeated. 'We stay!'

'Okay, mate, okay. I hear you!'

Grant was good with it. He didn't know my reasons, but he knew I'd have them. That was why Grant was such a great bloke to have in command.

Dolly's patrol was still in the thick of it. I could hear their guns hammering away. They needed light up over them pronto, for the last illume that I'd fired was well down by now. Turning to Cantrill I reached for another round, and within seconds I had it winging into the air high above Fern Gully. As it burst bright and angry in the dark night sky it was like a signal: *No one fucks us out of Lungi Lol; we're staying.*

The firefight raged on. I fired another illume and another, as the ones before them faltered. As a final flare round burst, throwing its harsh light down the length of the battlefield, the firing from the rebel side ceased abruptly. One moment, all hell was letting loose – the next, almost nothing. I could hear the odd *pop-pop-pop* of an SA80 firing from out of Dolly's trenches, but it was as if they were chasing after fleeting shadows.

In the near-silence I could hear Dolly yelling at his blokes, checking they were okay.

I heard Grant's voice from behind me again. 'Steve, I'm gonna move back to Tricky! I'm gonna send a full contact report!'

'Got it.' I gestured at Cantrill. 'Mate, go with him.'

Cantrill eyed me for a long second, before nodding his understanding. 'Yeah, okay, fine.'

I gestured for the daysack, and he thrust it into my hand. Taking the mortar tube in my left and the rifle in my right, I slung the sack of rounds over my shoulder. Like that I doubled over, sprinting in a crouch for H's trench. I needed to stay forward, but we'd been exposed in this position for far too long now. If I could make it to H's trench, I could get into some cover, rest the mortar on the lip, and still put up the light. Like that I could self-load, so I wouldn't need Cantrill any more.

As I thundered through the bullet-riddled bush I yelled out a warning: 'H, it's Steve! Steve! Steve! It's Steve! I'm coming in.'

H barely grunted an acknowledgement. His eyes were glued to the sights of his GPMG. To one side of H his wingman – Bucks – was likewise eyes-down his weapon. I tore across the last few yards and leaped in. Then I hunkered down, so I was sandwiched between the two of them. I threw the bag of remaining rounds onto the forward lip of the trench, laid the mortar tube next to the bag, grabbed my SA80 and took up a position leaning on the revetment, my eyes down the barrel of my weapon.

To my left H had the GPMG menacing the length of Fern Gully, but right now there were bugger all targets to fire at in there. Bucks was to my right, SA80 likewise in the aim. I could hear the odd burst of fire from the direction of the jungle, from where the latest rebel assault had been launched. Somewhat ominously, there was nothing much in terms of return fire from 33 Bravo.

For a moment I had this horrible thought: *What the fuck's happened to Dolly's lot?* I had visions of them being captured and dragged off into the heart of rebel hell.

The final illume round spluttered out into darkness, the last of the gunfire seeming to die with it. For a moment there was complete silence, and then I heard this new noise start up – these agonised groans and moans coming from the direction of the gully. No matter what a bloke's nationality the language of pain, agony and dying is pretty much the same. *Aaarrrgggghhh.*

For two minutes or so these horrible cries rent the darkness, before they too died into silence. All I could hear now was the *brrsst-brrsst-brrsst* of the basher-beetles, as they bumbled about in the vegetation to either side of us.

H let out this nervous laugh. It began as a faint chuckle deep in his chest, before creeping up out of his throat. He still had his eyes-down his gun, but from the corner of his mouth this thick Yorkshire accent went: 'Fooking hell, mate.'

'Yeah, fuck me,' I confirmed.

Silence.

Observation.

Watchfulness.

Where will they come from next?

And what the hell's happened to the lads at 33 Bravo?

I figured the QRF could only be minutes out, so we had to have a helo inbound. At the same time I figured the rebels had withdrawn with the aim of getting into our rear. They'd hit us left, right and centre and been smashed. That only left one avenue of attack. They'd probed our positions, in what amounted to a series of savage recces-by-fire, losing dozens of blokes killed and injured – but in doing so they'd discovered the limits of our defences and how to skirt around them.

That meant we had to get the QRF down on an LZ that was least menaced by the enemy. No point getting thirty-odd PARAs flown in, if their Chinook got blasted out of the sky and all the blokes were killed.

There was a bit of whispered chat between H and me as to where the enemy had gone to, and where to get the helo in. Wherever the rebels had pulled back to, we knew in our bones this was only a temporary lull. The rebel commanders had vowed to take

Lungi Lol and execute Operation Kill British. They'd keep coming.

They'd regroup in the jungle, patch up their wounded, and decide upon a new plan of attack. And here in H's position, plus in *33 Bravo*'s trench at least, we were down to less than a third of our ammo, and I figured we had to have wounded.

For a moment I wondered what we'd do with our casualties. Most minor flesh wounds we could treat in the field. But anything serious would have to get a casevac – a casualty evacuation back to Lungi Airport. It made sense to get any injured blokes out on the same Chinook that would fly the QRF in. In which case I figured it was time for me to get to the HQ ATAP, so I could get a sense of things, and liaise with the helo that was flying in.

'I'm going back to the HQ ATAP,' I grunted at H.

He nodded a silent acknowledgement.

I told him the obvious: to keep watching the track and the gully, scanning for movement. Grabbing the daysack of 51 mm rounds plus my SA80, I clambered out of the trench, retrieved the mortar from where I'd laid it, and began a hunched run the 70 yards back towards our HQ.

As I neared it, the village ahead of me seemed alive with figures. It was still dark, so I couldn't make out a great deal, but it sounded like complete chaos in there. I guessed we had to have dead and wounded villagers – those who'd been caught in the crossfire – and some of those might well need casevacing, alongside our blokes.

As I thundered into the HQ position I yelled out a warning: 'It's STEVE! STEVE! I'm coming in!'

I crashed through the foliage and sprang into the depression. Grant and Cantrill were there, with Wag and Tricky to the rear crouched over the Thuraya and the radio.

I locked eyes with Wag. 'Anything in from the patrol commanders? Wounded?'

I was expecting him to say: *33 Bravo* report three casualties, and so on and so forth all down the line of patrols.

He shook his head. 'No, mate, nothing yet.'

'Any update on QRF?'

'Yeah, initial contact report's gone and received. Sending more detailed one right now.'

We didn't need a confirmation message that the QRF were inbound. Our first contact report would trigger their launch, in which case they could only be bare minutes away now.

At that moment an unmistakable figure appeared from the direction of the village. It was Mojo, and following in his wake were his men. I counted eight blokes in all. I'd just presumed that Mojo's lot were in position in the trenches at the rear of the village. In which case, what were nine of them, their commander included, doing here?

Grant got to his feet and turned on Mojo. He simply exploded. 'What the fuck are you doing here? Why the fuck are you not in your positions? Get the fuck down to your trenches, or else!'

Mojo had a look on his face like he'd just shat his load. He didn't have a weapon with him, but then again he never seemed to carry one. At least his blokes appeared to be armed. I saw him bark some orders at his men. They turned almost as one and started sprinting down the road towards the rear of the village.

'Tricky! Wag!' Grant called over. 'Heads-up.'

We knelt in the HQ depression, the four of us facing inwards. We huddled together cheek to cheek in the cover of the earthen bowl. Cantrill was down in the prone position on the lip of the depression, looking back the way we'd crawled, his SA80 in the aim. But I could tell he had one ear cocked at the four of us.

'Right, guys, decision time,' Grant announced. 'What are we doing? Those attacks were most likely a probe, so there's still an argument that now is the right time to get out. Do you think we should go?' he queried. 'There's a lull in the battle. We're not under fire. So do we get out now? Steve?'

'No, mate, we stay.' I was adamant. 'We've repelled the attack. We've re-bombed our mags. We're in good defensive positions.

We've inflicted serious casualties. The plus points of staying out-weigh pulling out, putting half the blokes on the Pinz and running down an open track. Mate, I reckon in these initial stages we've stemmed the tide. I'm taking it that the QRF are inbound, and unless someone tells me different we haven't took any casualties.'

Grant shrugged. 'Too early to say.'

'Agreed, mate, but with our position being as it is I still reckon we stay.'

'Okay. Wag?' Grant prompted.

'Agree with Steve. For the time being we've held 'em off. But I need to get around the blokes and do ammo stats and check on casualties. But for me, for now, we stay.'

Grant glanced at Tricky. 'Tricky?'

'We stay.'

Despite doing an ace job as my mortar loader, Marine Captain Cantrill didn't – with all due respect – get to cast a vote.

Grant nodded. 'Okay, agreed, we stay.'

'Right, I need to get around the blokes,' Wag repeated.

'Coming with you,' I volunteered. 'Grant – you good to stay with Tricky and monitor the net?'

Grant confirmed that he was.

Wag and me crept through the trees that surrounded the HQ ATAP. We broke cover and sprinted across the dark void of the track, filtering into the bush on the far side.

Wag let out a yell of warning as we approached Dolly's position. 'Dolly, it's Steve and Wag! Coming in!'

We got the shout back: 'Okay!'

We scuttled up to the back of their battle trenches and Wag and me knelt down. Dolly turned to face us.

'We've made the decision to stay,' Wag whispered. 'You happy to hold your position?'

Dolly looked surprised that the question was even being asked of him. 'But fuck, yeah. Fucking right I am.'

'Right, any casualties? Plus what's your ammo stats?'

'No casualties. We're three hundred rounds remaining for the gun. Each bloke has around five full mags including the bandolier.'

'They were last seen at your location, so the fuckers could be going round the side and back of us,' Wag continued. 'They haven't fucking gone yet, mate. Keep a very close eye.'

Dolly nodded. 'Yeah. Got it, mate. No worries.'

Dolly had had the rebels practically on top of him, their fighters spewing out of the V-shaped gully to his front. It was amazing that no one had been wounded. We'd been incredibly lucky. It was equally amazing that they'd held the rebels off, yet still had some ammo remaining. There wasn't a great deal, but maybe enough for one more sustained firefight. Plus Dolly hadn't fired his Claymore yet, so they had one last layer of defence they could fall back on.

We did the rounds of the other patrols, moving across Nathe's, Ginge's and then Taff's, over at the railway line. As we flitted from one to the other, Wag briefed me in on what had happened with the comms, and the likely status of the QRF. The signaller back at Lungi Airport had been manning the 319 radio when the firefight had kicked off, so Wag's initial call via the Thuraya hadn't got an answer.

As a result, Tricky had been forced to radio through the contact report on the dodgy 319, with the added delay of having to encrypt the message (the 319 uses cryptographic coding to make the communications secure). The Thuraya, being a satphone, bounces the message up to an orbiting satellite and back down again pretty much instantaneously. By contrast, the 319 sends an HF signal up into the ionosphere, the idea being that it bounces off that down to the recipient. The transmission is very susceptible to climatic conditions: cloud cover, moisture in the air, and even a wet jungle canopy can stop the message getting through.

Eventually, even via the water-damaged 319, Tricky had got the message through, whereupon both sides had switched to using the Thurayas. In spite of the delays, by my and Wag's reckoning the QRF should be with us any moment now.

The news from *33 Alpha*, *33 Delta* and *33 Charlie* was that they too were well down on their ammo, but with a bit of cross-decking from one patrol to the other we should be able to hold on for a good while longer. More importantly, none of the patrols had taken any serious casualties. Amazingly, not one single bloke needed casevacing.

It was little short of a miracle.

With the QRF inbound, someone had to get down to the landing zone and clear the Chinook in.

'We'll go back via Grant and I'll make for the LZ,' I said to Wag.

'Got it, mate.'

We headed back to the HQ at a crouching run. I told Grant what I was planning, then asked Tricky to get one bloke from each patrol sent across to me, as security. We'd chosen to use a clearing at the far rear of the village – so beyond even Mojo and his men in their trenches – as the LZ for the Chinook to come down on. We'd scoped it out as the safest place to get the QRF into, but with the rebels getting around and behind us maybe it wasn't any more.

There was just no way of knowing.

I gathered the blokes, then had a final word with Grant. 'Right, I'm off. We'll take the Pinz, mate, 'cause I don't want to head out of the village on foot facing the number of rebels that are out there.'

'No problem,' Grant confirmed. 'Call me if you hit any difficulties.'

The five of us ran for the Pinzgauer. As we scurried through the predawn village the square was a mass of confusion, with groups of shadowy figures screaming and wailing. I could see a body lying on the ground, surrounded by weeping women. Clearly, we had dead or injured amongst the villagers, but we had zero time to deal with that now.

We reached the Pinz and I told Marky – the guy who'd driven Donaldson when he'd bugged out – to get behind the wheel. I jumped into the passenger seat and the others climbed into the rear. The Pinz had been parked for days with the keys in the ignition, but thankfully it fired up first time. We screamed down the track heading west out of the village, passed by our rear battle trenches and there was Mojo in position with his men.

They'd got there . . . eventually.

We pushed on for another 250 yards, heading for the dark fringe of jungle, then came to a halt. We parked up and went into all-around defence, lying prone at the side of the track. I found myself looking back at the village, with the faintest hint of breaking dawn on the distant horizon. A tinge of fiery pink was just starting to touch the high clouds.

Bring it on, I told myself.

With sunrise the advantage would shift to us big time.

I told the guys to listen out for any noises from the jungle. If, as I suspected, the rebels were moving to outflank us, now was when we'd detect the signs of their presence.

We lay there in utter silence, straining our ears for the faintest hint of any movement in the tree line. It was quiet. Deathly quiet. It reminded me of the seconds before the firefight had first kicked off, when the air had been thick with the tension of the coming battle. If we had a major contact here, we'd have to jump back in the Pinz and head hell-for-leather back to the village, and abort the landing.

I readied my night-time air-marker – an infrared strobe – to guide the helo in, and scanned the skies to the southwest of us. We'd yet to have a helo land on this HLS, so it was crucial I steered them in. I warned the blokes to keep focused on the jungle.

Last thing we needed right now was to get jumped, and just before we got the QRF landed.

20

We'd been waiting for ten edgy, nervous minutes when we heard the distinctive, juddering *thwoop-thwoop-thwoop* of a Chinook inbound. *Oh yeah.* There is no feeling like knowing the cavalry are on their way. The beat of that helo's rotor blades was the most welcome sound any of us had ever heard.

I spotted the helo silhouetted against the faint blush the coming sunrise had thrown across the heavens. Getting to my feet, I switched the IR strobe to pulse mode. I knew immediately that the pilot had spotted my marker – flying on NVG as he would be, my IR strobe would beat out like a lighthouse. He banked hard to starboard and swung the helo's nose around to my heading.

I brought the pilot in front-on to me, backing down the track away from the Pinz to give him room to land. He came in at real speed, and dropped the helo to treetop height with the aircraft's nose fifteen feet away from me. As it settled into the clearing, the thrashing rotor blades clipped the trees and the thick vegetation on either side. I could see the two pilots in the cockpit, the weird green light of their NVG casting their faces in a ghostly glow.

Going down on one knee, I switched off the IR firefly, and saw the pilot drop the arse-end of the helo onto the ground. There was a loud bang as it made contact. Orientated like this, the PARAs would be able to pile off the rear, and remain shielded from any enemy that were still to the east of us. But if we had rebels in the jungle around here now, the PARAs would be disgorging right into their line of fire.

I saw the ramp go down and waited for the surge. But nothing. I was thinking they should be off by now, so why hasn't the helo gone? After thirty seconds or so I ducked under the forward rotors, hurrying down the side of the Chinook to try to find out what was causing the delay. By rights, thirty seconds was more than enough time to get a platoon of PARAs off a helo.

I came around the back and glanced into the Chinook's dark hold. I spotted two lonely figures inside. One was the Chinook's loadie, the other was Captain Chris James, a guy I knew well. He was a former Second-in-Command of the Pathfinders. I'd taken him through Selection and for a while I'd had him in my patrol. He was now serving as 1 PARA's Adjutant.

I had one thought, and one only, crashing through my head right now: *Where the fuck are the fucking PARAs?*

Clambering aboard I closed in, so I could have words in Chris's ear. 'What the fuck is going on?' I yelled above the deafening whine of the turbines. 'Where's the fucking QRF?'

'Steve, I've been sent to have a look,' he yelled back. 'I've been sent to do a recce.'

I exploded. 'A fucking recce! Mate, we have just been in a fucking horrendous contact, we have no idea where they fucking are now, we're down to our last mags of ammo and there's *no fucking QRF*? What the fuck?'

'I hear you, mate, but I've been sent to have a look, to assess things.'

'Assess this, Chris: I don't give a fuck what you've been sent to look at, you need to get the fucking QRF in – *NOW*.'

I backed away in a seething cloud of rage, but he reached out and stopped me.

'Steve, we'll fly around and take a look! Fly over the village.'

'Mate, I don't give a fuck where you fucking fly – just get the QRF sorted.'

I stormed off the back. The red mist had well and truly come down. I felt waves of frustration and anger washing over me. We'd been promised a QRF on thirty-five minutes' standby. Those were the conditions on which we'd gone in. Instead, we'd just had possibly the entire RUF try to rush us, and they were very likely still out there getting us surrounded – and now this.

The Chinook took off.

I ordered my blokes back to the wagon. 'On the fucking Pinz! Let's go!'

The guys stared at me, confusedly.

'Steve, where's the QRF?' Marky queried.

'They ain't fucking coming,' I snapped. 'Let's go!'

We drove back in a taut silence. Not a single word was said. I had blokes in their early twenties with me, and I could sense their frustration and their anger. But what the hell was I supposed to say? *Yeah, lads, I know you've just given your all facing odds of 100–1, and we're running out of ammo, and we were promised a QRF and no one's fucking turned up; but wrong decisions get made; shit happens.*

That was about the truth of it, but it wouldn't exactly help much to give voice to any of that.

Above us the Chinook climbed to altitude, then followed the track out over the village, pushing east across the terrain from where the rebels had first hit us. It flew a circuit over that area, as I sat in the speeding Pinz trying to get my temper under some form of control. *But fuck me, Chris hadn't even brought us any re-supply of ammo . . .*

We parked up the Pinz and I ordered the guys back to their patrols.

As I headed for the HQ ATAP a local woman ran over and tried to accost me. In Pidgin English she started yelling: 'Ma dauter – she been shot! She been shot! She . . .'

The woman was trying to drag me towards the village square. I got both my hands up and forced her away: 'Get back! Away! Away!'

With no QRF having materialised, I couldn't deal with this kind of shit right now.

I stormed over to the HQ ATAP. I had had steam practically

coming out of my ears. The four of them – Grant, Wag, Tricky, Cantrill – were staring at me in amazement. I got lock-on with all four, and from a dozen yards away I yelled out the good news.

'There's no fucking QRF!'

I could see the looks of total disbelief on their faces. They had these blank expressions, as if they couldn't comprehend what I'd just told them; as if this couldn't be for real. They'd heard the helo come in. They'd expected me to come storming back with thirty paratroopers in my wake. And now this. It just didn't compute.

Tricky held up his hands, almost in a gesture of surrender. 'Mate, I fucking sent the contact report. I got confirmation . . .'

'What, they think we sent a contact report 'cause we were fucking homesick?' Wag snarled. 'Wankers!'

'When you say there's no QRF, d'you mean it's delayed or it's never coming?' Grant asked. The voice of reason, he'd posed the million-dollar question.

'No fucking idea. It was fucking Chris James on the helo, and he'd been sent out to *take a look*.'

'A look!' Wag exploded. 'A look at fucking what?'

I held my hands wide. 'I have no idea, Wag, mate, no fucking idea.'

Right at that moment you could cut the atmosphere with a knife.

I tried to get my anger under control. I tried telling myself that wrong decisions did get made at all levels of the chain of command. God knows, I'd made a good few in my time. The strength of a unit like the Pathfinders lay in how we responded to such bad decision-making. If we sat and stewed in our anger, spitting vitriol at whoever had fucked up, we'd fester and spoil. What we had to do now was deal with it, get over it and get sparking.

'Right, what the fuck do we do now?' Grant prompted.

We got our heads together for our second Chinese parliament of the morning. Decisions had been made in the first one based on the assumption that we only had to hold out until the QRF got here, with bucket-loads of fighting men and extra ammo. Grant laid it out for us how things had changed.

'Right, we have to work on the assumption there may be no QRF. They may not be coming.' He paused, letting the words sink in. 'On the upside, it's nearly first light and we can already see a good way into the jungle. This being the case, what do we do? What are our options?'

This was it now: life or death decision time. We'd had no further information from headquarters, and not the slightest hint that any help might be on its way. We had to call this for ourselves: *do we stay or do we go?*

'Option one is to stay and defend,' I volunteered, 'in the knowledge there may be no QRF at all. In my opinion, okay – there's no QRF. But on the ground nothing's really changed. We've got the same number of blokes, same ammo stats, the same defensive positions. We just readjust the plan. We've got the added advantage of daylight, plus no serious casualties. Let's stay and do this.'

Wag nodded. 'I've got a good handle on the ammo situation, so I can get it redistributed across the patrols.'

'For me we stay and defend this place,' I reiterated.

'Agreed, I reckon we stay,' said Wag.

Tricky nodded. 'I say we stay.'

Grant eyed the three of us for a long moment. 'Okay, I'm happy with that.'

I turned to Cantrill. I figured he'd earned the right to have a say, now we had no QRF heading our way any time soon.

'Mate, you've really got nowhere else to go, other than staying with us lot. But you've earned a say. What d'you reckon?'

Cantrill managed a thin smile. 'All I know is I'm safer with you lot than I am on my own.'

'So, we're unanimous,' Grant concluded. 'We stay.'

Wag shared ammo stats. We could cross-deck ammo to H, Dolly and Nathe's positions, and even things up a little. But we were still on the cusp of being two-thirds down across the entire unit.

One more probing attack like the one we'd just suffered and the ammo would be exhausted, and we'd very likely get swamped.

But there was also a kind of logic to staying, warped though it might sound. We had great cover in the trenches. The rebels did not. Come sunup we'd be able to see properly to ensure one round made one kill. With a hundred-plus rounds per man, that still gave us a good 2000 potential kills. And in the next few hours we were sure to get some sense out of headquarters in terms of ammo resupply and reinforcements.

Tricky got on the radio and called in the patrol commanders. Apart from the crying and wailing from the direction of the village square, it was quiet as the grave out there. Even the moaning of the rebel wounded out in no man's land had died down to nothing. Either the RUF had pulled back taking their injured with them, or their injured were now very dead.

I told Tricky about the wounded on the village square, and he radioed for Bryan Budd, our lead medic, to get over there to see what he could do to help. The villagers' thin-walled huts would have offered no protection from small arms and machine gun fire, and for all we knew some of the RPGs unleashed by the rebels might have taken out entire buildings.

We got the patrol commanders in for prayers. They'd heard the Chinook come in, so they knew we'd got a helo down, but no QRF seemed to have materialised. We had to nip this in the bud, and get everyone's focus back on the task in hand.

'As you've probably realised, there hasn't been the response from Lungi that we expected,' Grant started. 'No QRF has come in. That being the case, we've got to make the best of a bad job. The decision here is that we stay: we stay and defend the village.'

There were grunts of agreement all around.

Nathe: 'Fucking right we stay.'

Dolly: 'Yeah, we stay.'

Ginge: 'I'm for staying.'

Taff: 'Yeah, bud, that's it.'

It was around 0600 hours, and the course of action had just been endorsed by all.

Decision made, I heard a yell from our front ringing through the half-light. 'Steve! Steve! Steve!'

It was the unmistakable voice of H. I ran forward in a low hunch until I reached his trench. H pointed north up the track. In the dim light I could just make out three bodies lying there, maybe forty yards away from us, with a fourth in the ditch beside the road. H had killed them with his first burst of fire. That was how close the rebels had got – crawling through the ditches that lined the roadway – before H had opened up on them.

The corpses were dressed in a mishmash of fluorescent shell-suits, plus combat fatigues. One had been armed with an RPG-launcher, plus there were AK47s, and a belt-fed RPK light machine gun. There was no movement from any of them and they looked very, very dead.

I gave H my SA80, and took charge of the GPMG, so I could give cover while he and Bucks pepper-potted forward to the bodies. With Bucks's SA80 aimed at the nearest rebel's head, H moved the fighter's weapon out of reach. He searched the body, spending twenty seconds doing so, before moving onto the next one.

H and Bucks returned, confirming four dead: the rebels were riddled with 7.62 mm and lying in huge pools of their own claret. The lads brought back one RPG, complete with two rockets, plus a couple of AK47s, each with a few mags of ammo. But best of all they had the RPK – a Soviet-era 7.62 mm machine gun, equivalent to the GPMG – with a full belt of ammo. We are trained to use just about any weapon money can buy. H grabbed the RPK and placed it by his side. The Death Dealer had just added significantly to his firepower.

I returned to the HQ ATAP and put out word to scavenge weapons and ammo off any dead rebels in the vicinity. With no QRF and no ammo resupply, it was time to get our hands on whatever we could retrieve off the enemy. At the same time I ordered the lads to keep scanning their arcs, and to be prepared to unleash hell if the rebels showed themselves.

We got a bit of a morale boost from the extra rebel weaponry. Every little helps. As the sun crept above the ragged tree line the village started to come to life. There was this weird, eerie calm about the place. After the chaotic insanity of the firefight, it was like a bizarre and unreal comedown.

Whenever a villager passed us by, they threw us this look like they could not believe we had given it to the rebels. But we knew the enemy were still out there somewhere. It was just a question of where and when they'd hit us next.

Time passed.

We cleaned our weapons. I took the opportunity to recharge any empty magazines, using the spare ammo from my bandolier. I was back up to six full mags now, and I was good to fight. We resupplied the patrols that had taken the heaviest fire with what ammo we could spare, and the lads settled down to watch and wait.

I did a short walkabout with Wag, checking on the village wounded. Bryan Budd was on the edge of the square, and one of the girls he had treated was cradled in her grateful mother's arms.

Bryan gave a smile. 'I've treated the girl. Took a through-and-through. She's fine now. She'll live.'

The girl was a teenager, and she'd taken a round in her left shoulder, but luckily it had passed clean through. Bri had managed to stop the bleeding and get her stabilised, and needless to say her mother was overjoyed. She wanted Bryan as her son-in-law.

As Wag and me walked around the place I could feel the villagers staring at us. They watched us pass, eyes glued to our every move. It was almost as if they were desperate just to get sight of us and believe we were for real – their great protectors. Their expressions said it all: *You fought the rebels; no one fights the rebels; you fought them and won; we're alive; we're alive.*

There was this feeling of total euphoria about the place. I didn't want to burst anyone's bubble. For now at least we were all still here and breathing – Pathfinders and the villagers of Lungi Lol. Operation Kill British hadn't quite succeeded as the rebel commanders had planned it. Not yet, anyway.

And right now, that was about as good as it got.

21

At 0830 hours Tricky took a call on the Thuraya. Apparently, finally, the QRF were inbound. Better late than never was our attitude. I headed out once more to guide the helo in, taking Grant with me for company. This time we made our way to the regular resupply LZ, to the south of the village. This was where the radio message had told us the Chinook would put down.

We grabbed a few lads, secured the LZ and settled into all-around defence. The wait went on and on. I told myself to have zero expectations, which meant zero disappointments. If the QRF arrived, so be it. If they didn't we'd scavenged just about enough weaponry and ammo to put up a good, solid fight.

Twenty-five minutes went by before I heard the Chinook. It was hours since the first rebel shots had been fired and our contact report had gone in to headquarters. They needed to rename this lot the SRF – the Slow Reaction Force. Well no, that wasn't fair. The 1 PARA lads had nothing to do with the delay. I had every faith they'd have jumped on the helo and ridden to our rescue with gusto. There had been confusion that night; delay and breakdown in the chain of command. Responsibility lay at the highest levels, not with the bayonets.

The Chinook came thundering in over the jungle. I wandered out so they could see me on the ground and know it wasn't a hot LZ. The helo came in low and fast, went down with the rear ramp open – and *bam*!

Almost before it touched the ground figures bomb-burst out to left and right. My feeling was one of massive relief and euphoria: *Great; at last they're here. We don't have to fight alone any more.*

The Chinook was on the ground for maybe sixty seconds before all thirty blokes were out and it was gone.

We now had a circle of guys from C Company, 1 PARA, ringing the LZ. The bayonets were decked out in webbing and daysacks with helmets on and ammo hanging off them everywhere. They'd come for a fight and they didn't care who they were up against. It was a great sight to see. Nothing beats thirty heavily armed PARAs spoiling for a punch-up – fire-pissers the lot of 'em.

To every side of the LZ guys were darting all over the place, hard targeting it from tree to tree, ready for the rounds to come from anywhere. In the midst of the melee was the distinctive figure of Major Bob Bryant, a guy I knew from Kosovo ops. Bob had his radio operator knelt beside him, plus his company sergeant major and platoon sergeant. Grant and me made our way over towards them.

Bob opened with this. 'Right, right! What's fucking happening? Where are we at?'

Grant held out a hand in greeting. 'Captain Grant Harris . . .'

Bob waved him into silence. 'What's the sit on the ground and where are the enemy?'

Grant started to brief him, but Bob seemed to be only half-listening. The rest of him was itching to get on his way into the heart of the action, wherever it might be.

'Sir, this is it: during hours of darkness we were engaged by a large force of RUF. After a long and intense firefight we think the rebels are regrouping. We have no friendly force casualties; rebel deaths and casualties are unconfirmed at the moment, but there are four dead in the centre of the village.'

'Right, okay, take me to the village,' Bob announced.

With that he set off in the direction of the square at Olympic pace, leaving Grant and me floundering. We exchanged glances. The young PARAs were moving through the bush to either side of the major, darting from tree to tree and poised to unleash pure vengeance.

I broke into a half-jog as I tried to keep pace with the major, Grant doing likewise. We needed to brief him on the terrain and the positions, for the last thing we needed was a bunch of young PARAs charging about and stumbling into our punji fields.

'Sir, if you'll just look to your right we have two positions there, and the thrust of the attack came from the centre . . .'

Bob cut us off with a yell. 'Sergeant major, get the men spread out into cover! Get them digging shell-scrapes! I want the men in cover! Get them sparking! Get them going!'

'Yes, sir!' The sergeant major relayed the orders down the chain. 'Get the guys spread out. Take up arcs. Two-man shell-scrapes, and get the blokes down into the ground.'

Bob had come to a halt in the middle of the village track, his radio operator kneeling beside him. For a good five minutes he stayed where he was, barking orders. It reminded me of the scene from *Apocalypse Now*, when the American Marine Corps commander orders one of his men: 'See the way the waves break . . . Surf this beach!' The grunt replies: 'What about Charlie, sir?' – Charlie being the Vietcong enemy. 'Charlie don't surf!' the commander barks in reply.

Eventually, Grant managed to steer Bob towards the HQ ATAP. 'If you want to come this way, sir, this is the HQ. I can brief you fully in here.'

We got Bob in, whereupon Grant reached for the map, so he could properly talk him around our positions. Bob took up a stance in the centre of the depression, SA80 in one hand and the other jammed in his webbing.

'Right, tell me! What the fuck is going on? What happened?'

Grant gestured at the map. 'If you'll just close in I'll show you, plus talk you around . . .'

Bob gave a dismissive flick of the wrist. 'Never mind that! What's going on?'

Wag, Tricky and me inched away from the two of them. I got the strong impression that sparks were going to fly.

Grant stood up and put the map away. 'Well, sir, if you tell me how many men you've got we can start to look at bolstering our defences.'

Bob fixed Grant with a look. 'Right, Grant, let's be clear about one thing: I am the senior man on the ground here, so you now fall under my command.'

It was the first time Bob had addressed Grant by name.

Grant stiffened. 'I don't see it that way, sir. I am the commander of the ground force and until the CO of 1 PARA tells me otherwise, that's the way it stays.'

Bob turned to his signaller and barked. 'Get *Zero Alpha* on the net!'

Zero Alpha was the call-sign for Colonel Gibson.

Wag, Tricky and me were sat there thinking: *Well done, Grant, mate.* But I wondered what on earth Marine Captain Cantrill was making of it all. He'd just survived getting dragged into the teeth of a rebel onslaught only to be embroiled in this ... a scrap between the PARAs and the Pathfinders.

Bob was on the move again. 'Right, in the meantime, Grant – walk me around the positions.'

Grant and Bob disappeared in the direction of Dolly's trenches. Just then a message came in from headquarters. Our 'attached arm' – which had to mean Captain Richard Cantrill RM – was scheduled to get picked up by a helo at 1100 hours.

'Guess what, Rich, you're going home,' I told him.

Cantrill's face lit up like Christmas.

For a while we sat around chewing the fat and needling Cantrill about his getting out of here with the fight only half done. That got me thinking. Even now the rebels would be regrouping and trying to outflank us, so why not go out and hit them when they least expected it?

'What you thinking?' Wag prompted.

'I'm thinking we should take out a fighting patrol. They've been shot up, they've got injured, and they won't be moving very quickly, if at all. We have a chance to catch them on the hop, and that's the last thing they'll ever be expecting.'

Wag smiled. 'Yeah. Good one. Let's get after them.'

Grant was back some thirty minutes later, shaking his head in bemusement. I could still hear Bob's voice echoing through the trees, as he yelled out his orders. All around us PARAs were taking proper cover, using foldable spades to dig in. No doubt about it, as front line fighting troops these were about as good as it got.

Wag and me explained the idea to Grant – that we'd send out hunter patrols to track, follow and harass the rebels. 'We take everybody, push after them and try to pick up their trail.'

'Sounds like a plan,' Grant agreed. He smiled. 'Yeah, we'll all go.'

Wag shook his head. 'No, mate, not *all* all: you need to stay here and manage Bryant.'

Grant looked broken. 'But he's well and truly landed now, and the PARAs have a footprint on the ground . . .'

'No, mate,' Wag cut in, 'you need to stay here and manage this thing.'

'Well what about me?' Tricky piped up.

Wag shook his head again. 'No, mate, you need to stay here too.'

'You're fucking joking,' Tricky objected. 'What do I need to be here for? They've got a fucking signaller.'

'No, mate, you got to stay here and do our comms, relaying signals to HQ.'

Strictly speaking Wag was right. Our Clansman 349 radio only had about a 1.5-kilometre range. We'd need to be able to radio Tricky, so he could relay any urgent messages to Lungi Airport. Still, Tricky looked totally gutted and I couldn't say I blamed him.

Wag and I got the maps out and began to put flesh on the plan. We decided to push out two fighting patrols, one to the northern and one to the southern side of the main highway. The road would be each patrol's handrail – so helping lessen the risk of any blue on blue – friendly fire – incidents.

The ground from the village out to the fringe of the jungle

was ankle- or chest-high grass and bush. We'd change from open ground patrol mechanics to closed-forest drills once we entered the canopy. Each patrol would consist of twelve men, and we'd push out 1.2 kilometres from the village. That would be our agreed limit of exploitation (LOE). We'd follow the blood trails, track the enemy through the bush and hopefully put some rounds up their backsides.

With 1 PARA digging in all around our positions we were able to pull all the blokes back in, to brief them. Meanwhile, Grant was briefing Bob Bryant on what we were up to.

'We'll do it,' was Bob's reaction. 'We're the QRF. We're better suited to this. We're fresh on the ground ...'

'That's the reason you can't go,' Grant argued, with infinite patience. 'We're tuned in to the environment. Your guys aren't. We've had blokes out doing clearance patrols for days on end. We know the ground intimately; we understand the terrain; and this is what we're trained to do ...'

The argy-bargy went back and forth a bit, before Grant finished it.

'Look, it's a Pathfinder task and it'll be the Pathfinders that go.'

That decided, we sorted the orbat (order of battle) of the march. I'd lead one twelve-man stick, consisting of Dolly and Nathe's patrols. Wag would lead the other, made up of Ginge and Taff's lot. We'd go out with belt kit, weapons, ammo, medical kits and radios. We'd be light, agile and fast, which was key to the success of any hunter patrol – especially when the enemy was laden down with wounded.

The route march was simple. We'd move north through Dolly's position, then sweep east into the jungle, taking in Fern Gully as we went. From there we'd move ahead into the forest, then sweep south clearing as we went. Finally, we'd cross the main highway, sweep onto the railroad, and come back along that due west, which would bring us into Taff's position on the southern flank of the village.

When moving through close jungle the only way to navigate is with constant reference to a compass, and by counting footfalls – a process known as 'bearing and pacing'. You'd know that so many paces amounts to X distance covered, and that combined with a compass bearing meant progress could be plotted on a map. That's how we'd keep track of our position. If nothing else, this would be a proving patrol: by the end of it we would know where the rebels were located.

Most of the blokes had completed a Long Range Recce Patrol (LRRP) or a Jungle Tracker Course in the forests of Brunei, plus some of us had trained with the Kiwi SAS in Malaysia. The Kiwis are renowned for being the best bush-trackers in the world. They are even used by the New Zealand Government for tracking escapees from the nation's prisons, when they head for the mountains to try to evade recapture. The Kiwi SAS have unique skill-sets and are unbeatable.

Apart from the obvious – blood trails, dead rebels and discarded weaponry – we'd be searching for telltale signs of where the enemy were heading to regroup. We'd look for signs of ground disturbance, 'discardables', and 'transfer' – so where one piece of foliage might have caught on a rebel's clothing and been dropped in another location, betraying the direction of travel.

Before setting off, we agreed a set of verbal challenges and responses, should the 1 PARA lads see movement in the jungle and not know who it was. They would yell out 'Utrinque!' We would shout a response: 'Paratus'. 'Utrinque Paratus' is the Parachute Regiment's motto: it means 'ready for anything'. That way they'd know if it was us lot coming in, as opposed to the rebels . . .

The last thing we needed to do before setting out was to bid farewell to Captain Cantrill. A Sea King was inbound from HMS *Ocean*, an amphibious assault ship steaming off Freetown, and Cantrill was going to be on it. He'd spent a night with a bunch of renegade lunatics, and been dragged into the rebels' maw by yours truly. He'd more than earned his stripes out here.

I shook the bloke's hand. 'Good effort last night. Well done. It's a shame to lose you, but it's far too grungy out here for the likes of you, eh, mate?'

He laughed. 'Yeah, it was good while it lasted.' He went around shaking everyone's hand. 'Fucking hell, guys, outstanding. You've done the business.'

Cantrill had come in on a four-hour recce, and ended up in the battle of his life, fighting shoulder to shoulder with a bunch of hairy, stinking, unwashed Pathfinders, ones that he'd never even met before. Respect.

'Get yourself a nice hot shower and sing a fucking song in it for us,' Wag told him.

There was similar banter from the rest of the blokes. Then we formed up in our fighting patrols and set out through the village. We were pushing towards Dolly's position, when there was a load of yelling and shouting from the direction of the dirt track. We paused to get eyes-on whatever was causing all the commotion.

From out of nowhere a battered, light blue pick-up had rumbled into the village. The 1 PARA lads sprang out of H's position and yelled out a challenge: 'Stop! Halt!'

They had their weapons very much in the aim and were yelling for those in the cab to dismount. Draped over the vehicle's bonnet I could see something; a shape; a person maybe. As the pick-up got closer I realised it was a corpse. A guy was hanging out of the passenger window holding onto the dead body, and in the rear were several blokes waving weapons about and grinning foolishly.

Seeing the PARAs spring into action the blokes waving the weapons stopped doing so very quickly. They also stopped smiling. The pick-up juddered to a halt, the head of the dead man banging on the bonnet. There was more rust than bodywork on the vehicle, and it was a miracle that it was still driveable. With the PARAs doing their stuff, the guys in the pick-up threw down their guns by the roadside.

The 1 PARA lads surrounded the wagon screaming for everyone to get out. As soon as the guy let go of the dead body it tumbled onto the ground. The corpse was dressed in the ubiquitous shell-suit 'uniform' of the rebels, so I figured it had to be one of the RUF fighters. Once out, the PARAs hustled the blokes around, lined them up at the rear and began to give them a good pat-down.

That done the PARAs dropped them onto their knees, hands over their heads, and kept them covered. I knew the village chief would vouch for these guys one way or another, and we had a job to be getting on with here.

We gathered to the rear of Dolly's position, all of us Pathfinders minus Grant and Tricky. Wag had done a fine job of redistributing the ammo, so every man amongst us was well bombed up. H was up to 400 rounds for the GPMG, which was top news.

I'd left the 51 mm mortar behind. It was heavy and cumbersome and of no use beneath the forest canopy, plus we only had illume rounds and it was daylight now. But we did have one 94 mm LAW per patrol, just in case we came across any rebel vehicles. It hadn't escaped our notice that last night's attack had been minus any of the rebels' captured armour, plus their heavy 12.7 mm DShK machine guns.

We had to presume they were saving those up for round two.

22

By now the sun was well up and it was burning hot. As we moved off from Dolly's position, giving a thumbs-up to the lead sentry from 1 PARA, I caught the faint sound of a Sea King, flying in to rescue Captain Cantrill.

I'd formed up my stick with Steve Brown – 'Steve B', a cracking bloke from Dolly's patrol – as my lead scout. Super-fit and immensely strong, Steve B always started his day with 200 press-ups. He was robust mentally, and hugely capable, which was why I put him on point. I took up position immediately behind him, the blokes forming up in line to the rear.

Whatever happened while we were on this fighting patrol, the golden rule was not to break the line of march. That way, each bloke would know where the other was at all times, which was key to ensuring we had everyone with us, and that the heaviest firepower – the 2 GPMGs and the one LAW – could be used to best effect.

We pushed into the waist-high vegetation, moving silently as one, coherent, animal fighting unit. This is what we had trained and trained and trained for, and for the first time ever the Pathfinders were going out on an active seek-and-destroy mission. I could feel my heart pumping with the adrenaline. I knew with utter conviction that we would meet the enemy with deadly force.

This was no longer a peacekeeping mission, or OOTW. Each of us had our weapon in the aim scanning our arcs, and poised to unleash hell. The gun had become an extension of our head and shoulders: wherever the barrel moved our eyes were looking.

As lead scout, Stevie B's arc was 180 degrees to our front. Coming directly behind him, I covered an arc from his left shoulder ninety degrees to my rear, with the guy directly behind me covering the same arc but on the opposite side. This was replicated all down the snake, so that no part of the terrain we were moving through was missed. Steve B had no reason to look at me again now we were under way, and no one would make any verbal communications. It would all be done in silence, using hand signals.

We pushed ahead stealthily towards the canopy, moving through open terrain, with vegetation coming almost up to chin level, and at times head height. There were clumps of trees to skirt around, plus dips, depressions and small bushes to circumnavigate.

After ten minutes we came to the edge of a V-shaped ravine – the rear entrance into Fern Gully. Steve B went down on one knee covering the ground to his front, and I dropped to one knee covering my arc, the move cascading silently down the line. He placed his left hand on his head, the signal for me to close in on him, his right hand keeping a firm grasp of the pistol-grip of his weapon.

I moved up to Steve B's right shoulder. He indicated the footprints that criss-crossed the soft, loamy soil at his feet, leading into the gully bottom. Sure enough, scores of rebels had been through here. I could see by the direction of the footprints that they'd gone both ways – once as they tried to rush Dolly's position, the second when they were driven back under withering fire. In amongst the churned soil and crushed foliage were bright red strings of congealed goo: *blood trails*.

Further down the gully's length I presumed Wag's patrol was coming across more of the same, plus the rebel dead. I turned to Steve B, and indicated the bearing to push ahead towards the thick jungle. As we moved off I gave the bloke behind me a signal: two fingers into my eyes with one hand, then pointed at the gully. *Look in the ditch*. The signal was passed silently down the line, so everyone got to see the gruesome evidence.

We reached the edge of the trees, the shadows pooling thick and claustrophobic beneath the canopy. I glanced south, to check that Wag's patrol was entering the forest at about the same time as us. That confirmed, we nudged into the hot, musty interior, the smell of moist rot and decay heavy in our nostrils. The forest closed around us. Without the constant hum of the night-time insects, and the thwack of blundering basher-beetles, it was silent and foreboding.

Steve B paused again. He motioned to the ground at his feet. The leaves underfoot were thick with pools of congealed blood. No doubt about it, this was where the rebels had regrouped after we'd hit them in the gully. By the looks of things one hell of a lot of them had been seriously wounded and were bleeding heavily. Here and there a shaft of sunlight lanced through the canopy high above us, and where it hit the floor it formed a spotlight of bright, sickly red, like the hot point of a laser beam.

All we needed to do was track the blood trails, and we'd have them.

We pushed ahead, moving further into the ghostly silence. We moved due east for a good fifteen minutes, each footfall placed softly and with care, so as to cause minimum noise, or disturbance to the forest floor. When you're tracking an enemy in closed jungle you can't see very far, so you have to presume that an unseen force might be trying to hunt you. Or the enemy could be lying in wait, poised for you to move into their killing zone.

We'd lost sight of Wag's patrol as soon as we entered the jungle, but we knew where they were. Any movement to the north or east of us, and it was likely to be the enemy.

Steve B dropped to one knee again. Signalling the rest of the patrol to a halt, I closed up on his shoulder. He pointed ahead. About a hundred and fifty yards away I could just make out a group of small huts. There was smoke rising out of the centre of a cluster of buildings, from what had to be some kind of cooking fire.

I checked the map. I reckoned we were about 1.2 kilometres from the village, and via the Clansman 349 radios we had a range of 1.5 kilometres at best, less in thick jungle. We were on the limit of our comms, after which our only radio contact would be with Wag.

I lowered my mouth to my radio mic, which was strapped to my webbing. 'Wag, go firm. We've hit buildings.'

'So have we,' came back his hushed reply.

We remained where we were, totally motionless, for a good five minutes, studying the ground ahead. There were half a dozen mud and thatch huts grouped in a small clearing. Smoke hung beneath the trees like a haze of early morning mist, and I could smell its distinctive woodiness. I could see a huge cooking pot perched on the fire nearest to us, but not a soul could be seen.

This was the direction in which the blood trails – plus the scraps of vegetation ripped from the trees at the rebels' passing, – were leading us. We had to presume they had moved through this area, or maybe even used it as some kind of temporary base from which to launch their attack. More to the point, we had to work on the assumption that there were still rebels present, and very possibly this was where they were treating their wounded.

I radioed Wag: 'We've got six huts, no hostiles visible. But loads of blood trails leading in.'

'Three larger buildings,' Wag's voice came back at me. 'They look like kind of school halls.'

We agreed to go in and clear the areas simultaneously. Turning around so I was facing back down my patrol, I raised one hand showing two fingers. I closed it into a fist, before raising it to pat the top of my head. The fist was the signal that I needed the gun-group, the GPMG operators; two fingers indicated that I wanted both of them, and the hand on the head meant *on me*.

One of the GPMGs was positioned halfway down the patrol, to cover those forward. The other was second from last, to cover our rear. H and the other GPMG operator, Morgan Taff Hansen, a guy from Dolly's patrol, rose and came forward. I pointed out the buildings, speaking to them in a hurried whisper. We needed the short-barrelled weapons to go in and clear the huts – so the SA80s. I wanted the GPMGs positioned to provide cover, in case it all went noisy.

'You guys push forwards slightly left,' I whispered. 'Co-locate yourselves and cover us as we go in.'

They gave the briefest of nods, got to their feet and began flitting through the shadows. In a bent-over scurry they pushed 50 yards ahead, then got down into their fire positions, so we could move past them on their right.

I radioed Wag. 'Deployed a base of fire. Going in to clear buildings. H-hour fifteen.'

'Roger, out.'

Wag and I now had an agreed plan of attack. In fifteen minutes' time we'd each take our patrols in to clear the buildings, with a GPMG fire base set up to cover us.

I radioed Tricky: 'In canopy to north of village twelve hundred yards. Come across huts. Will move forward and clear. May go loud. Inform *Sunray*.'

'Roger. Out.'

Sunray was now Grant's call-sign, of course.

Poor Tricky. I could tell by the tone of his voice that he was sick to death with being joined at the hip to the radio. He was itching to get out here with us lot, taking the fight to the enemy. I spared a fleeting thought for what he was going through back there – with Major Bryant and Grant locking horns over command, and Colonel Gibson very likely inbound on a helo to bang heads together.

As I glanced forward at the smoke-enshrouded huts, I knew for sure where I'd rather be – out here on a hunter patrol.

I tapped Steve B on the shoulder and signalled for him to follow me. I moved back past each man, gesturing for him to converge on me. I dropped to one knee in the centre of the patrol. The others closed in so we formed a tight circle with our faces practically touching. It was another of the joys of working in a small outfit like ours: you grew so close to the blokes that you knew instinctively what each was about, and you weren't afraid of the intimacy.

I broke the patrol down into two-man assault teams, giving each a number to better facilitate my orders. Glancing at the faces ranged around me, I could see the excitement burning in the blokes' eyes.

A lifetime of training, leading up to this moment.

Let's not let it go to our heads, lads.

'Move silently into village,' I whispered. 'Assault Teams 1 and 2, move forwards under cover of fire base. AT 1, clear first building; once you're done go firm, signal to AT 2 it's clear; AT 2 move to clear second building. I'll move in with AT 3 and 4, and so on. We'll leapfrog across each other as we go, *but all on my orders*. Actions-on: SOP. Remember: weapons tight until we go loud.'

SOP stood for standard operating procedure.

I gave a final, searching look. 'Understood?'

I got nods of assent all around.

One of the greatest dangers now was of a blue on blue – one of the teams getting ahead of itself, and getting mistaken for the enemy. I needed to grip the lads, and keep it smooth, tight and controlled.

'Okay, AT 1 – go.'

It was deadly silent as the two blokes from AT 1 crept forward, threading their way between the trees. Two more blokes from AT 2 closed on their heels. We were now in Room Combat Mode, as opposed to Room Clearance Mode. Room Clearance is easy: you boot the door open, lob in the grenades, then open fire with max violence. You do that when you know for certain it is an enemy position.

But we couldn't be sure what this was, so we'd have to go in weapons at the ready and scanning the room for the bad guys. We'd go through the door with one weapon high moving right, and the other low sweeping left, to cover all angles. There could be women or children in there, or there could be rebel fighters or their injured. This was all about recognising the enemy before they got to open fire, and taking them out without killing any innocent bystanders.

I saw AT 1 scuttle across the sunlit clearing that stretched from the edge of the forest to the first of the huts. They reached the doorway, one behind the other tight against the wall. The forward guy stepped out and slammed a boot into the door, then both guys were piling inside, weapons at the ready.

Seconds later a head emerged. 'Clear!'

I signalled AT 2 forward to hit the next building. I moved forward at a low crouch, AT 3 and 4 at my heels, skirting by the GPMG gunners as we went. They had eyes-down their gun barrels and they didn't so much as nod at our passing. I heard a punching crunch as AT 2 went through the door of hut two, and an instant later there came a cry.

'Clear!' A pause. 'Ammunition! Blood!'

We'd found ammo already, plus blood trails. It looked like the rebels were here, or at least they had been very recently. I came up against the doorway of the first hut, joining the lads of AT 1. We were out in the open, the blinding sun burning hot above the forest clearing. The adrenaline was pumping, the sweat pouring into my eyes and trickling down my back in rivulets.

I glanced into hut one. It had a dark, damp, decaying feel to it. The roof was sagging with thatch that was semi-rotten. I didn't think anyone had been living here. Maybe this was just some sort of jungle camp, one where those gathering food or timber could temporarily shelter. It couldn't be a rebel base. That was inconceivable – not this close to the village. The chief of Lungi Lol would have known and he would have warned us.

Moving up to hut two I signalled to the next building: 'AT 3 – go!' I glanced through the doorway of hut two. Inside were several crates of what looked like AK47 rounds, plus belts of 7.62 mm ammo for their machine guns. Plus blood. Lots and lots and lots of it. In fact, it was like a charnel house in there.

I tried to get inside the rebels' heads; to imagine what sequence of events could have brought them here. From the blood trails in Fern Gully and the pools at the forest edge, I figured they'd retreated with their wounded that way, getting out of our line of fire. They'd moved through the forest heading east, and maybe paused at these huts to tend to their injured and take on water.

A lot of rebels had been bleeding profusely in this hut, so maybe they'd triaged their injured here – assessing who could be treated and saved, and who was beyond help. But if that was the case, where were the bodies of the dead? I searched with my eyes for any rebel fighters who had bled to death here, but there wasn't a single corpse.

It didn't make any sense.

Where were the rebels?

Where were their dead and their injured?

You didn't get blokes bleeding like this and surviving, especially not when you were in the jungle, presumably with no trained medics, no medical supplies and certainly no hospitals. So where were their dying and their dead? It was a total mystery. The only way to solve it was to keep going, and track them to wherever they had gone to ground.

They couldn't be far now.

Blokes bleeding profusely can't move far or fast, if at all.

As I moved on to the next hut, I reminded myself that an animal is at its most dangerous when it is injured. Human beings are basically animals – it's just that we have a thin veneer of civilisation laid over us. I urged the lads to remain ultra-alert, then sent them forward to hit the next building.

We pressed on through the clearing. In the very centre we came to a two-metre-wide fire-pit scooped out of the ground. The logs were still smoking and cooking pots were clustered all around it. There were tree stump seats to either side, plus a metal A-frame structure over the fire, for hanging pots. The smell of burning hung heavy in the air, with shafts of sunlight lancing through the lazy smoke.

Around the outskirts of the fire-pit was dark, hard-packed mud criss-crossed with footprints. Plus there was one massive, smoke-blackened cauldron lying on some hot coals. It was about three times the size of the one in which Nathe had brewed up his balti specials. In fact, it was so large you could have packed it with enough snails and fungi to feed the entire village of Lungi Lol.

Or you could have brewed up a dose of voodoo medicine large enough to 'treat' an entire rebel army. Back in Freetown we'd been briefed on how rebel fighters would bathe in a vat of voodoo medicine up to the neck prior to battle. It was via the total immersion method that you supposedly made yourself 'bulletproof'. Well, from all the blood I'd seen so far, they'd sure got the recipe wrong this time.

I placed my hand inside one of the smaller cooking pots and felt the remains of the food. It was still warm.

Where were the rebels?

Between the fire-pit and the far end of the settlement was eighty metres or so of open ground. I sent my teams pepper-potting across it. In the very centre was a huge pool of blood and body splatter, as if the wounded had been piled up there to die.

But where were the bodies?

We'd got all of the remaining huts cleared within ten minutes flat. More blood was found, plus piles of link ammo for the rebels' machine guns, and AK47 magazines. But still there were no wounded, nor any corpses – let alone any live enemy.

I sent my GPMG gunners east of the clearing to cover our onward movement. We formed up as a patrol and edged into the thick jungle again. As we went, I could hear the last of the cries from Wag's clearance operation filtering through the trees, as his team mirrored the actions of my own.

We exited the far end of the clearing, finding more blood and gore, plus piles of ammo, including bandoliers of AK47 rounds. There was a lot of freshly-crushed vegetation here, showing where a large body of men had moved through and very recently.

Via the damage to the foliage it was easy to trace the onward route they'd taken as they headed away from the village.

Having traced a wide arc north and east through the jungle, we were now around 1.5 kilometres north of Lungi Lol. This was further than we'd told Grant we were going to push. I spoke to Wag on the radio. He'd found similar signs of movement to us, and it was clear there had been wounded and dying rebels holed up in the larger buildings too.

So where the hell was everyone now?

We agreed to push east a further 1.2 kilometres, putting us a good 2.5 klicks or more out from the village. Hopefully, it would be far enough to catch the bad guys.

I informed Tricky over the radio. We crept ahead, hitting the densest terrain we'd yet encountered. It was approaching midday by now, so it had taken the twelve of us fit and very able blokes a good hour to reach this point. By the looks of what we'd discovered the rebels were laden down with scores of injured. They'd be moving at a fraction of our speed.

We should be right on top of them.

The terrain all around us was unerringly quiet. It was as if the very jungle itself was holding its breath, bracing itself for the next round of mayhem and carnage. I caught the odd animal and bird cry, but this time I was certain it was genuine jungle life, as opposed to rebel war cries. Occasionally, a fleck of sunlight filtered through the umbrella of leaves high above us, catching on a falling leaf or a speck of dust, but otherwise it was a network of shadow.

We moved silently across the jungle floor, pushing into a forest clearing. A giant tree had crashed to the ground sometime recently, bringing down a swathe of vegetation with it. After the musky dank of the forest interior the light in the open was blinding. I saw the glint of sun on something man-made. I bent to investigate. A crumpled cigarette packet had been dropped here. I retrieved it. It was smeared on the underside with dried blood.

Rebel wounded had been through this way, but how the hell were they managing to move so quickly?

We crept across the clearing, weapons in the aim, fingers on the trigger and safety catches very much in the 'off' position, scanning our arcs as we went. Every one of us was alert to the slightest movement or noise. The rebel dying and their wounded couldn't have gone much further.

Soon now.

23

I moved through the wall of vegetation on the far side, stepping back into darkness. Visibility fell to ten yards max with this level of light and the density of the surrounding greenery. This was close quarter battle (CQB) terrain par excellence, and we'd be on top of the enemy almost before we saw them.

When training for CQB in jungle as close as this you do so on a specially-designed Patrol Lane, and with your weapon held at the hip. Targets pop up from the undergrowth to either side, and the key is to hit them before they hit you. It's a given that you won't have the time in which to aim properly at such close quarters. Instead, you open fire from the hip instantly, working on instinct. The aim is to get the rounds down before the enemy has the chance to do so, in the hope of wounding them or at least putting them to ground – so giving you and your team the chance to pull back from the ambush.

That was exactly how we were patrolling now. Our aim was to move utterly silently and take the rebels by total surprise. By moving into the jungle to hunt them down, we were doing the completely unexpected. We were showing we had the battle skills to take them on in their own terrain, where they felt safest.

If we could smash them here from out of the blue – at a time and place very much not of their choosing – it would seriously deter them from launching a further attack on the village. Not only would they have got a bloody nose at Lungi Lol, they'd have got one when moving through the jungle – which they believed was their sanctuary.

We would instil total fear in their heads. Operation Kill British would start to look a lot less attractive. *If that's what twenty-odd British soldiers can do, what'll happen if we go up against 800 at Lungi Airport?*

As we moved ahead we kept picking up signs of the rebels' passing, but we reached the 2.5 kilometre mark still not having caught up with any. It didn't make the slightest bit of sense. Somehow, dead and injured rebels seemed able to keep moving through thick jungle . . . Maybe the voodoo medicine was working its dark magic, after all?

We went firm. I radioed Wag that we were there, no rebels seen.

'Roger, figures five,' Wag replied.

His patrol was five minutes behind us.

They arrived in the tree line on the opposite side of the dirt track. Wag and me linked up in one of the side ditches that lined the track and knelt for cover.

'Mate, lots of fucking blood in that village we cleared,' I whispered. 'Looks like they've been seriously shot up.'

'Yeah, maybe, but not so much on our side. We just patrolled up through, not really following anything much.'

'So, looks like they moved through my side after getting whacked at Dolly's position. But where the fuck are their wounded and their dead?'

Wag shrugged. 'Fucking search me.'

'Dead men walking?'

'Looks like.'

'Right, well, we've cleared to our front, mate. We've got to make the move back to complete a 360. Let's clear either side of the railroad as we go back through.'

By a '360' I meant a 360-degree clearance all around Lungi Lol – which was the ultimate aim of what we were doing now.

We crossed the highway, and with Wag's patrol on the far side of the railroad we started to move back towards the village, handrailing the metal tracks. Our pace quickened as we moved through more open terrain. We approached Taff's battle trenches,

Wag's lot stumbling upon more signs of rebel presence: a pile of hastily discarded weaponry and ammo.

We gathered up the hardware. There was enough here to start a small war, so it looked as if a serious number of rebels had tried to outflank us via the railway line. Following the tracks due west, we skirted by Taff's trenches, turned north to loop around the positions now manned by Mojo and his men, and finished off back at Dolly's position. That was it: 360-degree clearance patrol completed.

It had taken us two-and-a-half hours, and we'd collected up enough ammo and weaponry to arm a small insurgency. We'd also seen enough blood to sink a battleship, but the big mystery was – *where on earth were the rebel dead and injured*?

We made the village square and the guys filtered back into their patrol positions. Wag and me briefed Grant and Bob on what we'd found. That done we placed the captured weaponry in a pile on the main track, next to the growing heap of rebel corpses.

At 1430 hours – in an hour or so's time – we were scheduled to get a visit from Colonel Gibson. In the meantime, we noticed groups of villagers moving along the main highway into Lungi Lol. The expressions on their faces spoke volumes. They stopped and stared at the rebel bodies with these looks of sheer, unadulterated joy. *Finally, the rebels were getting their comeuppance.*

Mojo turned up looking inscrutable in his trademark immaculate dress. It was as if nothing much of any note had happened in the last few hours. How could he have been in his battle trenches alongside his men and have remained parade-ground smart? And how many bloody uniforms did the guy possess? Bob Bryant had no idea who Mojo was, of course, and I could see him staring at the Nigerian lieutenant suspiciously.

'Lots of people are now coming into Lungi Lol,' Mojo announced, speaking to Grant. 'They have come from outlying villages and they are going straight to the village chief. They have seen the rebels moving through, and they have come here in fear and seeking protection. Many villagers have been rounded up as work gangs and forced to carry the rebel wounded. And they are being forced to fetch them water and food.'

Right, so now we knew. That was how the rebels had managed to move their dead and their injured: they'd rounded up villagers to use as forced labour and stretcher-bearers. The riddle of their miraculous disappearance – the voodoo-dead-men-walking – had just been solved.

The new arrivals described how villagers had been forced to bury fourteen rebel dead here, ten there. They spoke of seeing strange wounds on the rebel bodies as if they had been *speared*. It looked as if the punji fields had done their work. Many villagers were still being held prisoner, and the fate of those so taken was an unknown. But at least we'd given the rebels a good pasting, and shattered the myth of their invincibility. And if this was the beginning of the end of their brutal rule here, then it had been something well worth fighting for.

Mojo gestured at the pile of rebel corpses out on the road. 'Those – I can take them? The dead? Take them to bury?'

Grant nodded. 'Yeah, get them in the ground, mate.'

Mojo scuttled away to his grisly task. It was a good idea to get the corpses buried, for they were attracting swarms of flies. I presumed Mojo would order his men to do it, for I couldn't imagine the man himself getting his hands – not to mention his uniform – dirty.

We used the opportunity of having the 1 PARA blokes on the ground to take a proper break. It felt fantastic not to have to be 100 per cent alert the entire time. Tricky was the brewmaster and since the girls had started their early morning water deliveries he'd been on permanent send on the brew front.

We'd ended up giving him all our brew kits so he could manage the catering. The Water Girls had got into the habit of collecting the empty containers at last light, and turning up just after first light with full ones. They'd deliver the water in silence, eyes downcast, as if they didn't want to be seen getting too familiar with the white men.

'Great, the Water Girls are here,' someone would announce. 'Thank you, girls. Biscuits? Sweets? Lancashire hotpot?'

The Water Girls had never taken a thing off us. They'd just smiled coyly and scurried away, delivery done. With a regular supply on hand we'd adopted a new water discipline. Tricky kept the brews coming from the Water Girls' supply, while each man kept one and a half litres of drinking water in his grab bag, plus two one-litre bottles in his belt kit. That was our E & E water, and we never made inroads into it.

But this morning after the battle there had been no sign of the Water Girls, so Tricky was forced to make the brews from our E & E supplies. He'd just got one going, when from out of the cloudless blue sky to the west of us a Chinook came thwooping in towards Lungi Lol.

We presumed it had to be Colonel Gibson, but it was taking a very odd approach route. It wasn't heading for the standard LZ. Instead, it hugged the length of the main track, swooping over the village square and going right over the top of us. By the time it reached the pile of rebel weaponry it was down to twenty feet, and spent bullet cases were getting blown all over the place in the downdraught.

The helo did a 180-degree about turn and put down on the track, practically on top of our forward trench position. The 1 PARA lads had to hold onto their helmets, as the downwash of the twin rotors practically tore them off their heads. The Chinook had come in with no warning, no one guiding it, no markers and no security. None of us could believe it. What the hell was going on?

Bob Bryant jumped up and hurried down the track, followed by his radio operator and sergeant major. I watched as the ramp went down, fully expecting Colonel Gibson and his retinue to be disgorged. Instead, out came the most ridiculous thing I have ever seen. Two gentlemen from the Royal Military Police (RMP) appeared, complete with spotless uniforms with knife-edge creases, gleaming pistols in their side holsters, and RMP berets clutched in their right hands.

As soon as they were off the helo took to the air again, banking south over Taff's position. The RMPs paused, put on their tomato-red berets and started marching up the track into the village. There is no other beret in the world like that worn by RMPs. You see one of those, you know immediately exactly who you're dealing with.

I turned to Wag. '*Fucking monkeys?* What the fuck are two monkeys doing here in Lungi Lol?'

Wag was speechless. He shook his head in silent disbelief.

It is a simple inalienable truth that all soldiers hate RMPs, and none more so than PARAs or ex-PARAs – hence the 'monkeys' nickname. Bob Bryant had got about halfway to the helo drop-off point, fully expecting it to be carrying Colonel Gibson. Now he was stopped dead in his tracks, staring in disbelief at the two RMPs.

They came to a halt beside the pile of rebel bodies – the ones that Mojo and his men were about to go and bury. The corpses had been blown half into the ditch at the side of the road by the Chinook's downdraught. The RMPs stood side by side, turning heads, nodding and pointing at the bodies, plus the ammo and the weaponry piled up beside them. Any second now I expected them to get out pens and notebooks.

Sure enough, one undid his shirt button, pulled out a pencil and paper and began making a note of the weaponry. Grant, Wag, Tricky and me exchanged these incredulous glances. If someone had asked me what had surprised me more – a newspaper reporter pitching up in a white Lada taxi, or these two muppets dropping in – well, there was no contest. The monkeys had it, every time.

After five minutes' comparing notes over the flyblown corpses, they pushed on towards us. I could see by their shoulder flashes they were sergeants. They passed by the young PARA lads they'd just flattened with their rotor wash without the barest flicker of an acknowledgement. As they neared Bob Bryant, they 'bent and drove' in perfect unison – ramming feet down into the ground and sawing the right arm up in a parade-ground perfect salute.

Bob managed a fly swat towards his helmet in response. I couldn't hear what was said, but by the gestures Bob was making it was obvious: *Yeah, I'm the senior commander on the ground, but we didn't do this – they did.*

As Major Bryant handed the monkeys over to Grant – he was still the ground commander, after all – Tricky, Wag and me moved well out of the way. The RMPs came to a halt before *Sunray*, looking seriously nonplussed. They were staring at him with his long black hair, thick growth of straggly beard and unwashed, grungy combats, searching desperately for some indication of rank.

'Sergeant Blick and Sergeant Block, from 160 Provost Company,' one of them announced. 'We've been sent out here to investigate the incident . . . sir?'

We left Grant to brief them: the joys of command.

If anything could encapsulate the ludicrous, misguided priorities of Her Majesty's Armed Forces this was it. We were twenty-six blokes who'd been denied a QRF when we most needed it, and were yet to have a proper ammo resupply. We were here with no body armour, no grenades, no HE mortar rounds, not enough ammo in the first place, not enough water until the Water Girls had taken charge, dodgy rifles, dodgy night sights, dodgy rations – the list went on and on . . .

Yet at the same time someone, somewhere believed it was a good and proper use of Army time, money and resources to fly these two idiots out to Lungi Lol. It was beyond comprehension. It was mind-numbingly messed-up. But most of all, after what we had just fought through and survived, it made my blood boil.

It was a combination of luck, plus sheer bloody-minded good

soldiering that we hadn't lost a lot of lads when their SA80s jammed, or the GPMG ammo started to run dry during the long night's battle. Yet the fuel costs alone of flying those two wankers in would have covered the cost of each and every one of us getting M16s, with oodles of ammo to spare.

I could hear the CH-47 that had dropped the RMPs flying an orbit to the west of us. Presumably it was waiting for them to be done with whatever crap they were here for. It was scandalous. Lives were being put at risk due to the age-old excuse – 'lack of resources' – yet we could still fly two RMPs into Lungi Lol for a nice little jolly.

The RMPs had been on the ground for no more than fifteen minutes when they decided they were done. They saluted Major Bryant as smartly as before: 'Provost Company investigation complete, sir!' I had one thought going through my head: *as if anyone gives a damn, you self-important tossers.*

For a whole minute after their helo took off we just stared at it in stunned disbelief.

The silence was broken by Wag. 'Does anyone have the slightest fucking clue what just happened? Tell me I've been dreaming . . .'

'No, mate,' I told him, 'I saw them too. Two monkeys just rocked up, did whatever the fuck they do and now they're gone.'

Wag turned to Grant. 'So, are you going to jail or what?'

Grant rolled his eyes. 'No, mate, I think I'm all right on this one.'

I told Wag the obvious: it was time to get a feed and a brew on, plus clean our wanky SA80s.

The RMPs gone, Mojo came pottering down the track driving the same blue pick-up that had earlier carried the dead rebel into the village. He parked up by the corpses, and his men jumped down from the rear. Under Mojo's instructions they took hold of the rebel bodies, threw them into the back, and headed out west to bury them. Top news. At least now there were a few less rebel lunatics around to slice up Ibrahim, the Water Girls, Mojo, or Nathe's trench-digging boys.

Thirty minutes after the RMPs had left we heard another Chinook heading in. This one put down on the regular resupply LZ, and we had to presume it was Colonel Gibson. Bob Bryant and his head-shed went down to receive them. A few minutes later he was back at the HQ ATAP with the colonel, The White Rabbit, Jacko and a bevy of others in tow.

We got to our feet to welcome them. The tradition is that you do not salute a commanding officer if you're not wearing any form of headdress – a helmet, jungle hat or beret. We were all of us bareheaded, so Grant greeted the CO with a handshake.

Gibbo shot out his hand. 'Grant!'

Behind Gibbo were stood the others, and I got a few nods of greeting – but they couldn't come forward until the colonel and Grant were done with their meet and greet. At the same time Bob Bryant was bobbing about, anxious to be seen to be in control.

'Right, sir, this is what we need to do ...' he began, but the colonel waved him into silence.

'Hold on, Bob, I want to hear from Grant.'

The two of them had a good old chinwag, and then Grant motioned for the CO to take a walk around the positions. As soon as they were gone the others moved in. Jacko was typical Jacko – a shock of wavy, bouncy, bouffant blond hair above an old Second World War leather shoulder holster, with his pistol slung inside. He was like Lawrence of Arabia – a throwback to an older, more innocent age. Everyone loved Jacko, and especially his hail-fellow-well-met attitude.

'Fucking hell, Jacko, you'd get where shite couldn't,' Wag greeted him – referring to his having taken over command of us lot, Donaldson being gone.

Jacko held out a hand for Wag to shake. 'Hah, hah, hah. Well done. Bloody incredible. Excellent. Bloody well done.'

Jacko tried really hard to swear like a 'proper' soldier. He'd ·th bloody, damn and shit, escalating finally to a fuck, but even his 'fucks' sounded posh. We gathered in the HQ depression, passing a brew amongst us – sippers, naturally.

Jacko leant forward excitedly. 'The CO – he's fucking bubbling over! He's telling everyone – we gave those rebels a damn good shoeing. Right, tell me the story. What bloody happened here?'

For a good fifteen minutes or so we proceeded to relate most of it, and there was a real sense of decompressing here.

'How are the men?' Jacko asked me, once we were done. 'How are the men?'

'Mega,' I told him. 'They performed brilliantly. We couldn't have asked for more.'

Jacko nodded, vigorously. 'CO's bloody impressed. Bloody well impressed. Taught those rebels a thing or two.'

'Where did Captain Cantrill go?' I asked Jacko. 'Did he transit via Lungi?'

'Yes, and he looked as if he'd seen a bloody thing or two, I can tell you!'

After a good few minutes of us lot chewing the fat, Colonel Gibson, Bob Bryant, Grant and the rest returned from their walkabout.

Gibbo plonked himself down on the lip of the depression. 'Fucking Pathfinders . . . I knew I could count on you lot. I knew, I knew when I put you here it was a bloody good decision.'

We chatted for a while and then the colonel got up to go. But as he went to leave he turned back, and called over his shoulder: 'Steve, can I have a word?'

We walked out of the depression towards Wag's gym area. We stood there in the shade, out of anyone's hearing. The colonel pulled out his water bottle, took a good swig, then offered it to me.

'Nah, it's okay, sir, I've got some.'

'Tremendous action by the Pathfinders. Tremendous.'

'Thanks, sir. The blokes were fantastic. The right men for the right job.'

He fixed me with this look. 'Is that what you're telling me, Steve? The Pathfinders have got the right men on the ground now?'

I knew what he was driving at. 'Yeah. Absolutely, sir. Absolutely.'

'Good.' He screwed the top on his water bottle and slotted it into his belt kit. 'That's what I needed to hear.'

With that, we returned to the HQ ATAP. I made my way back into the depression, Colonel Gibson heading off to have words with Bob Bryant. The colonel signalled for Grant and Jacko to join him, and there was an animated discussion between the four of them – the CO, Bob Bryant, Jacko and Grant.

Everyone else was staring at me. 'So what was all that about, with Gibbo?'

I shrugged. 'He just said give the blokes a big chuck up. Well done. And he just wanted to check that we're the right men on the ground now. So I told him – yeah, we are.'

A few moments later Jacko rejoined us. He had a massive smile on his face.

'Bob was angling to stay,' he chortled. 'Said it was an ideal 1 PARA role, and they were fresh on the ground. The CO cut him short: "No, Bob, this is a Pathfinder tasking. Things can only get worse. I need soldiers on the ground who can look after themselves and move through and live in the jungle. Your force cannot do that. Bob, you will stay today, but I will withdraw you tomorrow morning. That's my decision – final." Bloody CO told it like it was!'

It made sense. By keeping the PARAs here for a day we'd get a twenty-four-hour break, before we were back in the hot seat.

It was also pretty clear that Gibbo was right when he'd said 'things could only get worse'. The White Rabbit had given us a heads-up on the flood of Intel they'd got in over the last few hours. The rebels had declared that 'the British troops at Lungi Lol will pay in blood for what they have done'. They had to take Lungi Lol and make good on Operation Kill British, or they'd lose all credibility.

And so the rebel commanders had declared an all-out onslaught.

24

We pulled the patrol commanders in so Grant could brief them. 'Right, guys, the decision's been taken that we stay. The CO's keeping us here. Period.'

'Good.'

'Great.'

'That's only right.'

'Fucking right, as well.'

'But there's a real chance now we're going to be facing an on-slaught,' Grant continued. 'The rebels have taken a beating and they're thirsting for revenge, so be prepared.'

'Yeah, fuck 'em.'

'Let 'em come.'

'I've been told 1 PARA will be staying the night and they'll be lifted out tomorrow morning. So take this oppo to get some serious rest, get some food inside you, and get personal kit squared away, 'cause tonight could be fun and games.'

All were good with that. We now had a platoon of 1 PARA lads in place, plus the twenty-six of us lot. That meant fifty-six all told, facing whatever the rebels intended to throw at us. Colonel Gibson had promised us all the weaponry and support we could wish for, so I sat with Wag drawing up our bucket list.

'Half a dozen Claymores,' I started. Wag noted it down. 'Grenades, if they're in-country, and 3500 rounds of 7.62 mm link for the guns; another two bandoliers of ammo each for the SA80s, plus 51 mm HE . . .'

Wag glanced up from his pen and paper. 'Tell you what, let's ask for a couple of 81 mm mortars.'

I grinned. 'Yeah, why not?'

We finished scribbling the list, then handed it to Jacko to get sorted. The CO and his retinue were flying out complete with the wounded girl – the one that Bri Budd had patched up – so she could be given some proper hospital treatment. The girl's mum was going with her, so it looked as if Bri wasn't going to be having a Lungi Lol wedding any time soon.

The colonel's retinue plus-some loaded up the Chinook and it took to the skies, which left us here for the duration.

With the 1 PARA lads manning our posts, we were looking forward to the first proper night's rest in eleven days – that's if the rebels didn't hit us tonight. We got fresh Intel in that evening, gleaned from intercepts of rebel mobile phone calls. They had taken a serious number of dead and injured. Their commanders were incandescent with rage: predictably, they were coming back at us with everything they'd got.

Just before last light Mojo rocked up.

'What, no bread tonight?' I joked.

He looked confused. 'No, no, not tonight – I do not think so.'

Mojo didn't really get the British sense of humour. He was incredibly formal and regimented, and wind-ups and piss-taking just weren't his thing.

'What happened to the bodies?' I asked.

'We took them into the jungle and we buried them.'

'Right, good work.'

Out on the darkening road a crowd of locals hurried past. I could sense their fear, and I knew instinctively they were headed for the village square. When I asked Mojo what was what, he confirmed what we'd suspected: all day long they'd had villagers turning up at Lungi Lol, reporting news of work parties being forced to bury the rebel dead and carry their injured.

Come nightfall, the inrush of villagers into Lungi Lol got the PARAs into a massive state of heightened alert. The tension was thick and greasy in the darkness – like you could cut it with a knife.

Bob was up and about, looking restless and twitchy. He jabbed an angry finger towards the villagers moving along the road. 'Right, we've got to fucking stop those people! They could be anyone!'

'How will you stop them, Bob?' Grant queried. 'They've been coming in for days now. Are you going to physically stop and search each one? They're women and children from outlying villages. They're coming here for sanctuary. That's why we're here.'

Bob snorted like a bull. 'Well, I'm not bloody happy there are people moving in and taking up residence in this village, and I don't know who they are.'

'What are you going to do about it then?' Grant repeated.

For a while longer Bob huffed, puffed and tried to blow the house down – before he gave up. The quiet descended over us again. It was so silent that I imagined I could hear a leaf falling in the forest. Even the insects seemed to have canned it for the night. We'd resumed our dark-hours sentry routine, because we didn't want to risk getting jumped by the rebels.

Wag and me took the first stag. 'You know what this is, don't you, mate?' I whispered to him.

'What what is?'

'This silence?'

'What, mate?'

'It's the quiet before the storm. They are out there at the moment, licking their wounds, and they are fucking mustering every man they can lay their hands on.'

Wag nodded. 'Yeah, I know.'

Silence.

By first light the feared onslaught hadn't materialised. We guessed it was taking a while to organise the kind of numbers they wanted to throw at us.

Meanwhile, we ripped the piss out of the PARAs, who were shortly going to be leaving. *They'll be back tonight; you can read about it in the newspapers.* Bob Bryant's face was as long as sin as he gathered his blokes to load up the incoming helo.

He had a few last words with Grant, then to everyone at the HQ ATAP: 'Good luck, Pathfinders.'

The Chinook came in at 0800 hours, ready to whisk the PARAs away. But first off the open ramp came these guys hefting the unmistakable forms of 81 mm mortars. The 81 mm is a seriously heavy piece of kit, and it comes in three lumps. First off the helo were what looked like three 81 mm tubes. Next came three base plates, like large steel dustbin lids, and finally the bipod legs.

Wag turned to me. 'Fuck me, we got the 81 mm mortars. Three of 'em!'

Next came the big green boxes of 81 mm mortar ammo – each round weighing some four kilograms. There were fifty illume rounds and fifty HE per tube. Even with the 1 PARA lads helping, it took a good fifteen minutes to unload all the ammo. *Shit.* With the mortars in position and this much ammo to hand, we really would have transformed this place into Sierra Leone's Alamo.

Mortars stacked up, we got our own ammo resupply off the helo. Once that was unloaded, we gave Bob the thumbs-up, the PARAs climbed aboard and the Chinook got airborne again. Wag and me were left surrounded by a massive pile of war *matériel*, plus eleven new guys – the 1 PARA mortar teams.

Each team consisted of three mortar men. They hailed from 1 PARA's Support Company, and their mortar teams are renowned throughout the British Army as being some of the best in the business. If we needed 81 mm HE rounds dropped down the rebels' throats, these were the guys to do it.

I knew the lead Mortar Fire Controller (MFC), ALPHA, a bloke called Mike 'Tommo' Thomson, plus his 2iC, Joe Caveney, from my 3 PARA days.

We shook hands. 'All right, Tommo? Joe?'

'Hear you was fucking mixing it up the other night?'

I nodded. 'Yeah, that's what you're here for.'

'Yeah, we're here to please.'

I did the intros with Wag. Then: 'Tell you what, you guys walk into the village with us, and leave a couple of blokes on stag, and we'll come back down with the Pinz for the ammo and the tubes.'

'Yeah, gleaming, mate, gleaming.'

As we made our way up the track towards the village square I briefed the guys. 'I'll leave it in your hands, Tommo, but what we need, mate, is a wall of protective fire – 81 mm rounds – all around village, and we'll talk you through a target list once we get you settled.'

'Okay, mate, okay.'

'Under your guidance, Tommo, let's look at the siting of the mortars and discuss marking and targeting.'

'You show me what you want, I'll site the tubes and we'll go from there.'

We got the resupply of ammo distributed around our patrols. By the time we were done, Tommo was already getting the mortars dug in. He was a total whirlwind of energy, and we could see him in the centre of the village getting his blokes wound up to speed. Mortar pit one was sited opposite the chief's house. Pit two was across from it, on the far side of the track, and pit three was staggered back from those two.

Tommo and his lads slotted together these collapsible shovels. They marked out each mortar pit, which would consist of a circular depression some seven feet across, and then they started to dig.

Wag nodded in their direction. 'Someone needs to tell them Ibrahim can get a work gang on that.'

We laughed.

Tommo struck me as being like the British Army's equivalent of Ibrahim, and he certainly drew the crowds. The villagers were keeping their distance as Tommo and his boys worked, for it all looked decidedly dangerous. But they were clearly thinking – *what are the British Army up to now?*

Wag grabbed one of the belts of 7.62 mm link that we'd been re-supplied with, and broke it down by snapping out the rounds. He piled the 200 loose bullets into an empty ammo box and handed it to Mojo, telling him to get his boys to properly bomb up their mags with the extra ammo.

'Make sure it's in their mags, not in their pockets loose,' Wag told him. 'Make sure it's loaded, okay?'

'Okay, okay,' Mojo confirmed. 'In the magazines for the rifles. Very useful for where we will go if there is a problem.'

By that Mojo had to mean the trenches to the rear of the village.

It took barely an hour for Tommo and his boys to dig the mortar pits. Then the mortar base plate went down in the centre of the pit, looking like a spoked wheel laid on its side. The tube went next, a ball-and-joint connection attaching it to the heavy plate. Finally, the bipod legs locked onto the barrel. An hour and a half in and we could see three large tubes poking skywards. Next, they stacked the ammo into the rear of the pits – one pile of illume and one of HE.

That done, they started filling these empty hessian sandbags with dirt, building up a two-foot-high, double-bagged wall all around the pit. It was 1200 hours by the time they were done, and they had never bloody stopped. We now had a fully operational mortar line. The three blokes in each pit would never leave their station, unless to piss or to shit. They cooked, ate, slept and fought from there.

After some rushed scoff, Tommo and Joe came to scope out some targets with us. We walked along the main track, passing the point where the rebel bodies had been piled up.

'Right, mate, you advise,' I started, 'but this is what we think the rebels did when they hit us, and what we reckon they'll do next time.'

Joe and Tommo got out notebooks and maps and held them at the ready.

I talked them around the maps. 'This, mate, is the point where we think they first broke cover and came across open ground to hit us. It's about 1.2 klicks out.'

Tommo nodded, vigorously. 'Where the track meets that feature, we'll mark that as the first target – Xray 1-1. Where else?'

'We think they broke out of the jungle there, mate.'

'Right – Xray 1-2.'

'Plus see where the train line drops into that dead ground there – that was another massing point.'

'Right – Xray 1-3.'

In this way we went around the maps and over the terrain, selecting all the obvious targets we could hit with mortar fire. We finished off with Fern Gully, the last point from where they'd tried to overrun us.

'Put one target at the far end of Fern Gully,' I told him, 'so we can bring fire down there, and one at the near end.'

'Right – Xray 1-7 and Xray 1-8,' Tommo confirmed. 'We'll give 'em all Xray numbers, to keep it simple-stupid. It needs to be so simple that under fire your guys can have a copy of this target list, and any one of them can call in the fire. All they need to say is: enemy movement Xray 1-5 . . .'

'Fantastic.' I paused, then glanced at Tommo. 'Mate, they got fucking close last time.'

'Yeah, mate, I 'eard.'

'So, we need an FPF.'

FPF stands for Final Protective Fire – in other words, calling in mortar rounds on top of your own position.

Tommo scrunched his face up. 'Right . . . You want an FPF?'

'Yeah, we do. What's the closest you can give us?'

Tommo scratched his shaven head. 'Officially, I can't come closer than 250 metres to friendly force troops. But you know how it is . . . The order to fire the FPF will have to come from Grant, though, mate, 'cause he's the senior man on the ground.'

I told him we were good with that.

'The mortar may get a drop-short, so you're pretty much dropping on your own men,' Tommo added. 'To be clear, mate, the FPF is pretty much only ever fired if we are about to get overrun: it's the last thing we can do. Once we've fired the FPF the mortars are pretty much useless. We'll have been overrun.'

'Okay, Tommo, yeah, I know ... So we need to build you into our withdrawal plans. How about this: you fire the FPF, throw what you can on the back of the Pinz, then you and your blokes jump aboard and get the fuck out of Dodge.'

Tommo grinned. 'Okay, mate, got it.'

'One other thing,' I added. 'We've lived here with the villagers and become like a part of the place. Tell your blokes they have to shit down at the crappers, over near Taff's position. Plus we'll be getting you an early morning water delivery sorted, plus a delivery of bread rolls in the evenings ...'

Tommo stared at me for a second. 'You serious?'

'I'm serious.'

'Right, bang on, mate, bang on.'

We ran through the plans in more detail, based on the fact that we expected a tidal wave of rebels. The eleven blokes in the mortar team were fit, robust PARAs, but they weren't trained to E & E or for jungle survival – hence the plan being that they'd take the Pinzgauer. In an ideal world they'd fire the FPF, collapse the mortar tubes and load them on the wagon, before hitting the road. That way we'd prevent the 81 mms from falling into rebel hands.

But Plan B involved blowing up the mortars, if they had to move real quickly. We used the last of the PE4 to make up three charges, each with a three-minute fuse.

'If we give you the signal to withdraw and there's no time to salvage the tubes, you simply light the end of the safety fuse,' I told them. 'Pile a dozen HE rounds around the mortar, for some extra umph, and you've got three minutes from the point of lighting the fuse to make your getaway.'

Tommo nodded. 'Got it.'

With the mortar positions and procedures sorted, Tommo and Joe moved up to co-locate with us in the HQ ATAP. That way they could get eyes-on the battlefront to better call in fire, plus they would be the relay between our patrols and the mortar pits. We'd just about got them settled in, when Mojo came to see us bearing an invitation to visit the village chief. We hadn't seen or spoken to him since the rebel attack, so a chinwag was long overdue.

'Yeah, we need to talk to him anyway,' I told Mojo. 'We need to tell him about the mortars. If they start firing it will be very loud and what we don't want is for the villagers to think they're getting hit. They need to know to stay in their huts and to expect some big explosions.'

We wandered over to the chief's place. Mojo rattled on for a while about the mortars, relaying what we'd just said, and then the chief spoke to Mojo at some length. He was about the most animated that I'd ever seen him.

Mojo turned to us to translate. 'The chief says he is very grateful to you British. You have saved his people and the village. And he says thank you for helping the girl who was badly injured and for taking her to safety.'

'We're here to help you and protect you,' Grant reassured him. 'That's what we're here for.'

'And we're here to stay,' I added.

The chief thanked us again, and with that we returned to our battle stations. We called the patrol commanders in and briefed them on all the Xray target co-ordinates that we'd sorted with the mortar teams. Pathfinders are trained to call in mortar fire anyway, so this was like second nature to us. I could see this light burning in the blokes' eyes. It was the extra sense of confidence that three 81 mm mortars, plus an extra bandolier or two of ammo each, brings.

If needed, we knew we could mallet the rebels with 81 mm HE

rounds. It's one thing being shot at by small arms, quite another being plastered with that kind of highly accurate and murderous heavy fire. The 81 mms would be a battle-changer, or so we fucking hoped.

'They're coming,' I warned the blokes, 'and the hammer will fall hardest here tonight. Any one of you, if you hear or see anything you can call for illume ... Be mindful HE will come if you call for it, but there are a lot of civvies out there trying to get in here to safety, so we need to be under rebel fire before we bring in HE. Last thing we need is to drop on the locals and destroy all the goodwill. So, we can't just call in HE on any movement. It's not ideal, but we need to be taking fire from a position before we can hit it. Put the call through, and Tommo and Joe will put up the illume, with HE to follow if and when it all goes noisy.'

That was it. Briefing done.

It was around mid-afternoon when Tricky got warning via the Thuraya to expect another set of visitors – only this time it was about as high-up as it could get. Brigadier Richards, the overall force commander, was flying in for a heads-up. I cast my mind back to the promise he'd made several days earlier, to Sierra Leone's embattled leader, President Kabbah – that the British military would end the war in Sierra Leone by knocking seven bales of shit out of the rebels.

Well, I guessed here in Lungi Lol we'd made a decent start.

Brigadier Richards flew in on a Special Forces Chinook, and Grant and me were there to do the meet and greet. He had with him his Military Assistant, Major Mark Mangham, plus his close protection (CP) team. He spent about an hour on the ground chatting with us, plus as many of the lads as he could get around. And he had a good natter to the locals, who couldn't have made it clearer how happy they were that we'd kicked the rebels' butts.

The Brigadier confided in us that it had been his ultimate decision to put us this far out and exposed in the jungle, and that he was mightily relieved we'd stood firm in the face of the onslaught.

In fact, he'd sited us here deliberately to lure the rebels out, knowing how vital it was that British force gave them a right bloody nose early on – to establish our moral and fighting superiority from the start.

What we'd achieved here was crucial to the Brigadier's overall game plan in Sierra Leone, and making good on his promise to President Kabbah. It came as a bit of a surprise to learn that we'd been used as the bait in a trap to snare the RUF. Still, all's well that ends well – not that this was over yet. Far from it . . .

The Brigadier's was of necessity a flying visit. With him and his team gone Mojo rocked up at the HQ ATAP. The same cardboard tray as always was balanced on his shoulder. His arrival was pre-announced by the whiff of . . . freshly baked bread.

'I have the bread!' he announced. He glanced at Joe and Tommo. 'Also, I have for your friends.'

Tommo and Joe were staring at Mojo, like they couldn't quite believe it. I'd warned them about the bread and water deliveries, but maybe they'd thought it was a wind-up. Tommo was a typical chirpy cockney type, but right now he seemed lost for words.

'Don't worry about it, mate,' I told him, 'you're gonna be scoffing on some nice fresh bread.'

Wag loved getting around the blokes doing the bread delivery. The oldest man amongst us, he was like the father figure of the unit. *Dad's here with the bread rolls.* I could hear him counting them out in the background.

'Mate, can you manage up to thirty-seven?' I needled him.

'Fuck off, Smoggy . . . Yeah,' he confirmed, once he was done counting, 'all your blokes got bread too.'

Tommo's grin split his face ear-to-ear. 'Fucking hell! Diamond geezer, that Mojo.'

Wag counted out the rolls for the mortar teams. ''Ere you go – take yours. Take your eleven.'

Tommo eyed the stack of bread. 'Where the fuck am I gonna put all that?'

'No idea,' said Wag.

'Tell you what, I'll open me daysack and fucking put it in there,' Tommo decided.

Leaving Tommo to make his bread delivery, Wag and me headed for Dolly's position.

'Yeah, I've got the bread,' Wag announced, as we neared their trenches.

Dolly chuckled. 'Oh, the bread's back. We thought the baker had done a runner.'

'Nope, he's still here.'

By the time we'd done the rounds of the battle trenches and got back to the HQ ATAP, Jacko had been on the radio with that evening's Sched. Grant made sure to read out the message to us all, Tommo and Joe included.

'Fucking standby, standby. Every, every source of info we have is that they're coming at you with everything they've got and most likely tonight.'

After Grant was finished there was a kind of collective rabbit-eyed stare from the blokes.

I broke the silence, doing my best impression of Michael Caine's accent in the movie *Zulu*: 'Zulus, sir.' 'How many?' 'Fucking thasands of 'em.'

Tommo chuckled. 'Yeah, fun and games tonight. Fucking going to get busy.'

As darkness descended on Lungi Lol we kept getting hourly up-dates from Jacko, via the Thuraya. With the rebels using mobile phones to co-ordinate their movements, and with our spooks having cracked the phone intercepts, I figured he was getting a live update on exactly what the RUF commanders were saying.

'They're advancing on your position and there are thousands,' Jacko relayed to us. 'They are coming to attack in great strength. Be ready for the onslaught.'

We figured every rebel and his dog would be in on this one, minus those we had already killed and wounded. As we stared down our rifle barrels into the gathering darkness, we were readying ourselves to get hit by a dark tidal wave.

All evening the tension rose, as villagers flooded in. It was like a mass influx of refugees now. But by around midnight the movement had died to nothing, and all went quiet. Then we started to hear the noises. It was a repeat performance of the night we were hit – unearthly, spectral screams and screeches echoing across to us. Amidst the ghostly cries we figured we could see fleeting movement, as shadows flickered back and forth across the tree line.

Dolly's patrol was the first to put out the call. 'Put up illume over Xray 1-4. Possible movement.'

Tommo and Joe relayed the radio message to their teams: 'Fire illume Xray 1-4.'

An instant later the first 81 mm mortar went up with a massive thump.

We waited the eight seconds or so it took to climb to the heavens and then: *fzzzztttttt!* It was like a giant party-popper being unleashed high above us.

The flare hung in the sky like a mini-sun. The cone of blinding light it cast was far wider than that of the puny 51 mm that Cantrill and I had been using. But despite its size and its brightness, we couldn't hear even the barest hint of the thing fizzing. It was utterly soundless as it drifted, sparked and burned. It struck me how eerie it was that so much light could fall upon us, but in total silence.

Everyone was awake now – those on stag and those not on stag. All of us were on a knife-edge as we waited for the first shots to ring out – signalling the onslaught was upon us. We'd agreed between us only to use '*maximise*' if we'd clearly seen armed rebels massing, or if we were under fire.

The silence lengthened as the flare floated earthwards, and still no shots hammered out from the tree line. Finally, the flare drifted behind the fringe of jungle and all went dark.

A short message came in from Dolly: 'Roger, out.'

In other words, nothing seen as yet to justify giving *maximise*.

The rebels had their own mortars, that we knew. We had to presume they'd brought them forward to hit our positions, plus their 12.7 mm DShKs and their 'United Nations' armoured personnel carriers (APCs). Each patrol had a LAW lying at the ready, in anticipation of seeing a rebel gun truck or one of those ex-UN APCs come lumbering out of the jungle.

Next up on the air was Ginge: '*33 Charlie*: put up illume over Xray 1-6.'

Tommo did a repeat relay, and the second 81 mm round went up. It too drifted into darkness with no shots having been fired.

Next, Nathe was on the air: 'That's not a fucking animal noise over at Xray 1-7. Get some illume up – let's have a look.'

Another 81 mm round lit up the heavens, this one to the front of *33 Alpha*'s battle trenches. Because the rebels had got so close in the first battle, we wanted to hit them and smash them as early and as far out from the village as we possibly could. We figured they were probing us again now, and testing our reaction times. Either way they seemed determined to keep us awake all night, allowing no one to get a wink of sleep.

Come first light, we'd fired a good twenty illume rounds all along our front. No one moved through the jungle between midnight and 0500 apart from the rebels. None of us had any doubts that they were out there in the cover of the trees, massing in serious strength, as their commanders put the final touches to their plan of attack. Still, sunrise brought a real sense of relief. We didn't figure they'd hit us during the daylight hours.

We'd had maybe a thousand extra villagers dossing down in Lungi Lol that night. They'd been terrified of what the darkness would bring. Well, tonight at least it had brought them no gunshot wounds, no horror of capture, nor the brutal torture and amputations that would follow. With the rebels' anger being such as it was, presumably they planned to wreak terrible vengeance. They would know by now how the villagers here were in league with us, and they would torture their very souls.

No ground assault had materialised that night, but it occurred to us that maybe we were being played by the rebels. In the Vietnam War the Vietcong had adopted a tactic designed to exhaust their American enemy: it was to probe and harass a position all night long, night after night after night. They had set up shifts to do so, making sure that the American soldiers got no sleep. Over successive nights the tension and the sleeplessness had proved exhausting, until finally the Vietcong had launched an attack from out of the darkness.

We figured the rebels were doing the same now, hoping that sooner or later they'd catch us napping.

25

There hadn't been the slightest hint of what was coming. It hit us like a bombshell.

For night after night now we'd been probed by the rebels, and night after night we'd put up the 81 mm rounds to deter them. We'd pushed out foot patrols during the day into the jungle, and found all the usual signs that the rebels had been there massing to attack, but still the expected onslaught hadn't come.

After so many sleepless nights we'd more or less lost track of how long we'd been here. We were counting out the days in bread and water deliveries. But of one thing we had been certain: *we were here for the duration.* No rebels were fucking us out of Lungi Lol, or wreaking havoc on this village.

Not our village.

Not on our watch.

Not while we still had ammo and men to fight.

We'd been expecting a normal evening's Sched: *rebels are poised to hit you; be ready; stand firm.* I could see Tricky beavering away with his notepad as he scribbled down an extra-long message, so I guessed we'd got some extra-juicy Intel in.

He stopped scribbling and stared hard at what he'd written for several seconds. Then he turned and handed it to Grant, his face like death.

'Fucking hell, mate,' he muttered, 'you'd better read that...'

This wasn't Tricky. He wasn't the melodramatic type. He was calm, cool, collected and laid-back to the point of horizontal. We were all sat up now, listening hard.

Grant ran his eye over the message: 'Fuuuuuck...'

Me and Wag both said it at once. 'Fucking hurry up and read it, then.'

Grant stared at us for a long moment. Then he flicked his eyes down, and started to read: 'PF withdrawal, plus 1 PARA, DTG 250800MAY00. Full stop. Resupply HLS. Full stop. No relief in place.'

'Read it again,' I rasped.

Grant repeated it word for word. Twice. Then he glanced up at me. 'Basically, from the resupply HLS at 0800 tomorrow we're all to withdraw. There will be no relief. Isn't that what it means?'

We sat there staring at each other.

For ages.

In utter silence.

Finally, Grant repeated the question: 'Isn't that what it means? Or am I missing something? So what are your thoughts on that?'

'I'll tell you what my thoughts are on that, Grant, mate: it means we're being pulled out, and no fucker's coming in to take our place.'

The reality of what this meant was just starting to hit us. 'But d'you really think . . . D'you really think they can just . . . ?' Grant's words petered into silence.

'Look at it this way, mate: for us to be relieved, some other blokes would have to come in to do a handover, like we half-did with Cantrill. They'd need to get boots on the ground and scope out our positions, and only once they were in would we pull out. That's how a RIP works. There's no way we're getting on a helo tomorrow and when we've left the village unoccupied a bunch of Marines will fly in and reoccupy. It just doesn't work that way.'

Grant was ashen-faced. 'But . . .'

'Steve's right,' Wag cut in. 'It looks like they're pulling us out and no fucker is coming in. We bail out. Village abandoned. End of.'

Grant shook his head, disbelievingly. 'No. No. They wouldn't just pull us out? After so many days manning these positions and with the threat still out there, surely they'd put someone back in?'

'Well, maybe all units are being pulled out of country,' I suggested. 'Op over. Endex. Or maybe we're being pulled out onto another task. You never know.'

'Yeah, but they wouldn't just pull us out and leave the village unoccupied,' Grant repeated. 'Surely they wouldn't do that?'

'Yeah, 'cause that's pretty much leaving the village unprotected. Undefended,' Tricky added.

Wag nodded. 'And especially now we've poked a stick into the hornet's nest big time.'

Grant glanced around at our faces. 'They wouldn't, would they? Surely?'

For twenty-odd minutes this went around and around and around. At the end we decided that based on the scanty information provided we had no option but to conclude the unthinkable: we were being pulled out of Lungi Lol, and no force was coming in our place.

We called the patrol commanders in to brief them. I didn't envy Grant's position as he stood up to face the blokes.

'Right, guys, we've just got orders over the net,' Grant began. 'Us lot and the 1 PARA mortar lads are being pulled out tomorrow morning at 0800. We're heading back to Lungi Airport.' Long, heavy pause. 'At the moment I have no more info on whether it's a retasking. All I do know is that right now there's no RIP by the Marines.'

Grant's words were met with utter silence.

It was broken finally by Nathe. 'So why aren't the fucking Marines coming?'

Grant shrugged. 'I don't know, Nathe. This is all we've got.'

'So who *is* coming, then?' Nathe probed.

'As I've said, Nathe, at the moment the message indicates that nobody is.'

A few seconds' silence for the words to sink in; a long, heavy beat.

'*Fucking nobody is?*' Nathe snorted, in disbelief. 'So who is going to protect the village, then? Who's gonna fucking look after them?'

'Well, I presume, Nathe, when we're gone the Nigerians will stay. So, it's over to them.'

'*The fucking Nigerians.* Get real. What the fuck're the Nigerians gonna do?'

'Look, Nathe, I am just telling you what we've got over radio, mate. Whatever decisions have been made, it's way above my pay grade. It's already been decided, mate.'

'Well, it's total fucking bollocks.' Nathe was so angry his two false front teeth had started to rattle about. 'It's utter bloody fucking bollocks that is.'

The other patrol commanders were murmuring their agreement. Nathe was right, of course. It *was* utter bloody fucking bollocks. But there was sod all we could do about it right now.

'Okay, okay, *guys*,' Wag tried to calm it. 'Fully understand emotions are running fucking high. We feel the same here, but the decision's been made, so we gotta get on with it. End of.'

There was a lot of angry muttering from the blokes. I tried to focus minds on what lay ahead – the logistics of organising the withdrawal – for none of us had had the slightest inkling this was coming.

'Right, guys, minds on admin, 'cause we've got a fuck load to do before now and 0800 tomorrow. Make sure shortly after first light you bring in and dismantle the Claymores. Do not leave anything one of the villagers could hurt themselves with. Plus make sure you do a hundred per cent kit check; when you get the order to-morrow, move direct from your positions to HLS. Any questions?'

Silence.

Nothing.

Angry, dark silence.

'Make sure you say your goodbyes before then,' I continued. I figured Nathe needed a tasking to take his mind off the shit sand-wich that was being forced down everyone's throat right now.

'Nathe, there'll be no room on the Chinook for everyone plus the Pinz, so I want your team to drive it back pretty much after first light tomorrow.'

He grunted an acknowledgement.

I turned to the two mortar lads. 'Tommo, make sure you take care of your blokes and dismantle your mortars when you see fit to do so.'

'Okay,' Tommo confirmed, quietly.

'Right, guys, just before we wrap.' I glanced around the faces before me: Nathe, Dolly, Ginge, Taff and H. I'd never seen the lads like this before. There was bitter anger and defiance seething just below the surface. 'None of us wants this. None of us has asked for it. But, for better or worse, this is our last night. So, let's keep everything wired tight and let's get out of here in one piece.'

Without a word of acknowledgement the five of them turned and melted away. I knew what they faced now. They were returning to their patrols to brief their blokes that we were leaving Lungi Lol to its fate – and that meant leaving the villagers, plus the thousands more who'd come here seeking sanctuary. It wasn't exactly how I'd ever imagined us leaving this place ... or how I wanted us to go. Granted, we'd been here for days since the main attack, and still the rebels hadn't hit the village – but that didn't make it any easier on any of us.

No sooner were the blokes gone than the familiar figure of Mojo pitched up, tray-load of bread rolls perched on his shoulder. Grant glanced up at him, dejectedly.

'Mojo, mate, I need a word.'

Grant was sat on the lip of the depression with a face like death. Mojo was standing. He'd never once sat down with us all the time we'd been here. He was a stand-to-attention man through and through.

Grant gestured at a spot on the ground beside him. 'Mojo, take a seat.'

'No, no – I stand, I stand.'

'No, Mojo, sit down.'

Mojo sat down. He still had his Foster Grant shades on of course, but from behind them he was eyeing Grant nervously.

'Mojo, I've got some bad news,' Grant announced.

'Huh?'

'We have had a radio message this evening. We will all be leaving in the morning.'

'Leaving?'

'Yep.'

'All?'

'Yep.'

'And when will you come back?'

'We won't be coming back, Mojo.'

Mojo shook his head, confusedly. 'You won't come back?'

'We won't be coming back, no.'

Mojo tried a hopeful smile. 'And other British – they will come?'

Grant glanced at him. 'I honestly don't know – but I think not.'

'Nobody will come? Nobody?'

'Nobody will come. Mojo, you'll be here on your own until you have to leave.'

It was then that Mojo took his sunglasses off. For the first time in so many days we actually got sight of his eyes. He twisted the shades around in his hands, nervously, as he tried to take in all Grant had said.

'But what will happen now?'

'I don't know.' Grant's tone was very soft now. Wrapped in emotion. He shook his head. 'Mojo, I don't know.'

For several long moments we sat there, all of us enveloped in this heavy silence.

Then Grant said to Mojo: 'Will you take me to speak to the chief?'

'I will take you to speak to him,' Mojo confirmed.

He got up and put his sunglasses back on. I stood up and put my hand out. 'Mojo, thank you. And thank your men. Take care.'

As we shook hands I could tell he was still in shock. 'Thank you,' he replied. 'Thank you – for everything.'

Wag and Tricky likewise said their goodbyes.

As Grant and Mojo stepped away, Wag turned after them. 'I'll be coming with you, mate.'

Wag hurried after Grant, leaving Tricky and me alone in the HQ depression, staring at the tray of thirty-seven bread rolls, lying white and skull-like in the moonlight. I'd happily have faced another rebel onslaught, crawling forward with 51 mm mortar and SA80 in hand, than have to do what Grant and Wag were about to do now – tell the chief we were bailing out of his village.

Their willingness to do that – *to do the right thing* – was the real test of a soldier. Grant could have chosen the easy path – to sneak away quietly. The decision to withdraw wasn't his, and it would have been so much easier to melt away. But he displayed the mark of a real man and demonstrated incredible moral courage, when he chose to take the hardest road possible, and Wag had volunteered to stand with him.

They were back fifteen minutes later. I glanced up at them, guiltily. 'Fucking hell, guys, how did that go?'

Grant shrugged. 'Emotional.'

'What . . . What did he say?'

'Well . . . when we told him, it was pretty much a repeat of Mojo; "You will go and come back? You will go and new British will come?" I told him I didn't think so: most likely no. He didn't rant and rave. He just said; "So, no one will come?" I confirmed most likely no one. I thanked him for all that he and his people had done. Told him how we felt a part of the village . . . His people took us in . . . Grown close to them . . . Felt real close . . . At that point I had to pull away . . . Just leave it at that.'

'Fucking hell. Fuck me. Heavy.'

Grant turned away. 'Yeah, mate. A bit emotional.'

Last light was almost upon us by now, after which we slipped into our night routine. Only, tonight wasn't like any night that had gone before. All across our positions blokes were somehow having to get their heads around the fact that we were out of here come morning, leaving the village all but defenceless.

It lay across us all, dark and heavy like a death shroud.

Grant and Tricky took first stag. I lay on the I-bed, gazing up at the heavens. It was an absolutely crystal clear night. Directly above me were fingers of wispy tree branches, and above those a skein of stars so close I felt I could reach out and touch them. A thousand villagers were bedded down on the square tonight – as they had been for so many nights before – gazing up at that same sky, feeling ... secure. Secure because of us. And little did they know that tomorrow we would be gone.

I lay there with my senses on hyper-alert and praying for the rebels to hit us. If the onslaught came tonight, at least we could smash seven bales of shit out of the bastard rebels, and maybe deter them forever from trying to take this village. Or, we could use the attack to argue for a change of plan – to allow us to stay, or at least until a replacement force was flown in. But all I could hear from the forest was the rhythmic *breep-breep-breep* of the night-time insects and the odd animal cry.

Tonight, I couldn't detect the barest hint of the rebels' presence, and come daybreak no illume would have been fired. But as I lay there on the I-bed unable to sleep, I realised something. I couldn't seem to remember coming into this village – our arrival. It was weird, but I felt like I'd always been here. As if it had always been like this. Life before Lungi Lol felt like a whole universe away.

I couldn't seem to remember any other life before this, but tomorrow we would be gone.

At first light the Water Girls arrived. But this time it was us lot who had our eyes downcast as they made their delivery. We tried telling them we didn't need the water, but the girls just stared at us like it didn't compute. *This was our early morning water delivery. We got it every day. What were we saying?*

At around 0630 Nathe led his patrol up to the HQ ATAP. He was trying to act businesslike and soldierly, but I could tell he was having a difficult time keeping a lid on things.

'Right, Steve, that's us,' he announced, gruffly. 'That's everything accounted for. We're gonna head back . . .'

With that he led his guys over to the lone Pinzgauer, they loaded up their kit and he got the wagon under way. I could see the mortar teams dismantling their tubes, and emptying the sandbags into the pits they'd dug. By now Dolly and Ginge's teams had collapsed their positions, so I asked them to help lug the mortars down to the LZ.

The village was a hive of soldierly activity, and all around I could see the locals pausing to stare. They had to be wondering what the hell was happening. As the mortars were manhandled towards the LZ there was a lot of serious kit on the move, and it wouldn't take the brains of an archbishop to realise what was happening.

It came the time for the four of us to move out from the HQ ATAP. We headed onto the track. All around us people had stopped doing whatever they had been doing, and were staring at us. I paused for an instant, gazing back into our position: the I-beds, Wag's gym, the path I'd crawled with Cantrill the night of the main battle. I tried to commit those things to memory, and then the four of us joined on the end of the long line of blokes heading south to the LZ.

We were the last guys out. Word had clearly spread like the plague, for by now we had scores of villagers lining the track, silent and watchful. I felt as if we were marching through a corridor of staring, fearful eyes. Many of the faces we knew by sight if not by name. We'd sat with them, played with their kids, shared their food and water; they'd built our beds and dug our trenches, cleared our arcs of fire and planted our punji fields.

They'd stood firm with us in the face of overwhelming enemy numbers.

And now we were just walking out of here.

I'd half expected Mojo, or Ibrahim, or the village chief to come and see us off, but there was no one. Instead, there was just a crowd of confused and bewildered villagers.

At 0820 the Chinook came in and landed. The patrols moved up the open tail ramp in two files, and Wag and me were the last to board. We walked into the helo side by side and took a pew. The turbines started to scream to a fever pitch above us, as the ramp whined closed.

As the helo took off the top half of the ramp was open, and when we turned westwards towards Lungi Airport I could see down into the village, barely fifty feet below us. My eyes traced the track leading up to the village square, and I could make out this wide sea of faces, all turned skywards and staring at us.

I glanced at Wag, who was seated opposite. Our eyes met. I could tell he was feeling as shitty as I was. His eyes said it all: *this is not right.*

I glanced along the row of blokes. A couple returned the look. But most had their heads leant back against the helo's side, eyes wide shut in the comedown of it all, and the exhaustion.

As the helo levelled out for the flight to the airport, I had conflicting thoughts crashing through my head. *Why were we not getting RIP'd? Why were we getting withdrawn after stirring up such a hornet's nest? Why were we on this helo, leaving the entire village in the shit . . . ?* I felt some relief that we'd got all the blokes out alive, but that was buried under an avalanche of fear and guilt for those we were leaving behind us.

And leaving behind, I feared, to the mercy of the rebels.

EPILOGUE

The men of the Pathfinders were flown back to the UK some forty-eight hours after withdrawing from the village of Lungi Lol. Upon returning to the UK they sought out information on the welfare of the villagers, by searching through British military post-operational reports, Sierra Leone government bulletins, local and international media reports and other intelligence sources.

Thankfully, no further rebel push came through Lungi Lol after they were withdrawn, and there was no attack on Lungi Airport. Those twenty-six Pathfinders had held Lungi Lol for sixteen days. They were not replaced by the Royal Marines, or any other troops for that matter. In the final analysis the Marines had decided they did not have a unit capable of deploying to such an isolated, deep-jungle location, one bereft of escape routes, or means of relief or back-up. Accordingly, no unit took over the Pathfinders' positions.

The 1 PARA battle group was relieved by 42 Commando at Lungi Airport and in Freetown. The back-to-back deployments of two extremely capable fighting units had sealed the fate of the country, bringing an end to a horrific civil war that had lasted for over a decade and cost so many lives. Of course, a very large part of that success was due to a small force of Pathfinders and their extraordinary actions at Lungi Lol – the only significant military action fought against the rebels.

It was that action that broke the backbone of the rebel army in Sierra Leone. Having got the measure of the British forces at Lungi Lol, the rebels had lost the appetite for the fight. Even as the Pathfinders lasted out their final days in the besieged village, Foday Sankoh, the overall commander of the RUF, had been taken captive by British forces. He was captured in Freetown itself, and that, coupled with the crushing defeat of the rebels at Lungi Lol, left the remaining RUF commanders in hopeless disarray, and at loggerheads with each other.

The Pathfinders had been at the tip of the spear in Sierra Leone, and the action they fought at Lungi Lol was the decisive battle. In due course the mission received the recognition it deserved. Nathan Bell, the commander of *33 Alpha*, received a Mention in Dispatches, and amongst other honours Steve Heaney was awarded the Military Cross, in recognition of his role in taking the initiative during the heat of battle.

His citation reads: 'On hearing the first shots, Sgt Heaney immediately ran forward past the trenches, and against the axis of the attack, and under automatic tracer fire from the enemy machine guns. Armed with his personal weapon and 51 mm mortar, Sgt Heaney then proceeded to coordinate fire of the forward positions, while putting up illumination with the mortar, despite being out in the open and completely exposed to intense enemy fire...

'He continued to provide light across the frontage as the enemy conducted a fighting withdrawal, before mounting three subsequent assaults. Sgt Heaney's quick reactions and his part in winning the firefight were crucial to the successful repulsion of the enemy attacks. With complete disregard for his own safety he moved to a position from where he could put up accurate illumination for each enemy assault. His influence over the soldiers around him during the attack was considerable, displaying immense physical courage.'

In due course the Nigerian peacekeepers in Sierra Leone were replaced by an Indian contingent, but the RUF were by then already a broken force. They were never again to mount a significant operation in the country. The British military intervention had put a stop to them, and by the end of 2000 Sierra Leone was finally at peace.

The British military campaign in Sierra Leone was one of the most successful ever. A force of less than 1000 British soldiers brought to an end a decade-long conflict that 17,000 UN peace-keepers had failed to stop. It proved that interventions in war-torn Africa did not always have to end ignominiously – as had the 1993 US intervention in Mogadishu, Somalia.

Today Sierra Leone as a nation has known peace, democracy, development and progress – at least compared to the decade-long civil war that went before – for approaching fifteen years. The rebels have been disarmed and demobilised, and many of their leaders have stood trial for war crimes. Sadly, Foday Sankoh, the RUF's founder and overall leader, died in captivity before he could be put on trial to face his crimes.

Happily, Lungi Lol today is a peaceful, thriving village.

POSTSCRIPT TO THE PAPERBACK EDITION

Hearts and Minds

In the years following the events of May 2000, and then more recently with the publication of *Operation Mayhem*, I have been asked on countless occasions a raft of questions concerning the operation. Of these, one stands out more than most: 'How did you manage to defeat the rebels?' The answer is difficult to sum up in just a few words or sentences, but fundamentally it was down to two main reasons.

Firstly, it was because of the men who defended the village for those sixteen days. It was their daring, tenacity, selflessness and raw courage in the face of insurmountable odds that won the day. They believed so strongly and passionately in not only themselves as individuals, but also in the men to their left and right, and, moreover, in the justness of the cause, that they were willing to risk everything. Every man present made a conscious, informed decision to stay, fully accepting the very real possibility of failure. Their purpose was to defend the men, women and children of Lungi Lol from the barbaric fate that awaited them at the hands of the RUF.

Secondly, the defence of Lungi Lol would doubtless have proven untenable without the help of the villagers themselves. However, there is more to that statement, and I feel the detailed answer lies in the very fabric of the story: in the relationships and bonds that were formed between the soldiers and the villagers, which resulted from a battle to win their hearts and minds as much as the shared intention to fight against evil.

The UK military is envied throughout the world and has the reputation of being able to form effective, productive and lasting relationships with the local population within an operational area. The UK military is regarded as a force for good, which is justifiably deserved; this is due to having personnel who both understand and are capable of conducting a hearts-and-minds campaign. The ability to understand local culture and apply a sympathetic, light-handed approach is classed as a military strength, and this hearts-and-minds mentality is central to successful counter insurgency (COIN) operations.

The initial deployment to Sierra Leone in May 2000 was categorised as a non-combatant evacuation operation, but after the first three to four days in the country – and once all of the entitled personnel had been safely evacuated – the mission quickly evolved into a COIN operation. A COIN operation is essentially a battle to win support from the local population. Experience has taught us that if the affected population is not protected from insurgents by its government (as was the case with Sierra Leone's brutal RUF rebels), and it is left exposed to violence and intimidation, then it will have no choice but to side with these groups. History is littered with examples of campaigns that failed because the local people were left to the mercy of insurgents; however, campaigns that ensured the security of these people have inevitably succeeded. It is about understanding not only the geographical terrain of a conflict but also the human terrain.

In our case, success came from dominating the ground. Since security can really only be achieved by maintaining a presence in the conflict area, the aim was to disrupt rebel activity whilst reassuring the local population. By living amongst the villagers, we not only provided them with a blanket of protection whilst marking a footprint on the ground, but we also demonstrated that we were willing to share the same risks as they were. Becoming part of the village and being adopted by its residents was a direct result of our behaviour towards them, demonstrated through a respect for their beliefs, values and traditions. We laughed, joked and played with their children, offering what limited luxuries we had in the way of chocolate and biscuits; we shared their meagre food supplies, buying their goods, such as cigarettes and soda, that were at least ten years past their sell by dates; and we generally conformed to their way of living. It was this that set us apart from an occupying force. It was this acceptance of us by the village that led to the chief or village elder offering his hand in friendship and assigning work parties to participate in the active defence of the village.

Stopping the rebel advance whilst protecting the villagers became our single mission statement, and it could not have been achieved without our presence in the village. At the very core of COIN operations lies the belief that only a permanent static presence will create the conditions for a local population to become sufficiently trusting and confident in you. This cannot be achieved by forces which surge in and out of the area, leaving gaps in the level of protection afforded to them. The villagers understood beyond doubt what would happen to them if and when the RUF marched through Lungi Lol, but this demonstration of our commitment to them and our willingness to share the risks in facing the rebels created an unbreakable bond, and they embraced us as their own.

In any conflict, the best form of intelligence is local knowledge. However, that knowledge will not come readily until a population feels safe, and they will not feel safe until they are convinced that the rebels' stranglehold on power has been broken. Once the villagers felt sufficiently confident in our mission, they began to feed us information on rebel sightings, dispositions and movements. Any rebel or insurgent group cut off from a readily available source of manpower has to resupply, during which time information quickly becomes weak; this may lead to possible surrender or even destruction at the hands of government forces. The RUF relied totally on fear tactics, intimidation and unprecedented brutality to control the population, meaning news of the presence of British soldiers in Lungi Lol would make their power base look weak and diminished. The rebels needed to demonstrate very quickly that this was not the case and that all opposing forces were impotent against the ferocity of their might.

Operation Kill British, as it was termed by the rebels, was to be their response to this union of British soldiers and local villagers. There was to be clear, decisive action against the village outpost we occupied, which would crush any thoughts of future resistance once and for all by any villages in the area, and the killing or capturing of British soldiers would humiliate the governments of Sierra Leone and the UK. What could be better than dragging the bodies of British soldiers through the streets as a show of strength and victory? This was to be their Somalia, when the world watched helplessly as the dead, mutilated, beaten and naked bodies of US servicemen were dragged through the streets of the capital Mogadishu by the insurgents fighting to destabilise the country – events that were immortalised in the book *Black Hawk Down* and the subsequent movie adaptation.

I have been asked on several occasions about any correlation between our role and actions in Sierra Leone and those undertaken by US forces in Somalia in 1991 to 1993.

In 1991, Somalia was in the grip of severe fighting. Its president, Mohamed Siad Barre, had been overthrown by a coalition of opposing clans. In the civil war that followed, up to 20,000 people were killed by the end of that year. The war resulted in the destruction of Somalia's agriculture, which in turn led to starvation in large swathes of the country. The international community responded and began sending aid supplies to halt the starvation, but with any conflict where power is dictated by those who control what the population needs for survival, this aid was intercepted and then directed to the local clan leaders, who used it as a currency to buy weapons from neighbouring countries. Rough estimations suggest that around 300,000 people died between

1991 and 1992, with at least another 1.5 million people suffering from the effects of starvation.

Throughout 1992, the USA launched several attempts to bring aid to the starving masses, and in an attempt to create a stable environment within Somalia, began launching attacks against the warlords. In June 1993, a UN contingent made up of Pakistani troops was attacked, resulting in the deaths of 24 soldiers and leaving 57 wounded. In October 1993, in a final attempt to restore a legitimate government to Somalia and bring an end to the vicious, criminal rule of the clans, George H. W. Bush (snr) ordered a task force consisting of Tier 1 Special Operations troops into Mogadishu to arrest the warlord Mohamed Aidid and his top lieutenants who controlled the city. Operating out of the airport located on the outskirts of the city, a task force consisting of nineteen aircraft, twelve vehicles – of which nine were heavily armed Humvees – and 160 men began its assault.

The similarity between Sierra Leone and Somalia lay in the fact that both countries were in the midst of a civil war, and both had governments which had either been deposed or were under threat of being deposed. Rebel militias had seized power and were bleeding each country of its wealth for their own gain. The people of both countries were suffering from a lack of food, basic amenities and medical care. They were also being beaten, mutilated, raped and murdered on an industrial scale. Children were taken from the arms of their dead parents, marched into a life of drug-induced servitude and forced to pledge their allegiance to the leader of the gang: in Sierra Leone, this was Foday Sankoh of the RUF, and in Somalia, Mohamed Aidid of the disbanded Somali National Army rebel factions.

The action taken by the USA in Somalia was well intended but missing a vital component, in that the more you protect your force, the less secure you are. Ultimately, success in COIN operations is gained by protecting the population, not by force protection. A population will give their allegiance to the side that best protects it. It is a matter of survival, and the population knows that a failure of security could result in death or brutal punishment. They will support their government if and when they are convinced that the state can offer them a better life, and that it can and will protect them against the enemy for ever. The US troops could not offer that protection, nor could they reassure the population. Aidid had a stranglehold on them by controlling the UN aid that was coming into the country and never allowing it to reach the people of Mogadishu.

The USA could not operate outside of the confines of their secure base. By failing to provide a static presence, they were therefore unable to bring any comfort or reassurance to the people. This in turn prevented any build-up of trust, confidence or local disruption of rebel activity, which resulted in the USA having to fight the entire population of the city. The US forces were never in a position to win over the hearts and minds of the population of Mogadishu; their approach was always with a heavy hand, and they never benefitted from reliable, accurate local information or intelligence.

After the failed attempt to arrest Aidid – which resulted in the deaths of eighteen US soldiers and seventy-three wounded, plus the unconfirmed deaths of over 200 Somalia civilians and a further 700 injured – President Clinton stated it was a mistake for the USA to play the role of police officer in Somalia and immediately announced a plan to remove all US forces from the country within six months. Subsequent observations of the pullout identified that by withdrawing from Somalia, the USA had left a lawless region ripe for an Al Qaeda takeover, handing over a whole generation of Somalis to be educated and groomed by Islamist fundamentalists.

So why did 'Operation Kill British' fail to do to British forces in Sierra Leone what Somali militias did to US forces in Somalia? I think it goes back to the very essence of the British military's modus operandi, and its unique ability to win over a population through compassion, understanding and acceptance of diverse cultures, plus the application of a light-handed approach. In 1901, it was Theodore Roosevelt who said his own foreign policy as president of the USA was to 'speak softly, and carry a big stick'. Our relationship with the villagers was amplified by our constant presence among them, through which they developed a fondness for us, trusting in our mission and confident in our ability to not only defend them but also to defeat the rebels. They understood we shared the same risks as them and that we were all putting our lives on the line. The respect and humility demonstrated by each operator when in direct contact with the villagers showcased that we did not place ourselves above them or value their contribution any less than our own. Add all of these things together in a bowl and stir, and you have the beginnings of a resistance.

WHERE ARE THEY NOW?

Richard 'Rich' Cantrill OBE MC

Richard Cantrill is now a Lieutenant-Colonel in command of 42 Commando Royal Marines. In 2010 he was awarded the MC for his time as Company Commander in Afghanistan (HERRICK 9). He was appointed OBE in the 2014 New Year Honours list for two busy years spent in the Operations Directorate of the MOD. He lives in Devon with his wife and three rowdy children.

Eddie 'The White Rabbit' Newell MBE

Eddie Newell went on to replace Wag as the Ops Warrant Officer of the Pathfinders, a job in which he remained until he left the military in 2006. On completion of his 22 years' service he was awarded an MBE. His citation reads: 'For distinguished and exceptional service in five operational theatres, and unstinting dedication to the unit'. He currently lives in the UK with his wife and son.

Mark 'Jacko' Jackson

Mark Jackson left the military in 2003 and trained as a professional sculptor and painter. In 2012 his sculptures dedicated to the Airborne Forces were unveiled by HRH Prince Charles at the National Arboretum. The two sculptures represent a Standing Paratrooper in full jump equipment and Bellerophon astride the winged horse Pegasus. Mark has his own studio in France, where he presently resides.

Darren 'Taff' Saunders

Darren Saunders left the military in 2004 after being involved in a helicopter crash that left him with a broken neck. After making a full recovery he went on to become a private security consultant working in both the UK and abroad. He is presently employed as a consultant for a major UK oil company. He lives in the South of France.

Joe 'H' / 'Tackleberry' Harrison

Joe Harrison remained with the Pathfinders until he left the military in September 2002. He re-enlisted in the Pathfinders for the 2003 deployment to Iraq and again left the military in 2004. After a few years working in the private security industry he joined the reservists and deployed three times to Afghanistan. On one such deployment in 2010 he was awarded an MID (Mention in Dispatches). H lives in the UK where he grows his own fruit and vegetables. He is currently seeking employment, and is a self-confessed *war junkie*.

Neil 'Tricky' Dick

Neil Dick left the Pathfinders and the military in 2003 after operational deployments to both Iraq and Afghanistan. He was subsequently employed by a high-profile US communications company that produces military grade radios. Tricky currently travels the world providing both practical and technical assistance to countries that employ those communications systems. He lives in Scotland with his wife and two children.

Dale 'Ginge' Wilson

Dale Wilson returned to his parent unit after the deployment to Sierra Leone. He remained there and undertook several posts as a senior NCO. Then he returned to the Pathfinders in 2010 as the

Ops Warrant Officer. In 2012 he again returned to his parent unit to finish his military service. He and his family currently live in the UK.

Sam 'Dolly' Parton

Sam Parton remained with the Pathfinders until 2003, before moving on to another unit in the British military in order to receive promotion. Dolly is still serving in the military and lives in the UK with his wife and two children.

Nathan 'Nathe' Bell MC

Nathan Bell went on to replace Steve Heaney as the Pathfinders' Platoon Sergeant where he remained until June 2004. During the Pathfinders' deployment to Iraq in 2003 Nathe was awarded the MC for his actions during the Qalat Sikar operation (the story of which is related in David Blakeley's book, *Pathfinder*). Nathe also served as an instructor at the UK Land Warfare Centre at Warminster before returning to 1 PARA. He left the Army in December 2011 having completed 22 years' service. He currently lives in the UK with his wife and daughter.

Grant Harris

Grant Harris remained with the Pathfinders until 2003 as its Second-in-Command. He then returned to his parent unit in order to receive promotion. Grant is still serving in the British military elite and lives in the UK.

Graham 'Wag' Wardle

Graham Wardle remained as the Pathfinders' Ops Warrant Officer until May 2002, when he left the military having completed 22 years' service. From 2003 until 2007 he worked in Iraq on numerous Personal Security Details (PSDs), providing security for visiting businessmen and reconstruction companies. In 2008 he began working on a residential security team based in the Middle East, in which capacity he remains to this day. Wag and his wife live in the UK.

Stephen 'Steve' Heaney MC

Steve Heaney remained as the Pathfinders' Platoon Sergeant until February 2001. He then took the decision to leave the military and move into the private security industry. Having trained as a Close Protection Officer (CPO) he went to work for a very high-profile businessman in London from April 2001 until January 2002, providing security and personal protection to the principal and his immediate family. In February 2002 Steve moved to the Middle East to provide military advice and training solutions across the full spectrum of close combat operations. He currently resides in the Middle East with his wife and two children.

Bryan 'Bri' Budd VC

Bryan Budd remained with the Pathfinders until June 2006. He returned to 3 PARA in order to receive promotion and then deployed to Afghanistan in July 2006. On 20 August 2006, during a patrol in the Sangin district of Helmand province, his section was ambushed by Taliban fighters. Bri led his men forward to clear the enemy position, which resulted in the section sustaining three casualties. He was wounded but continued the attack on his own. Spurred on by his actions the remainder of his men cleared the position, forcing the enemy to withdraw. Bryan died from wounds sustained during that battle. When his body was recovered it was surrounded by three dead Taliban fighters. He was awarded a posthumous Victoria Cross.

ACKNOWLEDGEMENTS

A number of people have provided me with assistance in clarifying details for this book and to those brothers in arms, my thanks: to the men I have stood shoulder to shoulder with on countless occasions – you shall forever have my respect. To my mother and father who undoubtedly sat by the telephone whilst watching news reports for a decade and a half, I apologise for those sleepless nights and offer you my eternal gratitude for your unwavering love and support. To my brother Neil, my confidant and best friend – thanks, mate, for always being my release valve and drinking partner when I needed to unwind!

Thank you to my co-author Damien Lewis for his belief and steadying hand on this project and in helping me to articulate my experiences during those long days at his home (not to mention down the pub!). Thanks also to his wife and family for putting up with my dragging him away to work on this book. A special thank you to Alan Samson, Lucinda McNeile, Jamie Tanner, Helen Ewing, Hannah Cox, Jess Gulliver, and all the sales teams at publisher Orion who worked tirelessly to ensure this book was a success. Thanks to Andy Chittock, military photographer, for your help sourcing images for the photo plates herein. To my literary agent Annabel Merullo and her assistant Laura Williams – thanks for your unflagging enthusiasm throughout. Thanks also to film agent Luke Speed, for your belief in the story getting told. Fantastic work, the lot of you!

A very special thank you to General Sir David Richards GCB CBE DSO, for the Foreword to this book: suffice to say, no better commander could a soldier ever have wished for in the field.

Last but not least I wish to thank my wife Lisa whose unfaltering support and encouragement over the past twelve months has been incredible, and to my children Maisie and Miles who have wondered why their father has been locked away in a room for so long and unable to play as often as they would have liked.

Steve Heaney MC
April 2014,
the Middle East

PHOTOS, IMAGE AND QUOTE CREDITS:

The authors and publisher are grateful to the following for permission to reproduce photographs:

Andy Chittock, 1–6, 11–12, 16–21, 30–7, 44
Peter Russell, 7–10
Kadir van Lohuizen/Noor/eyevine, 28
David Rose/Panos, 29
AFP/Getty Images, 31, 40
Travis Lupick, 38
Pep Bonet/Noor/eyevine, 39, 42
Fredrik Naumann/Panos Pictures, 41
Francesco Zizola/Noor/eyevine, 43
Malcolm Fairman/Alamy, 45

INDEX

African pouched rats, 170
air marker panels, 163
Air Mounting Centre (AMC), South Cerney, 24, 26–9, 31
airliners, civilian, 5, 33
AK47 assault rifles, 30, 59, 173–5, 188, 200, 237
Al Qaeda, 31, 48
Aldershot Training Area, 2
Allem, Captain Johnny, 94
alligators, 40
Altitude Decompression Sickness (ADS), 5
Amphibious Readiness Group, 160
'Amps Camps', 119
AR15 assault rifles, 215
Arctic Survival cadre, 18
Army Air Corps, 3, 15
Army Dental Corps, 19
Ashby, Major Phil, 98

B-1B heavy bombers, 6
bamboo, *see* punji sticks
Barnes, Bill 'Basha', 213, 215
'battle-sighting', 218
battle trenches, 104–5, 109, 119, 122, 129, 167
'bearing and pacing', 246
Belize, 60, 212–16
Bell, Corporal Nathan 'Nathe'
  and British withdrawal, 288–90, 294
  defensive preparations, 86, 109–10, 118, 126, 134, 159

and Donaldson, 53, 72, 92
food preparation, 129–33, 136, 144, 154–6, 166–7, 170, 212
and I-beds, 139–40
joins Pathfinders, 21–3
mentioned in dispatches, 297
and rebel assault, 182–5, 187–8, 198, 206, 210–11, 218, 221, 228, 284
Ben (dog), 3–4, 15, 26, 129–30, 157
Blair, Tony, 26, 48, 57
body armour, lack of, 181
Borneo, 102–3
bread rolls, 140–1, 170, 278, 281, 290, 292
Brecon Beacons, 2, 49, 164
Brewster, Pete, 24
British Army
  and kit procurement, 71–2
  and personal weapons, 30–1
Brown, Steve (Steve B), 75–7, 79, 249–51, 253
Browning machine guns, 24
Browning pistols, 34, 177
Brunei, 60, 246
Bryant, Major Bob, 241–5, 253, 262, 264–70, 273–4
Budd, Bryan, 236, 238, 272
buddy-buddy system, 117, 136
'bullet mantles', 68

Caine, Michael, 282
Cantrill, Captain Richard
  arrival in Lungi Lol, 163–8

Cantrill, Captain Richard—*contd*
　and decision to stay in Lungi Lol, 234–5
　departure from Lungi Lol, 243, 246–7, 249, 269
　and rebel assault, 172, 176–8, 180–4, 187, 189–90, 193, 197, 199, 201–6, 208–11, 217–20, 222–3, 225–7, 283
Carson, Lewis, 42, 58
casevacs, 225
Caveney, Joe, 274, 276–9, 281, 283
centipedes, 212
child soldiers, 46–7
China Lake, 4–6, 8–9, 14–15
CIA Special Activities Division (SAD), 59
Claymores, 55, 101–2, 107, 111–15, 167, 228, 271, 289
close quarter battle (CQB) terrain, 260
Combat 95 uniform, 164
common weapon sights (CWSs), 192
compassionate leave, 94

Dakar, 32, 41
defensive perimeter posts (DPPs), 38–9
dehydration, 89, 143
Delta Force, 59
detcord, 111–12
diamonds, conflict, 31–2, 47–8
Dick, Neil 'Tricky'
　and Brigadier Richards' arrival, 280
　and British withdrawal, 286, 288, 292–3
　and Cantrill's arrival, 166–8
　defensive preparations, 85–6, 159–60
　and Donaldson, 72, 90–1
　establishes communications, 39–40, 53, 66, 78–9, 93, 96, 142
　and fighting patrol, 248, 253, 258
　and Ibrahim, 123–4, 130

Pathfinders' brew-master, 100, 151–2, 263–4
and QRF, 234–6, 240, 242–4
and rebel assault, 171–2, 176–7, 184, 210, 223, 225–9
and RMPs, 265–6
Donaldson, Captain Robert
　appointed OC, 17–18
　and arrival of Mojo, 68–9
　and E&E issue, 51–3, 66, 73
　and forward patrol, 73–5
　granted compassionate leave, 94, 96
　and Pathfinder 'prayers', 72–4
　and Pathfinders' deployment, 29, 34, 42–3, 45–6, 58–9
　withdraws to airport, 79–80, 85–6, 91
drinking water, 89, 95, 141, 143, 145, 263–4, 278, 281, 293
drug-runners, 212–16
drugs, RUF and, 47–8, 115, 179–80
DShK machine guns, 94, 104, 248, 284

escape and evasion (E&E), 114, 169, 219, 221, 264, 278
　issue with Donaldson, 51–3, 66, 73

F-15 Eagle fighter pilots, 14
Falklands War, 120–1
Final Protective Fire (FPF), 277–8
FN assault rifles, 90, 107
'follow-on' bags, 29
'forced air' mixture, 6
Freetown, 31–2, 35, 257, 296
　British Embassy evacuation, 32, 42–6
　capture of rebel leader in, 297
　Mammy Yoko Hotel, 44–5
　rebel advance on, 41–4, 47, 50, 81–2, 91, 95, 97, 99
Freetown Estuary, 43, 45, 62

general purpose machine guns (GPMGs), 21, 24, 34, 54–5, 57, 87, 102

barrel-changes, 185–6
use against rebel assault, 173, 175–6, 178–9, 185–6, 188, 191–2, 194, 198, 201, 218–19, 223, 237, 267
use by fighting patrol, 248–9, 252–3, 255, 257
Gibson, Colonel Paul 'Gibbo'
briefs Pathfinders, 50–1
and Donaldson, 29, 43, 45, 77, 79–80, 91
and Kosovo mission, 26–7
and Pathfinders' deployment, 26–9, 31, 34–6, 41, 43, 45, 48, 50–1, 57–8, 62–3, 114
and QRF, 184, 243, 253
visits Lungi Lol, 262, 264–5, 268–72
Gow, Company Sergeant Major Andy, 121
Guatemala, 212, 214
Gurkhas, 212–13

hammocks, 71
Hansen, Morgan Taff, 252
HAPLSS (High Altitude Parachutist Life Support System), 5–9, 14, 23, 49, 162
hard tack biscuits, 123–4
Harris, Captain Grant
and Brigadier Richards' arrival, 280
and British withdrawal, 286–8, 290–3
and Cantrill's arrival, 163–6
defensive preparations, 66, 86, 96, 99–100, 109–10
and Donaldson, 43, 51, 53, 58, 72–3, 80, 91–2, 96
and fighting patrol, 248, 253, 258, 262
and forward patrol, 73, 75–7
and Gibson's arrival, 268–70
meetings with village chief, 82–4, 158, 291–2

and Mojo's arrival, 68–9
and Pathfinders' deployment, 22–3, 34, 37, 39, 42, 57
and Pathfinders' ethos, 127
and Pathfinders' humour, 3, 16
pre-battle briefing, 159
and QRF, 234–5, 240–5, 253
and rebel assault, 171–2, 176–7, 184, 210, 220–3, 225–7, 229, 271, 273–4, 282
and RMPs, 265–7
and snail stew, 132–3
Harrison, Lance Corporal Joe 'H'
and British withdrawal, 290
defensive preparations, 146, 159
friendship with Nathe Bell, 21–3
known as the 'Death Dealer', 21, 178
and rebel assault, 173, 175, 178–9, 184–8, 193, 196, 198, 200, 209–10, 217–19, 221, 223–5
retrieves rebel weapons, 237
and snail stew, 132–3
Harrison, Major Andy, 97–8
'hexy' stoves, 29
HIP helicopters, 44, 58
HMS Ocean, 246
Holt, Roger, 20
HOOK helicopters, 58
human shields, RUF use of, 88, 122

Ibrahim, 108–11, 116–18, 121, 123–8, 130–1, 134–5, 275, 295
and I-beds, 135–40
and makeshift gym, 147–8
Intelligence Preparation of the Battlefield (IPB), 42
Iraq War, 180

Jackson, Captain Mark 'Jacko', 94, 96, 268–70, 272, 282–3
Jackson, General Sir Mike, 94

James, Captain Chris, 232–4

Joint Air Transport Establishment (JTE), 8

jungle boots, US Army, 165

Jungle Tracker Courses, 246

Kabbah, President Ahmad, 48, 280–1

kidnappings, by RUF, 97–8

Kosovo, 26–7, 94, 156, 241

L2 fragmentation grenades, 55

L96 AW sniper rifles, 21

Lariam antimalarial pills, 96

LAW light anti-armour weapons, 24, 54–5, 115, 248–9, 284

Lewis, Mark 'Marky', 75–7, 79–80, 85–6, 93, 229, 233

'light order', 29

live fire exercises, 174

Long Range Recce Patrols (LRRPs), 246

Low's Gully, 165

Lungi Airport

British arrive at, 41–2, 44–5

and British withdrawal, 295–6

Donaldson returns to, 79–80, 86

rebel advance on, 113–14, 122

weapons dump, 54–7, 87, 111, 177

Lungi Lol

British withdrawal from, 286–95

civilian influx, 92–3, 114, 117, 159–60, 262–3, 272–3, 285

defensive preparations, 86–7, 99–110, 116–22, 125–31

Fern Gully, 205, 209, 218–20, 222–3, 245, 250–1, 256, 277

fighting patrol around, 243–62

latrines, 136, 278

meetings with village chief, 83–5, 99–100, 134–5, 158–9, 279, 291–2

Pathfinders' deployment to, 50–1, 62–6

Pathfinders' relations with villagers, 134–5, 143–4, 293–5

railway line, 101, 115, 128, 188, 193–5, 199, 201, 228, 261–2

rebel advance on, 91–2, 94–5, 99–101, 115–16, 142–3, 158–9, 163

rebel assault begins, 172–81

villagers and forced labour, 263, 272

villagers singing, 119

weapons captured at, 237–8, 262

M16 assault rifles, 30–1, 57, 71, 162, 213–14, 216, 267

Malaysia, 165, 246

Mangham, Major Mark, 280

maps, operational, 41–2

MI6, 31

Middlesbrough, 1, 119–20

Military Cross, 297

Minimi light machine guns, 57, 162

Ministry of Defence (MOD), 25, 31, 181

'mission command', 106

Mogadishu, 98, 298

'Mojo, Lieutenant', see Obasanjo, Lieutenant Oronto

morphine, 19

mortars, 51 mm, 54–6

illuminate rebel assault, 177–8, 187–94, 197–9, 204–5, 209, 211, 217, 219–20, 222–3, 225, 248, 283, 297

mortars, 81 mm, 271, 274–9, 283–4

motion sensors, 72, 105

Mountain Leaders, 165

mushrooms, 154

named areas of interest (NAIs), 23

NATO ammunition, 179–80

negligent discharge (ND), 172

net explosive quantity (NEQ), 55

New Zealand SAS, 246

Newell, Colour Sergeant Eddie 'The White Rabbit', 17, 22–4, 29, 34, 58, 105, 149, 167
  arrives in Lungi Lol, 93–5, 97, 128, 153, 268, 270
  and Donaldson, 43, 77, 91
Nigerian military, hierarchical nature of, 106–7
'night routine', 75
night vision goggles (NVGs), 37, 231
night-time air-markers, 230–1
non-combat evacuation operation (NEO), 16–17, 41–2, 44–5, 50, 94, 97
Northern Ireland, 93, 180

Obasanjo, Lieutenant Oronto ('Lieutenant Mojo'), 68–71, 80–5
  and bread deliveries, 140–1, 170, 281
  and British withdrawal, 290–2, 295
  and defensive preparations, 89–90, 99–100, 104–8, 158, 166–7
  and influx of villagers, 262–3
  and latrines, 136
  and rebel assault, 172, 181, 196, 226, 229–30, 276
  and rebel dead, 263, 265, 267, 272
  and villagers' gratitude, 134–5, 279
observation post (OP) kit, 23
'Operation Blind', 23
Operations Other Than War (OOTWs), 175, 249

parachute jumps
  high-altitude, 4–14, 25, 49
  tandem, 8–9, 16
  see also HAPLSS
Parachute Regiment
  author and 3 PARA, 121, 274
  deployment, 16–17, 26–31, 33–5, 41
  hatred of RMPs, 265–6
  Junior PARA, 120–1

Kosovo deployment, 26–7
medical provisions, 19
numbers, 47
P Company, 2
Quick Reaction Force (QRF), 51, 95, 97, 101–2, 107, 184, 210, 221, 224–30, 240–5
Support Company, 274
withdrawal from Lungi Lol, 270–4, 296
Parsons, Andy, 213–15
Parton, Corporal Sam 'Dolly'
  and bread rolls, 141–2, 282
  and British withdrawal, 290, 294
  defensive preparations, 67, 86, 109, 114, 117, 127, 129, 134, 159, 161
  and Donaldson, 53, 72
  and fighting patrol, 245, 247–9
  and I-beds, 139–40
  joins Pathfinders, 44
  and QRF, 235–6
  and rebel assault, 184, 196–8, 200–1, 204–5, 209–10, 216–19, 221–3, 227–8, 283–4
  and snail stew, 133
Pathfinders
  and bad decision-making, 234
  'black' identity, 9–10, 25, 162
  call signs, 22
  decision-making, 52, 72, 74–5
  deniable operations, 212–16
  esprit de corps, 20, 75
  first seek-and-destroy mission, 249
  formal role of, 145
  formation of, 25
  identity markers, 26
  Interest Room, 4, 18
  medical training, 19
  navigational skills, 42
  nickname, 10

Pathfinders—*contd*
  Pathfinder Selection, 1–3, 22, 40, 62, 75, 171, 232
  pay and conditions, 9, 162
  personal kit, 45–6
  'prayers', 72–4
  self-reliance, 133
Patrol Lanes, 260
Patrols Medics cadre, 19
PE4 plastic explosive, 55–6, 111–13, 278
ponchos, US Army, 45
Port Stanley, 121
'prickly heat', 145
punji sticks, 102–4, 107, 112, 116–19, 121, 125–7, 130–1, 166–7
  and rebel assault, 186–7, 205, 207–8, 263

radios, Clansman 319 HF, 39–40, 95, 128, 142, 144–5, 176, 228
radios, Clansman 349 VHF, 78, 144, 211, 244, 251–2
RAF Brize Norton, 8
RAF Odiham, 43
range cards, 86–7
rape, by RUF, 46, 121
Ready Status One, 15
Revolutionary United Front (RUF)
  Al Qaeda links, 47–8
  and animal cries, 143, 171
  battle chant, 179
  final defeat of, 297–8
  ideology and tactics, 46–7
  noms de guerre, 194
  numbers, 47
  Operation Kill British, 97–8, 113, 122, 195, 201, 211, 225, 239, 260, 270
  Sex The Child 'game', 194
Richards, Brigadier David, 48–9, 57, 114, 280–1
Robson, Mick, 54–7, 111, 177, 200

rocket propelled grenades (RPGs), 180–1, 200, 203–4, 236–7
Roebuck, James 'Bucks', 198, 200, 223, 237
Room Clearance Mode, 254
Room Combat Mode, 254
Rowland, Lieutenant-Commander, 98
Royal Marines, 160–1, 163, 165, 287–8, 296
Royal Military Police, 27, 265–7
Royal Regiment of Wales, 67
RPK light machine guns, 200, 237
rules of engagement, 105, 175

SA80 assault rifles, 30–1, 54, 71, 74, 87, 128, 133, 162, 253
  tendency to jam, 30, 192, 267
  use against rebel assault, 173, 176–80, 182, 185, 187–8, 191–2, 195, 198, 200–1, 204, 206–10, 212, 216–18, 222–3, 225–6, 237
Samsonoff, Major Andrew, 98
Sankoh, Foday, 46, 297–8
Saunders, Taff
  and British withdrawal, 290
  defensive preparations, 67–8, 86, 115, 134, 146, 159
  and Donaldson, 72
  and fighting patrol, 245
  and I-beds, 139–40
  joins Pathfinders, 67–8
  and QRF, 236
  and rebel assault, 184, 194–6, 201, 204–5, 221, 228
  and snail stew, 133
SEALs, 4, 6, 9, 40
Secret Intelligence Service, 32
Senegal, 34
shell-scrapes, 68, 242
Sierra Leone Army, 47
sleeping bags, 45
Smith, Johno, 213, 215

snails, 129–33, 212
Somalia, 98, 298
Special Air Service (SAS), 31–2, 41–2, 47, 63, 165
  recce at Lungi Lol, 95, 161–2, 168–9
  selection, 2
  training, 25, 102, 162
  weaponry and body armour, 31, 57, 162, 181
Special Boat Service (SBS), 25, 31, 41, 51–2, 165
standard operating procedure (SOP), 254
stand-to, 74–5
Swedish Special Forces, 18

tactical air landing operations (TALOs), 33
Thomson, Mike 'Tommo', 274–9, 281–4, 290
Thuraya satphones, 95–6, 128, 142, 176–7, 210, 228, 240, 280, 282
trip flares, 105
tropical kit, 38–9

UK Special Forces, 9, 162
UN peacekeepers, 33, 47, 97–8
  Nigerians at Lungi Lol, 68–71, 81–2, 89–90, 100, 104–8, 115, 196, 226, 229–30, 289, 297
US Marine Corps, 40

Vietnam War, 179, 216, 285
voodoo, RUF and, 47, 116, 179–80, 194–5, 257

Wardle, Warrant Officer Graham 'Wag'
  acquires weapons, 54–7, 87, 111–12, 177
  and bread rolls, 141–2, 281–2

and British withdrawal, 287–9, 292, 295
and Cantrill's arrival, 166, 168
and Cantrill's departure, 247
defensive preparations, 68, 86–90, 92, 96, 100, 111, 117, 129, 132, 159, 161
and Donaldson, 18, 46, 51–3, 58, 72, 77, 80, 96
and fighting patrol, 243–5, 248, 250–3, 257–8, 261–2
and Ibrahim, 108–10, 123–7, 130–1, 135–9
joins Pathfinders, 15–16
makeshift gym, 146–9, 153
meeting with village chief, 83–6
and Mojo, 105–8
and Pathfinders' deployment, 22–3, 33–4, 42, 57
and punji sticks, 102–3
and QRF, 234–5, 238, 242–3
and rebel assault, 172, 176–7, 184, 196, 210, 225–9, 271–6
and RMPs, 265–7
washing and shaving, 95–6
water purification kits, 19
Wattisham, Norfolk, 3, 15, 19, 25
Wilson, Dale 'Ginge'
  and British withdrawal, 290, 294
  defensive preparations, 67, 86, 110, 118, 134, 159
  and Donaldson, 72
  and fighting patrol, 245
  and I-beds, 139–40
  and QRF, 236
  and rebel assault, 184, 194, 196, 221, 228, 284
  and snail stew, 133

'yaffling irons', 155